CHILD LABOR

Recent Titles in
A World View of Social Issues Series

Child Abuse: A Global View
Beth M. Schwartz-Kenney, Michelle McCauley, and Michelle A. Epstein, editors

Crime and Crime Control: A Global View
Gregg Barak, editor

Domestic Violence: A Global View
Randal W. Summers and Allan M. Hoffman, editors

HIV and AIDS: A Global View
Karen McElrath, editor

Migration and Immigration: A Global View
Maura I. Toro-Morn and Marixsa Alicea, editors

Substance Abuse: A Global View
Andrew Cherry, Mary E. Dillon, and Douglas Rugh, editors

Teenage Pregnancy: A Global View
Andrew L. Cherry, Mary E. Dillon, and Douglas Rugh, editors

Teen Gangs: A Global View
Maureen P. Duffy and Scott Edward Gillig, editors

Teen Violence: A Global View
Allan M. Hoffman and Randal W. Summers, editors

Women's Rights: A Global View
Lynn Walter, editor

CHILD LABOR

A GLOBAL VIEW

Edited by
Cathryne L. Schmitz,
Elizabeth KimJin Traver, and
Desi Larson

A World View of Social Issues
Andrew L. Cherry, Series Adviser

Greenwood Press
Westport, Connecticut · London

Library of Congress Cataloging-in-Publication Data

Child labor : a global view / edited by Cathryne L. Schmitz, Elizabeth KimJin
   Traver, and Desi Larson.
       p. cm. — (A world view of social issues)
    Includes bibliographical references and index.
    ISBN 0-313-32277-5 (alk. paper)
    1. Child labor. I. Schmitz, Cathryne L., 1946- II. Traver, Elizabeth
KimJin.   III. Larson, Desi. IV. Series.
HD6231.C453 2004
331.3′1—dc22   2003057132

British Library Cataloguing in Publication Data is available.

Library of Congress Catalog Card Number: 2003057132
ISBN: 0-313-32277-5
ISSN: 1526-9442

First published in 2004

Greenwood Press, 88 Post Road West, Westport, CT 06881
An imprint of Greenwood Publishing Group, Inc.
www.greenwood.com

Printed in the United States of America

The paper used in this book complies with the
Permanent Paper Standard issued by the National
Information Standards Organization (Z39.48–1984).

10 9 8 7 6 5 4 3 2 1

CONTENTS

SERIES FOREWORD

Why are child abuse in the family and homelessness social conditions to be endured or at least tolerated in some countries while in other countries they are viewed as social problems that must be reduced or eliminated? What social institutions and other factors affect these behaviors? What historical, political, and social forces influence a society's response to a social condition? In many cases, individuals around the world have the same or similar hopes and problems. However, in most cases we deal with the same social conditions in very dissimilar ways.

The volumes in the Greenwood series A World View of Social Issues examine different social issues and problems that are being faced by individuals and societies around the world. These volumes examine problems of poverty and homelessness, drugs and alcohol addiction, HIV/AIDS, teen pregnancy, crime, women's rights, and a myriad of other issues that affect all of us in one way or another.

Each volume is devoted to one social issue or problem. All volumes follow the same general format. Each volume has up to fifteen chapters that describe how people in different countries perceive and try to cope with a given problem or social issue. The countries chosen represent as many world regions as possible, making it possible to explore how each issue has been recognized and what actions have been taken to alleviate it in a variety of settings.

Each chapter begins with a profile of the country being highlighted and an overview of the impact of the social issue or problem there. Basic policies, legislation, and demographic information related to the social issue are covered.

A brief history of the problem helps the reader better understand the political and social responses. Political initiatives and policies are also discussed, as well as social views, customs, and practices related to the problem or social issue. Discussions about how the countries plan to deal with these social problems are also included.

These volumes present a comprehensive and engaging approach for the study of international social conditions and problems. The goal is to provide a convenient framework for readers to examine specific social problems, how they are viewed, and what actions are being taken by different countries around the world.

For example, how is a problem like crime and crime control handled in third world countries? How is substance abuse controlled in industrialized countries? How are poverty and homelessness handled in the poorest countries? How does culture influence the definition, and response to, domestic violence in different countries? What part does economics play in shaping both the issue of and the response to women's rights? How does a national philosophy impact the definition of and response to child abuse? These questions and more will be answered by the volumes in this series.

As we learn more about our counterparts in other countries, they become real to us, and our worldview cannot help but change. We will think of others as we think of those we know. They will be people who get up in the morning and go to work. We will see people who are struggling with relationships, attending religious services, being born, and growing old, and dying.

This series will cover issues that will add to your knowledge about contemporary social society. These volumes will help you to better understand social conditions and social issues in a broader sense, giving you a view of what various problems mean to different people and how these perspectives impact a society's response. You will be able to see how specific social problems are managed by governments and individuals confronting the consequences of these social dilemmas. By studying one problem from various angles, you will be better able to grasp the totality of the situation, while at the same time speculating as to how solutions used in one country could be incorporated in another. Finally, this series will allow you to compare and contrast how these social issues impact individuals in different countries and how the effect is dissimilar or similar to your own experiences.

As series adviser, it is my hope that these volumes, which are unique in the history of publishing, will increase your understanding and appreciation of your counterparts around the world.

Andrew Cherry
Series Adviser

INTRODUCTION

*Cathryne L. Schmitz, Elizabeth Kim Jin Traver,
Desi Larson, and Pamela Pieris*

Child labor is a complex social and political issue with a long and evolving history. This phenomenon has moved to new dimensions over the last couple of centuries. The work of children is a global issue. The manifestations vary widely in impact depending on the conditions (Boyden, 1991) of poverty, economy, history, and position in the global social and economic systems. Children's work can be paid or unpaid; it can be family or employer labor. Poverty is the major precipitating factor, but education, rigid social and cultural roles, economic greed, family size, geography, and global economics all contribute.

Child labor is found in poor and wealthy economies. While no clear or universal definition exists, in general the term child labor refers to work that impedes children's access to education and is harmful to their physical, mental, moral, developmental, and social well-being. Child labor is reported in terms of varying degrees of exploitation, from oppressive to hazardous.

Central to this discussion is the definition of child labor. Questions many countries struggle with include: What is a child, what is labor, and what entails work? It is globally recognized that there is a period during the life span when a person is a child. Nevertheless, the world debates at what point in life childhood actually ends and what the capacities and responsibilities of children are along the road to adulthood. The dominant perception of childhood is a modern Western phenomenon based on the child's biological structure and cultural information. This perspective colors our ideas about child's play and the notion that childhood should be carefree. It is a view that sees the modern child as lacking "the capacities, skills and powers of adulthood" (Archard, 1993, p. 30). According to the Convention on the Rights of the Child 1989, a child is a person under eighteen years of age. This definition, however, is seen as emerging from a Western concept of child as well as a political premise (Ennew, 1994). Other cultures interpret childhood across other parameters. Cultures worldwide mark the upper age limit of the child at various ages. This age can be different for girls and boys in the same culture. Defining childhood can be tied to age as well as performance, comprehension, and capabilities. Most Western cultures also establish childhood in terms of developmental periods: infancy, child, and adolescence (Archard, 1993).

The work of children can be helpful to the child, family, and community. Paid and unpaid child labor can support the family or it can provide the child with money. It is possible for children to continue their education, to benefit economically and socially, and to contribute to family income if they work limited hours in nonabusive conditions (Siddiqi and Patrinos, 1995; World Bank, n.d.). However, such ideal work conditions are unequally available throughout the world depending on the country's culture, political stability, social values, and position within an emerging global economy. For example, children in poor countries contribute more to family income in paid and unpaid labor than children in wealthy countries. They are not the economic "burden" they have become in wealthy countries (Siddiqi and Patrinos, 1995).

Child labor can also be developmentally, emotionally, and physically abusive. Child workers are more vulnerable than adult workers, leaving them at risk for exploitation, dangerous conditions, and abuse. The impact is dependent on the age of the child and the conditions of employment. Child labor can interfere with the child's education and lure children away from family into conditions of "slavery." In many parts of the world, it too often involves confinement, bondage, and forced labor; it frequently involves dangerous and unhealthy working conditions. Children work longer hours and have lower pay than adults (Bequele and Boyden, 1988). Some children are sold into labor with no hope of getting out. Some are abducted. Children as young as four and five years of age are forced into servitude.

FAMILIES AT THE MARGINS

Poverty is recognized as the major reason for child labor. The economic gain from the labor of children can be vital to the survival of all family members in the poorest of families. Strategies to reduce child labor focus on poverty reduction and related issues, including education, support services for children and families, and the elimination of gender oppression.

Persistent poverty fuels the perpetuation of abusive child labor. When the income level of a country increases, the incidence and proportion of child laborers decreases. In countries with a per capita income of $500 or less,

30 to 60 percent of children ten to fourteen years of age work; in countries with a per capita income between $500 and $1,000, the rate for children in the labor force decreases to 10 to 30 percent (Siddiqi and Patrinos, 1995; World Bank, n.d.). Child labor has decreased in the parts of Asia where poverty and fertility rates have decreased.

In Latin America many children who work do so for wages in direct response to issues of poverty. In places like Senegal, India, Ghana, and Indonesia on the other hand, most child laborers work with their families without pay. Child labor afflicts marginalized groups such as indigenous people, and in Latin America, the Afro-Latin Americans. This plight of oppressed populations advances the cause of the privileged classes. In Europe it is immigrant and Roma children who are more likely to work and more likely to work under abusive conditions (Dorman, 2001).

The rapid migration of families from rural to urban environments has increased child labor rates, with new poverty arising from the growing urban population (Siddiqi and Patrinos, 1995). In 1950 only 17% of the population in poor countries lived in urban areas. By 2000 an estimated 40% lived in urban areas. The number continues to rise and is estimated to be 57% by 2025. In urban areas, children work predominantly in the trade and service industries, but also in domestic service, construction, and manufacturing (Human Rights Watch, 2003; Siddiqi and Patrinos, 1995; World Bank, n.d.).

DEFINING THE ISSUE

International conventions that direct national laws and policies on child labor are the United Nations Convention on the Rights of the Child (1989), the International Labour Organisation's (ILO) minimum age conventions, and the Convention on the Worst Forms of Child Labor 182 (1999). In addition to these instruments, ILO Recommendations 146 and 190 present proposals that enhance the previous ones. Interestingly, these international standard-setting instruments do not provide a definition for child labor. Together, however, these instruments discern general instructions for: a) setting a minimum age to enter employment, the parameters for light work, the number of work hours for the age, and the boundaries for defining economic exploitation; b) the occupations, work activities, work conditions, and employment agreements of worst forms of child labor; and c) programs for child laborers, with special attention regarding girls in employment.

These instruments are based on Western understandings of childhood, generating concern in other countries about culturally grounded definitions that view child work and child labor from different perspectives. In most countries child work is viewed as an apprenticeship or other form of training, which prepares children for future occupations. With the changing economic conditions shifting the majority of the population into dire poverty, children are often compelled to supplement the family income. As a consequence, children work more hours for less money, in deplorable work environments, and are subjected to economic and sexual exploitation.

ILO Minimum Age Convention 138 stipulates children's minimum age to enter employment "as the age of completion of compulsory schooling and, in any case, shall not be less than 15 years of age" (ILO, 1999). In countries where the economies and educational facilities are not fully developed, fourteen years is allowed as the minimum work age. Further, the convention stipulates that national laws and policies delineate that children from the ages of thirteen to fifteen years be allowed to do "light work." This means work that is not harmful to children's health or development and that does not hinder their attendance at school or participation in vocational programs or training (ILO, 1999).

The ILO Recommendation 190 of 1999 describes areas and conditions of hazardous work in section II, part 3, entitled "Hazardous Work." This includes work that: a) is abusive physically, psychologically, or sexually; b) is performed under dangerous conditions, including work underground, on water, at great heights, or under confined conditions; c) involves machinery or equipment that is dangerous or heavy; d) is environmentally risky due to potentially hazardous substances, noise, vibrations, or temperatures; or e) involves long or night hours (as cited in Human Rights Watch, 2000). Children worldwide encounter these work conditions on a daily basis. Many continue to be entrapped against their will and/or without their consent.

The worst forms of child labor exist in both wealthy and poor countries and are identified in ILO Convention 182 in article 3:

a) all forms of slavery or practices similar to slavery, such as the sale and trafficking of children, debt bondage and serfdom, and forced or compulsory labor, including forced or compulsory recruitment of children for use in armed conflict; b) the use, procuring or offering of a child for prostitution, for the production of pornography or for pornographic performances; c) the use, procuring or offering of a child for illicit activities, in particular for the production and trafficking of drugs as defined in the relevant international treaties; and d) work which, by its nature or the circumstances in which it is carried out, is likely to harm the health, safety or morals of children. (Human Rights Watch, 2000, pp. 89–90)

Children are involved in a variety of exploitative occupations, jobs, and work activities, often under agreements their parents make with employers. Children are found in occupations such as carpet weaving, cooking, and tailoring. They work at jobs in agriculture, entertainment, the hospitality industry, trading, and light industry. They carry out a multitude of activities such as hauling wood and water, brick making, wrapping cigarettes, domestic chores, and child care. Children work as bonded labor paying back parents' or family loans, or as apprentices working to learn a trade. Some children live and work on the streets in order to survive day to day. They are exploited in the commercial sex industry and engaged in the drug trade. Girls in certain cultures are compelled to take care of household tasks and may drop out of school as early as the fifth grade. In some parts of the world, girls may be forced into early marriage, where they continue to work for the husband's family.

DATA ESTIMATES

To determine child labor estimates, the International Programme on the Elimination of Child Labour, in conjunction with its Statistical Information and Monitoring Programme on Child Labour (IPEC/SIMPOC) (2002), adopted an internationally accepted definition of employment. This definition delineates economic activity as children's paid and unpaid work in the formal and nonformal sectors of rural and urban areas. Although children's employment as maids and domestic workers is considered economic activity, children working in their own households do not fall into this category.

The IPEC/SIMPOC (2002) found that 352 million children ages five to seventeen years were engaged in economic activities in the year 2000. Of these, 211 million were between the ages of five and fourteen years; 73 million were under ten years of age. The Asian-Pacific region had the largest number of children from the ages of five to fourteen years at work, an estimated 127.3 million. In the same age category, sub-Saharan Africans accounted for 48 million. In Latin America and the Caribbean, 17.4 million children were at work. In wealthy countries, including the U.S., it was estimated that there were 2.5 million children at work in the age group of five to fourteen years. Child labor rates are higher in rural areas, where the work is predominantly agrarian; 90 percent of child laborers are engaged in agricultural work. Urbanization and the presence of a female labor force also affect the rates of child labor (Drenovsky, 1992).

The IPEC/SIMPOC (2002) report found that 171 million children are involved in hazardous employment, which translates to 48.5 percent of economically active children. There were 8.4 million engaged in the worst forms of child labor. Since illegal activities such as drug trafficking and the commercial sexual exploitation of children are clandestine in nature, data collection is difficult and estimates are conservative. These estimates do not include children involved in domestic chores, stirring concern among child advocates around the world.

Wealthy Nations

Expanding the definition of economically active children, the numbers in wealthy countries, including the United States (U.S.), New Zealand, Australia, and most of Western Europe, increase dramatically. The work of children has not been eliminated in these countries; this includes those child labor practices considered most abusive. In spite of the high level of participation in school, child employment rates can be high.

In the U.S., child labor means young workers at work. By age fourteen years, 57% of youth are involved in formal or informal paid work; by fifteen years of age it rises to 64% (Dorman, 2001). In Western Europe the employment rates for youth ages fifteen through nineteen range from 5.3% in Belgium to 56.3% in Denmark. The employment rate in Australia is 45.6% and in the United Kingdom it is 52.2%.

Education

Child participation in education increases as the availability and quality of the education improves. It is estimated that 50 to 70 percent of child workers also attend school (World Bank, n.d.). Additionally, childhood education rates are correlated with family income, parent educational level, social class, and gender. Children from the "lower" classes are less likely to receive an education. In some countries families cannot afford to educate all of their children, so they decide which children will attend school and which will work to help support the family.

Gender

While some of the literature indicates that gender does not appear to impact the overall participation in work for children, other literature points to statistical difficulties. This leads to the problems in showing the extent of female involvement in work. Officially, boys in the older age group (fifteen through eighteen years) are more likely to work than girls. When girls work, however, they tend to work longer hours than boys (World Bank, n.d.). Data on female children are underreported for a number of reasons. By fifteen years of age, girls in some regions are given in marriage, especially in many Muslim and traditional cultures (Boyden, 1994); this includes sub-Saharan Africa, where the dominant religion is Islam. When married, girls are considered adults. Also common to many cultures is a cultural norm that identifies girls age fifteen and older as "women." In Nicaragua, for instance, a girl of fifteen years is considered an adult (Hodgkin and Newell, 1998). Further, the involvement of girls in domestic work is not acknowledged as employment (Salazar and Glasinovich, 1996). Three-fifths of girls are involved in domestic chores. By high school age the participation of girls in domestic chores is 91 percent (ILO, 2003). Girls in both rural and urban environments spend significantly more time involved in household labor than boys. This is true even when comparing girls who work with boys who work.

Gender stereotyping and roles result in increased vulnerability and the perpetuation of female poverty (ILO, 2003). In some parts of the world, gender affects educational choices (Bequele and Boyden, 1988). This lack of education and other resources decreases the long-term prospects for employment opportunities. This leaves girls more vulnerable to commercial sexual exploitation. The risk of exploitation faced by girls results from a combination of vulnerabilities including poverty, race, lack of educational and training resources, and no viable employment opportunities (ILO, 2003).

Child prostitution and trafficking are singled out as two of the most abusive forms of child labor (IPEC/SIMPOC, 2002). Unfortunately, accurate statistics are not available. While boys are also vulnerable to sexual exploitation, the vast majority of victims are females (ILO, 2003). The consequences of these forms of child labor are tragic not only in the physical harm to children but also in the emotional abuse inflicted by pimps and captors. Additionally, these children face the severe debilitating consequences of the health risks of HIV/AIDS and other diseases. Child prostitution is a pervasive problem in all nations (IPEC/SIMPOC, 2002).

Child Soldiers

As many as three hundred thousand child soldiers as young as eight years of age have recently been used in at least thirty-three armed conflicts globally. Poverty, isolation, and upheaval contribute to a child's vulnerability. Refugee and orphaned children face perhaps the greatest risk of conscription. Although boys are used more often, girls are also used and face the added danger of rape. These children serve not only in service roles but also in combat. They are at times forced to commit atrocities against family and neighbors, separating them further from a potential future in those environments (Human Rights Watch, 2003).

Global Economy

The economic policies established by Western governments and financial institutions foster the development of global systems in which parents in poorer countries must rely on the labor of children (Seabrook, 1999). Consumers have the power to undermine the use of child laborers in both the agricultural and manufacturing sectors. While there are efforts to label and block the import of goods produced by children, this approach has the potential to create unintended consequences, including the layoff of children who desperately need the money for their own and their family's survival. These children might then be forced into even more hazardous forms of employment.

It is the responsibility of wealthy industrialized nations to question and challenge their position of privilege in the international economy. To bring about a safe transition in the reduction of child labor, consumers play a critical role in the direction of the world economy and its subsequent impact on the labor of children. The wealthy nations, including the U.S., dominate the world economy and carry much of the responsibility to work toward the development of more equitable international trade relations. A shift from the misnamed "free trade policies" to fair trade approaches would provide just opportunities and living wages to workers in poor nations. It would also be more effective in attacking child labor than boycotting isolated imports. Western nations and international lending institutions advocate free trade and neoliberal economic reforms. These structures perpetuate their control and superior economic position while protecting strategic industries (such as steel and agriculture) with tariffs and subsidies. In many cases these policies and international aid only exacerbate the economic challenges of poor nations.

TOWARD THE FUTURE

Globally, the movement against abusive child labor is growing rapidly. Proposed strategies for eliminating child labor are multifaceted, addressing the overlapping issues of poverty reduction, economic development, improved access to education, and ending gendered oppression. The United Nations Children's Fund (UNICEF), International Labour Organisation (ILO), the World Bank, and other children's and human rights groups are working together to develop a strategy to prevent child labor from interfering with the education and childhood of children and from placing children in danger of bonded labor (Human Rights Watch, 2003; Siddiqi and Patrinos, 1995; World Bank, n.d.).

International laws and conventions are establishing new norms. On June 17, 1999, an international convention was established that prohibited the most abusive forms of child labor, including child slavery, bondage, prostitution, pornography, drug trafficking, forced military conscription, and work that is harmful physically and psychologically. This was ILO Convention 182, which calls for a ban on abusive child labor. It was ratified by 132 nations in just three years (ILO, 2003).

The 1989 Convention on the Rights of the Child states that children have the right to be "protected from economic exploitation and from performing any work that is likely to be hazardous or to interfere with the child's education, or to be harmful to the child's health or physical, mental, spiritual, moral or social development" (UNICEF, 1989, Article 32, paragraph 1). The U.S., along with Somalia, are the only two nations that have not ratified the 1989 United Nations Convention on the Rights of the Child.

Most countries have policies and regulations regarding minimum work age and working conditions. They are, however, difficult to enforce. Regulatory and legislative interventions are perhaps the most effective in addressing bonded labor, hazardous working conditions, and child prostitution. Stricter enforcement of laws against bonded child labor and trafficking is a significant component in addressing the abuses encountered by street children.

The path to eliminating child labor in the future requires ongoing, multiple, coordinated strategies. Increasing public awareness, changing norms and values in opposition to abusive child labor, and increasing the education and support of females outside marriage are all critical to permanent change (Siddiqi and Patrinos, 1995; World Bank, n.d.). An increasing role of nongovernmental organizations (NGOs) in raising awareness and supporting social activism can have powerful repercussions in collaboration with the engagement of all media sources.

Support services—such as literacy programs, food and shelter assistance, and other resources—help children and families improve their current conditions and long-term prospects. Support services have been provided particularly for children working in the informal urban sector. They have also been provided in rural areas and for young domestic workers, who are primarily female.

Helping children remain in school decreases the risk of the more abusive forms of child labor, including bonded labor. Reducing the costs of education and making schedules flexible are additional factors in increasing accessibility. Flexible scheduling of school is particularly important in rural areas where children are needed to work in the fields. In addition, increasing the participation of females in education and economic development are recognized as effective strategies in the reduction of abusive child labor.

OVERVIEW OF THE CHAPTERS

The chapters that follow provide an examination of the diverse issues and possible solutions that surface in the examination of child labor through the lenses of fifteen countries, representing four continents. The focus and emphasis of each chapter varies as the issues and needs of the country and region differ. Each examination of child labor is placed within the historical, social, political, and economic context globally and nationally. The book starts with a review of child labor in Bangladesh, which is abysmally poor. This country is home to a myriad of abusive and often deadly child labor practices, including trafficking in children, which is one of the most challenging of child labor issues. The plight of children in the garment industry provides a significant focus for this chapter. In examining Brazil, a country experiencing increasing economic stress, a view is provided of families marginalized economically and physically. Within the context of abject poverty, families are excluded from the "normal" world of work, and the human rights of children are violated.

China's rich agricultural heritage and complex political history are reviewed. This nation's rich history contributes to a child labor landscape that is highly legislated, with numerous regulations and laws, but struggles like many countries with enforcing these laws. Communist China's central planning economy and the Cultural Revolution had major influences on child labor. Abusive child labor in the Dominican Republic has grown as globalization has increased and become responsible for decreasing the jobs and wages available to adults. Children participate in the formal and informal economic systems and work to contribute to the income their families need for survival. Among the most abusive conditions of child labor in the Dominican Republic is the growing commercial sex industry, including sex tourism. The reemergence of child labor in the Republic of Georgia parallels the political and economic shifts following the collapse of the former USSR. The work of children on the streets and farms supplements the income of families struggling with poverty. It also places children at risk for exploitation from abusive child labor. These children are vulnerable to poor health and disadvantaged in education.

Although Guatemala and Honduras are both in Central America, different political circumstances influence each country's unique struggle to combat child labor. The worst forms of child labor in Guatemala are tied to that nation's history of sustained civil and political turmoil along with persistent poverty. Child soldiers and the trafficking of child workers in sex tourism remain serious issues in a nation struggling to survive economically. Historically, many children have worked in Honduras, a highly agricultural country. Across the past few decades, however, there have been marked changes in labor with severe and profound social implications as young girls are lured off farms to work in factories *(maquilas)*.

More children work in India than in any other country. Estimates place the number of working children at 100 to 150 million. A significant number are engaged in bonded labor, a form of servitude that often passes from generation to generation. Political changes, economic instability, poverty, a population shift to the cities, and an influx of foreign refugees have contributed to the increase of child labor in Iran. Some of the worst conditions are found among children weaving carpets under intolerable conditions, with a new and growing population of street children. The pattern of increasing child labor in Mexico follows a pattern typical of Latin America. As poverty has increased, so has child labor. In order to survive, poor families are forced to draw upon all family members to contribute. Free trade policies and the North American Free Trade Agreement (NAFTA), as structured, have exasperated the dilemmas.

A cultural mix of black African, white, Indian, and colored people is the context for child labor in South Africa. The issue is further marked by the lingering effects of apartheid and institutionalized racism. Although apartheid was outlawed in 1994, black African children are still most likely to be caught up in the web of oppressive child labor. The chapter on South Korea illustrates the invisibility of child labor typical of industrialized nations. The prevalence and specific forms of child labor in South Korea are interwoven with the trafficking of women as sex workers in Southeast Asia. Thailand is a poor country with a long history of children in the labor force. Struggling against the cultural belief that children should work to pay back their parents for their support, Thai children are commonly employed as domestic and agricultural workers. In the United States it is assumed that children work in order to make spending money. It is a wealthy country with many resources. Yet child labor, including abusive child labor, continues. The book ends with the chapter on child labor in Zimbabwe. In this nation, child labor is entrenched in the legacy of colonialism, which institutionalized racism. Zimbabwe has a large youth population that cannot be accommodated in the formal workforce. African children and families are hardest hit by poverty, marginalization, and disenfranchisement.

BIBLIOGRAPHY

Archard, D. (1993) *Children: Rights and childhood.* New York: Routledge.

Bequele, A., and J. Boyden. (1988) Working children: Current trends and policy responses. *International Labour Review* 127(2): 153–72.

Boyden, J. (1991) Working children in Lima, Peru. In W. E. Myers, ed. *Protecting working children.* London: Zed Books.

———. (1994) *The relationship between education and child work.* Innocenti Essays No. 9. Florence, Italy: UNICEF International Child Development Centre.

Boyden, J., B. Ling, and W. Myers. (1998) *What works for working children?* Stockholm: UNICEF.

Dorman, P. (2001) *Child labour in the developed economies.* Geneva, Switzerland: International Labour Office.

Drenovsky, C. K. (1992) Children's labor force participation in the world system. *Journal of Comparative Family Studies* 23: 183–95.

Ennew, E. (1994) *Street and working children: A guide to planning.* Development Manual 4. London: Save the Children.

Hodgkin, R., and P. Newell. (1998) *Implementation handbook for the convention on the rights of the child.* New York: UNICEF.

Human Rights Watch. (2000) *Fingers to the bone: United States failure to protect child farmworkers.* New York: Human Rights Watch.

———. (2003) *Child soldiers: Facts about child soldiers.* Retrieved March 24, 2003, from http://www.hrw.org/campaigns/crp/facts.htm.

Images of child labor: Child labor and the global village. (n.d.) Retrieved March 24, 2003, from http://www.childlaborphotoproject.org/childlabor.html.

International Labor Organization. (1999) *Convention No. 182 concerning the prohibition and immediate action for the elimination of the worst forms of child labour.* Geneva, Switzerland: International Labour Office.

———. (2003) *Has your country ratified?* Retrieved June 30, 2003, from http://www.ilo.org/public/english/standards/ipec.

International Programme on the Elimination of Child Labour. (2003a) *Eliminating hazardous child labour step by step.* Geneva, Switzerland: International Labour Office.

———. (2003b) *Good practices: Gender mainstreaming in actions against child labour.* Geneva, Switzerland: International Labour Office.

International Programme on the Elimination of Child Labour/Statistical Information and Monitoring Programme on Child Labour. (2002) *Every child counts: New global estimates on child labour.* Geneva, Switzerland: International Labour Office.

Otis, J., E. M. Pasztor, and E. J. McFadden. (2001) Child labor: A forgotten focus for child welfare. *Child Welfare* 53(5): 611–22.

Salazar, M. C., and W. A. Glasinovich. (1996) *Better schools: Less child work and education in Brazil, Colombia, Ecuador, Guatemala and Peru.* Innocenti Essays No. 7. Florence, Italy: UNICEF International Child Development Centre.

Schlemmer, B., ed. (2000) *The exploited child.* New York: Zed Books.

Seabrook, J. (1999) Reproach of child labor. *Financial Times* (August 24).

Siddiqi, F., and H. Patrinos. (1995) *Child labor: Issues, causes and interventions.* HCOWP 56. Human Capital Development and Operation Policies. World Bank. Retrieved November 27, 2002, from http://www.worldbank.org/html/extdr/hnp/hddflash/workp/wp_00056.html.

UNICEF. (1989) *Convention on the Rights of the Child.* Retrieved June 29, 2003, from http://www.unicef.org/crc/crc.htm.

United Nations. (2002) *Concluding observations of the Committee on the Rights of the Child: Lebanon* (January 2). Retrieved May 14, 2002, from http://www.unhchr.ch/tbs/doc.nsf/3.

World Bank. (n.d.) *Child labor: Issues and directions for the World Bank.* Retrieved June 30, 2003, from http://wbln0018.worldbank.org/HDNet/Hddocs.nsf/0.

1

BANGLADESH

Shelley Feldman and Desi Larson

PROFILE OF BANGLADESH

Bangladesh is among the most fertile countries in the world, with a rich cultural heritage of poets and musicians, and a tradition of struggle. East Bengalis were crucial support for the partition of India in 1947 when it became part of Pakistan. As East Pakistanis, they struggled for its independence in a civil war in 1971. In the popular imagination of many, however, Bangladesh is perhaps better known for its natural tragedies—floods, cyclones, and famines—that shape its agriculture and patterns of rural survival and provide the basis for what former U.S. Secretary of State Henry Kissinger termed "the basket-case of the world." Despite this popular understanding, Bangladesh is recognized for its cultural and social resilience and is credited for its ability to dramatically alter its population growth rate (presently 1.8 percent annually) and its rapid rise as a major site for garment production. Garment production accounts for a major portion of the country's export earnings. It has led to a spectacular expansion of women's urban wage labor force participation and is a site often associated with child labor. In the U.S., the Harkin Bill, the Child Labor Deterrence Act introduced by senator Tom Harkin (D. Iowa), was at least in some measure a response to a concern with child labor in Bangladesh, a country that is a major source of low-end apparel for the American market.

Today Bangladesh remains the eighth-most-populous country in the world, with a current population of almost 133 million, a land area of 55,598 square miles, and a population density of 2,401 per square mile. Forty percent of the population is under the age of fifteen, life expectancy is fifty-nine years, and infant and child mortality stand at 66 per 1,000 and 94 per 1,000, respectively. Reliable estimates put maternal mortality at 377 per 100,000 live births (Bangladesh Maternal Health Services and Maternal Mortality Survey, 2001, cited in USAID, 2003) although Asian Development Bank (ADB) estimates are notably higher, 440 per 100,000 live births (ADB, 2001, p. 7). Bangladesh is one of only four countries in the world where males outnumber females. In 1995–96, sex ratios for rural and urban areas were estimated at 104 and 106 respectively down, from 106 and 129 in 1974 (ADB, 2001, p. 7).

Bangladeshis are predominately Muslim (83 percent), with the remaining population primarily Hindu followed by Christians and tribal groups. The language spoken is Bangla and the most common ethnic identity is Bangladeshi. In 2003, annual per capita income was approximately equal to US$375. The economy is market-based, with the government owning most utilities, transport companies, and large manufacturing and distribution firms. A small elite controls most of the private economy, including the large export processing section, which accounts for most of the country's foreign exchange earnings. A middle class is growing in Bangladesh. Notwithstanding these changes, foreign aid continues to be an important source of national income.

Today Bangladesh has a parliamentary democracy. The prime minister was first elected in 1991 following a broad-based social movement calling for the ouster of Gen. Mohammed Ershad (1981–90). The formal institutions of democracy in Bangladesh function with limited accountability and public input. These forms include a parliament, an active opposition, a free print media, a judiciary, open elections, and the right to free speech. Such democratic institutions and practices follow two decades of military rule, which began in 1975 with the assassination of Sheik Mujibur Rahman, but today remain incomplete with only limited accountability. Human rights, for example, are guaranteed by law but not always protected in practice.

As a predominantly rural country, two major river systems, the Padma (Ganges) and the Jamuna (Brahmaputra), enrich the alluvial soil. Except for the Chittagong Hills, Bangladesh is low-lying, with approximately 6 percent of its total land area permanently under water. Two-thirds of the land experiences flooding, which contributes to soil fertility. However, it often results in the loss of life and accounts for significant losses of crops and property. Marked by mild winters and hot monsoon summers, Bangladeshis also endure periodic droughts and cyclones. Such dramatic changes in weather are especially devastating for the rural poor and landless, who are among the least able to fight against the high prevalence of waterborne diseases, water pollution, groundwater contamination by naturally occurring arsenic, soil degradation and erosion, and deforestation.

Despite these constraints, Bangladesh has been able to dramatically increase crop yields from one to often three cycles per year, particularly in the production of its staple food, rice. Other primary agricultural products include jute, sugarcane, tobacco, and tea, which complement reserves of natural gas, some coal and petroleum, and an industrial sector focused on jute, textiles, cement, ceramic, and garment manufacturing. Significantly, the country renewed its export regime following the dramatic decline of the world market for jute in the early 1980s. A 1982 industrialization policy contributed to the rapid development and expansion of garment manufacturing and fish production, two commodities that account for the majority of foreign currency earnings. In addition to apparel and fish production, other industries include cotton textiles, jute, and tea processing. Almost two-thirds (63%) of the employed population work in agriculture, 26% work in services, and 11% work in industry.

Changes in the social and political economy of Bangladesh have had contradictory effects on women. In some respects women have been beneficiaries of new labor market opportunities, the diversification of rural and urban production, the increase in education, health, and nutritional resources, and NGO investments. These have led to women's expanding participation in the wage economy, in the public sector, and in social and political decision-making as well as in the use of social services. A contributor to rural women's economic power has been their increased access to microcredit. Because of the rapid growth of the garment industry over the last two decades, employment opportunities have increased faster for women than for men. These patterns are reported mostly in the capital city of Dhaka and the port city of Chittagong. Today, approximately 85% of the 1.6 million garment sector workers are women. But in other wage-earning jobs, women continue to be grossly underrepresented. Moreover, women continue to have less access to education than men. For instance, the literacy rate for men is approximately 52% while for women it remains at 29% despite recent improvements in girls' rates of enrollment. In 2003 it is estimated that approximately 50% of all school students were female.

OVERVIEW OF CHILD LABOR

Bangladesh's economy increasingly relies on the garment industry and the export of manpower for its foreign currency earnings. Currently it is one of the largest apparel exporters in the world; it is the sixth-largest exporter to the U.S. and the fifth-largest to the European Union. Bangladesh exports labor to Saudi Arabia, Kuwait, the UAE, Oman, Qatar, and Malaysia. In 1998–99 alone the country earned an estimated $1.71 billion in remittance income. In addition to contributing to foreign exchange earnings, the export of labor also contributes to reducing the demand for employment. This is especially important in a context where unemployment is estimated to account for 35% of the labor force (Central Intelligence Agency [CIA], 2002). In 2001, 64.1 million people were estimated to be unemployed (CIA, 2002).

Bangladesh's child labor force "accounts for approximately 5 percent of the world's working child population under age 14" (Skolnik, Hiraoka, and Hussain, 2000). Of children fifteen years of age and under, 12% are in the Bangladesh labor force. Of all children five through fourteen years of age, 18% are active in the labor force. This includes an estimated 10,000 to 30,000 children in Bangladesh's garment factories alone. While illegal child labor in export industries has received considerable attention in recent years, since the passage of the Harkin Bill, most child laborers work in agriculture and domestic service. These parts of the economy are less visible to public scrutiny and are usually unregulated, and because production is often carried out on individual land holdings, it is difficult to monitor.

Child labor can take a variety of forms. These forms include bonded labor, quasi-slavery, or a feudal relationship. For example, parents who are in-debted to another person might bond their children to them in order to repay the debt. According to the International Labour Organisation (ILO) and UNICEF, child labor can include those who work below a certain age, those who work too many hours, or those who perform the kind of work that imposes excessive physical, social, and/or psychological strains on children in ways that hamper development.

Bangladesh has a tradition of legal codes that prohibit child labor even though such practices continue to occur. This is because some families de-pend on their children to contribute to family income. In families unable to provide food, clothing, and shelter for their offspring, children may be of-fered as domestic servants, child-minders (ayahs), or agricultural workers to other families or persons. These children do not receive wages but may be provided the means for their own subsistence. In other cases, especially where agriculture and home-based production are critical sources of family income, children may be forced to work long hours in these enterprises without recompense. Under these conditions, a family's reliance on child labor may take priority over their children attending school. In still other cases, children are stolen, marketed or trafficked as laborers, entertainers, or prostitutes, and often taken to other countries where they have few pro-tections or resources to manage their return.

Vignette

Shonali is a quiet and serious twelve-year-old who lives with her family in Shibpur, on the outskirts of Dhaka, the capital city of Bangladesh. Her father is a ricksha driver and leaves their small one-room home before the sun rises each morning. Sometimes he works late through the night as well. Shonali's mother has been ill since her youngest brother was born last year. Everything in their lives got worse after her sister Meena died at twelve years of age in a big fire at the garment factory where both Shonali and Meena worked. At the factory they made about 1,200 taka a month, which is about US$.86

a day or US$5.15 a week, working 8:00 A.M. to 8:00 P.M. each day six or seven days a week.

Shonali relives her experience of the fire over and over. The fire broke out on the top floor of the factory building and spread quickly. It was hard to think. Shonali hadn't seen Meena since they had arrived for work early that morning. It was late in the evening, and Shonali was working on the first floor while Meena was on the top floor. They worked sewing sweaters for export to a company in Europe. When the fire broke out, the building quickly filled with smoke. Everyone around her started choking and panicking. It was pitch dark since the electricity and lights went off. In the darkness everyone was screaming and ran for the exit door, but it was locked. The workers, all women and girls, were locked in. As it got hotter and smokier in the factory, some women jumped to their deaths from the fourth floor. Before it was over, hundreds were injured and at least fifty people died. Most were girls in their teens. Among the dead were five girls ages ten through twelve, and three were fourteen years old.

HISTORY OF CHILD LABOR

Bangladesh is a very young country that has faced problems similar to India's. As in most dominantly agricultural countries, children have historically worked alongside their parents and extended family members on farms, in fishing, and in trades. There is also a long history of children working as domestic servants and in light manufacturing. In its broadest terms, child labor has been an accepted practice. It has long been a response to severe poverty.

CHILD LABOR TODAY

In Bangladesh, some conditions of poverty are so extreme that many children work because of their family's economic status (Skolnik et al., 2000). The Bangladesh Bureau of Statistics (BBS) estimated that there were 5.7 million children from the ages of ten through fourteen who worked during the 1990s. Other estimates run even higher. In addition to working in the garment industry, children can be found working as brick chippers, construction workers, domestic servants, and tea stall servers (International Labour Organisation, 1998). Children drive rickshas, carry goods for shoppers at markets, roll cigarettes, work in shrimp processing, and are exposed to hazardous conditions in the leather industry.

POLITICAL VIEWS AND PUBLIC POLICIES

As Siddiqi and Patrinos (1995) point out, the gap between compulsory education age and minimum work age in Bangladesh is problematic. This is because children are required to be in school only until age ten, but then are legally excluded from employment until after the age fourteen.

Numerous laws prohibit child labor. Children under fourteen years old are prohibited from working in factories by the Factories Act. In commercial sites, the Shops and Establishments Act prohibits the employment of children younger than twelve. These laws establish inspection mechanisms against forced labor but, due to scarce resources, they are not consistently enforced. For children under the age of fifteen, the Employment of Children Act prohibits work in railways and ports. Prohibitions of child labor laws notwithstanding, such laws are rarely enforced outside of the export garment sector and, even when enforced, penalties for child labor violations are nominal. Along with ineffective law enforcement, the Ministry of Labor is significantly understaffed, with less than 110 inspectors responsible for monitoring 180,000 registered factories and establishments. Such a lack of staff support makes it impossible to ensure the enforcement of labor laws to protect the more than 1.5 million workers.

While the Factories Act is comprehensive in establishing occupational health and safety standards, the lack of enforcement and only limited penalties for their abridgement means that employers often choose to ignore the law. Similarly, many fire safety codes exist but are regularly violated, including when factories are located in inappropriate structures or industrial sites or when building access or exit is constrained. This has been a consistent problem in garment factories where doors are locked or blocked in order to control workers' movements. As a consequence, numerous lives have been lost to fires because doors have been locked and workers could not escape. While Bangladesh's Constitution prohibits forced or bonded child labor, locking doors and requiring women to work overtime to meet a production deadline continue to shape conditions in the garment sector.

For people eighteen years and over, prostitution is legal only with government certification. However, this minimum age requirement is ignored by law enforcement, and those who employ child prostitutes are rarely prosecuted. Large numbers of child prostitutes can be found working across the country in brothels. Moreover, despite the fact that trafficking for purposes of prostitution carries penalties varying from a ten-year prison sentence to the death penalty, police and local authorities can be easily bribed. Authorities too frequently ignore trafficking in women and children. Girls who are forced to migrate against their will end up in the sex trade. Some are coerced to urban areas as domestic workers or as illegal child laborers in the industrial sector. For these girls, returning to their places of origin is often not possible given the associated reputation, even if false, and harassment that can accompany females who take off on their own, whether through coercion or not.

It is worth noting that Bangladesh is a signatory to most international human rights conventions, including the Child Rights Convention and

International Labor Organization Convention 182 against the worst forms of child labor. Eight laws related to child labor are on the books, however, these have not yet been implemented, and no child labor cases have been filed.

Trafficking of people from Bangladesh is not new, as the movement of kidnapped or bonded laborers taken by force or coerced has been going on since well before the turn of the century. Contemporary understandings of trafficking, however, focus more narrowly on young women, girls, and young men who are kidnapped or recruited under false pretexts and forced or coerced into labor. An estimated 10,000 to 20,000 Bangladeshi women and children are trafficked each year to major cities in India, Pakistan, and the Middle East. They end up as laborers in the sex trade, as domestic workers, and as camel jockeys and beggars (Global March against Child Labour, 2003; U.S. Department of State, 2003). Estimates place as many as a thousand underage South Asian camel jockeys working in the United Arab Emirates. While many come from Pakistan and India, increasing numbers are coming from Bangladesh. While many of these young boys have been kidnapped for this kind of work, others work with the knowledge that their parents may have received up to US$200 (Taka 10,000) for their labor. In recent history, those who work as domestic servants are increasingly found to do so in conditions that resemble servitude. Many suffer physical abuse and, in some cases, even death. A 2001 study of forms of violence against domestic workers found that seven children were tortured, three died from physical torture, two were raped, and nineteen were victimized in other ways (U.S. Department of State, 2003).

Women and children are lured into prostitution and other forms of forced servitude by promises of good jobs or marriage. Women and children who live in persistent poverty and destitution and those who live without a family support system, like orphans and widows, are easy prey to the seduction of traffickers. Unfortunately, regulations, if they exist, are only weakly enforced. Illegal border crossing to support trafficking is easier around the cities of Jessore and Benapole, where border monitoring is lax (Global March against Child Labour, 2003). For these reasons, the repugnant practices of child abandonment, kidnapping, and trafficking have become increasingly serious and pervasive during the past few decades.

The age of most trafficked women and girls ranges from seven through twenty-four years. The Annual Report of the Lawyers for Human Rights and Legal Aid, Pakistan (1991) revealed that estimates of about 200,000 young women and girls have been trafficked to Pakistan alone, and continue at the rate of 200 to 400 women per month; most end up in prostitution, as do those trafficked to brothels in Kolkata, Mumbai, and Goa. Figures from the Centre for Women and Children Studies in Bangladesh (CWCS) confirm similar patterns; most trafficked boys are under the age of ten while most trafficked girls range from eleven through sixteen years old. While international trafficking in children carries severe penalties, few perpetrators have been punished.

The child labor issue that received considerable national press during the 1990s was the Harkin Bill, which aimed to restrict the import of goods made by child labor into the U.S. This issue shook up Bangladesh's garment industry and precipitated, in 1994, the Labor Law, which consolidated and superseded a series of previous laws. However, government efforts to implement labor reforms were irregular at best. In 1993, Bangladesh garment industry exports were worth over $1.2 billion, accounting for over half of the country's total exports. Half of these exports went to the U.S., which meant that the Harkin Bill was a serious threat not only to garment manufacturers, but to the foreign exchange earnings of the country. At this time it was estimated that fifty thousand children fourteen and younger were working in the garment industry. After the bill was introduced, many mill owners were reported to ban child employees. The Bangladesh government, Bangladesh Garment Manufacturers and Exporters Association (BGMEA), the International Labour Organisation, the United Nations International Children's Emergency Fund, and other international agencies, including NGOs, sought alternatives in education and training for children displaced by the industry's move to comply with the provisions of the Harkin Bill (International Labour Organisation, 1998). The BGMEA began inspections of factories as part of the effort to eliminate child labor in the garment industry. During one year the team found seventy-one member factories employing a total of one hundred and fifty-five children among the 3,340 garment factories they inspected. "According to the ICFTU, there was a significant reduction of child labor in the garment industry; while 43 percent of exporting factories used child labor in 1995, by 2001, the figure had fallen 5 percent. The BGMEA fined each factory about U.S. $100 (Taka 5700). Additionally, former child employees were offered a small monthly stipend to help replace their lost income while attending UNICEF-sponsored schools" (Economic Research Institute, 2003).

SOCIAL VIEWS, CUSTOMS, AND PRACTICES

In poor agricultural countries such as Bangladesh, child labor remains a critical source of income for many poor families despite government efforts to combat poverty through education, health, and nutrition. Government investment in the social services sector, although modest, has been augmented by the work of nongovernmental organizations (NGOs) since the 1970s. For example, one of the country's largest NGOs is the Bangladesh Rural Advancement Committee (BRAC). Providing primary education to more than 1.2 million children, BRAC's efforts have combined with those of numerous other NGOs to support approximately 70 percent of all children who successfully complete grade five. And, even though primary education for children six through ten years of age has been mandatory since 1991, an estimated 20 percent of all children in this age group have yet to attend school. Of those who do attend, conditions in the schools and the resources available for school programs are deplorable. Moreover, because school construction fell behind population growth decades ago, most schools run two shifts to accommodate more students, most rural teachers are inadequately trained and difficult to recruit because of very low salaries, and many are not sufficiently motivated to provide regular and consistent opportunities for rural children. In addition, to increase girls' school attendance, the government has organized a Food-for-Education program to provide food subsidies for families that send their daughters to primary school.

In 1990, 16.7 million children were enrolled in primary school, 77% of boys and 66% of girls of the total number of primary school–age children. This reflects a decline in gender differences in school attendance, a decrease from 22% in 1985 to 3% at the end of the 1990s (ADB 2001). While 42.5% of rural and 53.6% of urban girls attend school, only 12% of girls were enrolled in secondary school in 1996 (UNESCO 2000). Structural gender inequalities are perhaps most pronounced in women's participation in postgraduate, college, and university training.

Most noteworthy about education statistics are the increases in women's literacy rates over time. In 1961 female literacy stood at 16.0% and reached 35.1% by 1996. The rate of illiteracy among women over fifteen, however, remains at 72.2%, one of the highest official rates in the world (UNESCO 2000). The dramatic rise in female literacy is due largely to NGO support, particularly the Bangladesh Rural Advancement Committee's Non-Formal Primary Education Program, introduced in 1985, that provides flexible learning hours and competitive scholarships for girls. Beginning with 22 experimental schools, the program now exceeds 34,000 and serves over 1.1 million students, 70% of which are girls. BRAC teachers are among the most educated village dwellers, with at least nine years of schooling, and presently 97% of all BRAC teachers are women. With women teachers as role models, each year almost 90% of the students who graduate from BRAC schools attend formal schools. Since the mid-1990s, the education sector has developed numerous partnerships with other NGOs, and this too contributes to improving both rural and urban women's access to and participation in literacy training.

THE FUTURE OF CHILD LABOR

Child labor in Bangladesh is a complex and multifaceted issue shaped by cultural practices that are associated with the value of women and children. It is also shaped by poverty and economic need on the one hand and the demand for cheap labor on the other. The ramifications of child labor in Bangladesh are local and global. In response to this complexity, the responses to the issue have been varied. Globally, some organizations and governments focus on forbidding products made by children. This, however, can have a devastating effect on the economy of Bangladesh.

Recently progress has been made addressing the trafficking of children. The government of Bangladesh and many NGOs have developed a plan of action to address the trafficking issue regionally (U.S. Department of State, 2003). Part of this plan includes promoting economic growth, which would include increased access to education and decreased abusive child labor.

In 2000 the government of Bangladesh and the Norwegian government aid organization NORAD developed an infrastructure for addressing trafficking of children. A goal of the project was to increase the government's involvement in arresting and prosecuting traffickers. This project also increased shelter capacity and rehabilitation programs for children rescued from trafficking.

Many NGOs and community-based organizations in Bangladesh are using multiple methods in various combinations to eliminate child trafficking. These methods include: prevention efforts, research, data collection, documentation, advocacy, creating awareness, networking, cross-border collaboration, legal enforcement, rescue, rehabilitation, reintegration, income generation, low-interest loan programs, vocational training, and legislative reform. Action against Trafficking and Sexual Exploitation of Children (ATSEC), a national antitrafficking network, has launched several antitrafficking activities. These activities included bringing NGOs and government entities into partnership, establishing a resource center to disseminate data on the subject, and providing technical support to grassroots NGOs. The program has developed and tested materials used for a culturally sensitive national multimedia campaign around prevention and awareness regarding child trafficking. ATSEC has aggressively worked to increase public awareness in all areas by using diverse strategies (ATSEC, 2003).

Another grassroots NGO, the Bangladesh National Women's Lawyers Association (BNWLA), has also worked to raise awareness, particularly for poor people. In addition to providing legal assistance to victims and legal action against traffickers, BNWLA operates a shelter home where trafficked women and children received health care, counseling, and training. The Centre for Women and Children Studies in Bangladesh (CWCS) monitors trafficking across Bangladesh, conducts meetings to educate the public, and teaches police about of the rights of women and children. These sorts of efforts along with frequent press coverage are raising the public awareness of trafficking in Bangladesh.

Another response to the issue of child labor has been increased education and vocational training for poor children. One example of this is the World

Bank's Underprivileged Children's Education Program (UCEP), established in 1972. UNICEF similarly provides education to 350,000 children working in urban slum areas. In collaboration with the government of Bangladesh, NGOs, some trade unions, and the ILO's International Programme on the Elimination of Child Labor (IPEC) are working to increase access to education for 6,000 children. For these children, IPEC does not focus on removing them from work, but rather is focused on seeing that these children, who work in hazardous settings, have access to education. The IPEC project has focused primarily on children working in the cigarette *(beedi)* rolling industry, construction, leather tanneries, match factories, and the domestic work sector. The ILO has contracted with twenty-four NGOs to monitor child labor from community resource centers. Of working children, so far over 18,000 are attending nonformal education classes and 2,000 have been mainstreamed to formal schools. Additionally, the success of these collaborative efforts can be seen in 1,681 children who have been withdrawn from hazardous work, and six *beedi* factories signing memoranda of understanding with local communities, identifying themselves as "child labor free."

Today Bangladesh is seeing growing unrest in the region, with the politicization of religious fundamentalism giving rise to the increased voice of religious parties in the democratic process. This has been institutionalized through alliances with secular parties that have solidified constitutional changes that constrain women's behavior in ways that are in conflict with women's growing need for economic and social participation. Such political alliances and the criminalization of the political process have led to a failure to provide and implement policies and programs that would ensure social justice and rights for women. As well, secular parties and public discourse has increasingly infused religious symbolism that inhibits women's sense of economic and social security as they work, attend school, or visit the marketplace. This new symbolic environment has led parents to circumscribe daughters' behavior, not out of belief but out of fear, and has led women to fear the loss of state protection of their rights.

Because the prevalence of child labor in Bangladesh is intricately tied to the plight of women, some see that effective strategies addressing child labor would also include decreasing violence against women, including family violence; curbing class inequalities; strengthening rural economic security; controlled urbanization with necessary infrastructural support to manage the increasing demands of housing, sanitation, and education; and revising the Multi-Fiber Agreement, which threatens to reduce Bangladeshi garment exports to the U.S., her largest market, and in turn reduce the demand for women garment workers. They believe that without these changes, the lives of rural and urban women will remain insecure in a context where opportunities for participation and voice have been hard-won victories.

CONCLUSION

Western governments and financial institutions shoulder a responsibility for fostering development models that make child labor a necessity for many families in poor countries. In the example of Bangladesh the garment industry earns 70 percent of the country's hard currency and benefits from the cheap labor of it's workers. This means many families are left dependent on child labor because the industry fails to provide all its workers with sufficient income. This creates contradiction demands on families, especially those in need of resources sufficient for subsistence.

BIBLIOGRAPHY

Action against Trafficking and Sexual Exploitation of Children (ATSEC). (2003) Home Page. Retrieved June 27, 2003, from http://www.atsecbangladesh chapter.fws1.com/atsecbangladeshchapter/index.html.

Asian Development Bank (ADB). (2001) *Women in Bangladesh: Country Briefing Paper.* http://www/adb.org/Documents/Books/Countr...ng_Papers/Women_in_ Bangladesh/default.asp.

Boyden, Jo, Birgitta Ling, William and Myers. (1998) *What works for working children?* Florence, Italy: UNICEF ICDC.

Central Intelligence Agency. (2002) *Bangladesh: The World Factbook.* Retrieved June 27, 2003, from http://www.cia.gov/cia/publications/factbook/geos/ bg.html.

DeGregori, Thomas. (2002) *Child labor or child prostitution?* Washington, D.C.: Cato Institute. http://www.cato.org/dailys/10-08-02.html.

Economic Research Institute. (2003) Bangladesh: Compensation & Benefit Legislation. Redmond, Washington: Economic Research Institute. Retrieved June 27, 2003, from http://www.erieri.com/freedata/hrcodes/index.htm?bangladesh.htm.

Global March against Child Labour. (2003) Worst forms of child labor data: Bangladesh. Retrieved June 27, 2003, from http://www.globalmarch.org/ worstformsreport/world/bangladesh.html.

International Labour Organisation. (1998) Remarks of Tom Harkin, senator, Iowa. *Teach-In on Child Labor.* Retreived May 27, 2003, from http://us.ilo.org/ teachin/harkin.html.

National Labor Committee. (2001) *Factory fire in Bangladesh kills fifty-one.* New York: National Labor Committee. Retrieved June 27, 2003, from http: //www.nlcnet.org/bangladesh/0401Chowdhury/main.htm.

Siddiqi, F., and H. Patrinos. (1995) *Child labor: Issues, causes and interventions.* HCOWP 56. Human Capital Development and Operation Policies. World Bank. Accessed November 27, 2002, from http://www.worldbank.org/html/ extdr/hnp/hddflash/workp/wp_00056.html.

Skolnik, R., R. Hiraoka, and Z. Hussain. (2000) *Child Labor.* World Bank. http: //lnweb18.worldbank.org/sar/sa.nsf/Attachments/Child+Labor+in+SA/$File/ CLNote.pdf.

Sweatshops and child labor web page. http://www.rcan.org/schools/sweat.html.

United Nations Educational, Scientific and Cultural Organization (UNESCO). (2000)
     Women and Girls: Education, not Discrimination! Accessed July 13, 2004
     from (http://www.unesco.org/education/.
USAID. (2003) Bangladesh Population and Health. Retrieved June 30, 2003, from
     http://www.usaid.gov/bd/pop.html.
U.S. Department of State. (2003) *Country Reports on Human Rights Practices:
     Bangladesh.* Bureau of Democracy, Human Rights, and Labor, Washington,
     D.C. http://www.state.gov/g/drl/rls/hrrpt/18309.htm.

2

BRAZIL

Elizabeth KimJin Traver

PROFILE OF BRAZIL

Following three centuries under the rule of Portugal, Brazil became an independent nation on September 7, 1822. With the greatest land area and the most people of any South American country, the Federative Republic of Brazil has overcome more than half a century of military conflict in the governance of the country. Abundant with vast natural resources and a massive labor pool, Brazil leads South America in economic power.

The native South American peoples originally thrived in what is now Brazil, including the Arawak and Carib groups in the north and the Tupí-Guaraní in the east and Amazon River valley. These groups were mostly seminomadic. Their existence came from hunting and gathering and simple agriculture. Up until the late twentieth century, people in the very remote areas of the interior maintained traditional ways of life.

At the time of the Europeans' arrival in Brazil in 1500, it is estimated that one thousand indigenous nations existed comprising 3 to 4 million people. Since the Europeans' arrival, scholars have identified that 85 percent of native languages have become extinct.

The Brazilian Social-Economic Institute (ISA) recently released a study of the indigenous people. According to this study, in 2000, the population of indigenous groups grew by 3.5 percent. Among 216 indigenous nations, there were about 350,000 persons. Today Brazil's indigenous peoples are threatened by disease, poor health care, loss of native culture, illegal mining on indigenous lands, road construction, and deforestation.

Occupied at different periods and in different regions by the Portuguese, French, Dutch, and Spanish, economic expansion southward was stimulated by a hunt for mineral wealth (gold and diamonds). Various treaties served the colonial occupations to retain the natural resources. The successful revolution, which freed Brazil from Portuguese rule, ushered in a series of autocratic imperial rulers of Brazil. In 1889 a military revolt followed the emancipation of all slaves. Forcing an abdication of the emperor, a republic was proclaimed along with reforms such as the separation of church and state. Due to the lack of national democratic traditions, political turmoil, revolts and uprisings, military rule, and dictatorships marked the first century of the new republic.

Today Brazil is a constitutional federal republic. Its twenty-six states and the federal district are administered from the capital, Brasilia. Beginning in 2003, Brazil elected the country's foremost labor leader and founder of the Workers Party, President Luis Ignacio da Silva (Lula). His vice president is José Alencar. Brazil has a bicameral National Congress (Congresso Nacional) that consists of the Federal Senate (Senado Federal) and the Chamber of Deputies (Camara dos Deputados). The Senado Federal has 81 seats, for three members from each state and the federal district, elected by majority vote to serve staggered eight-year terms; the Camara dos Deputados has 513 seats, for members who are elected by proportional representation, to serve four-year terms. The last important administrative branch is the Supreme Federal Tribunal, whose eleven ministers are appointed by the president and confirmed by the Senate (all judges are appointed for life). Brazil has many major political parties.

The country's population, approximately 172.8 million, lives on 3,265,076 square miles, an area larger than the continental United States (U.S.). Argentina, Bolivia, Colombia, French Guiana, Guyana, Paraguay, Peru, Suriname, Uruguay, and Venezuela are all immediate neighbors bordering Brazil. Brazil's climate is mostly tropical and more temperate in the south. Brazil's land is characterized by plains, hills, mountains, and an ocean coastline.

Brazil's people are heterogeneous. In the population today, 55% are white, with Portuguese, German, Italian, Spanish, or Polish heritage. People who are mixed white and black make up 38% of the population, black 6%, and other heritages, including Japanese, Arab, and Amerindian, 1%. Portuguese is the official language, while many citizens also speak Spanish, English, or French. In terms of faith traditions, 76% of the population identify as Roman Catholic, 11% as Protestant, and 13% as other.

Brazil has a diversified open market economy that dominates South America. Agriculture accounts for 7% of gross domestic product (GDP), mining and manufacturing for 36%, and services for 57%. Brazil is expanding its presence globally, exporting both manufactured and primary goods. Principal exports include iron ore, coffee, airplanes, and soybeans. Brazil is the world's largest producer and exporter of coffee and orange juice, second in soybeans.

Amidst Brazil's thriving trade, unequal income distribution is a critical problem. Distributions of income are dramatically skewed. Government statistics reported that in 2000, the poorest half received only 10% of the national income while the richest tenth received 48%.

OVERVIEW OF CHILD LABOR

In a country of 172.8 million people, 59.9 million are under the age of eighteen. Statistics about the number of working children in Brazil are uneven and vary according to the reporting source and the years under discussion. According to government figures released in 1999 and confirmed by UNICEF, the number of child laborers has decreased by over 26 percent since 1993, while the number of children attending school has increased. The U.S. Department of State reported that more than 2.9 million children under the age of fifteen years worked in 1999; of those children, 583,000 were between five and nine years old. The International Labour Organisation (ILO) reports that 7.5 million children between ten and seventeen years old work in Brazil, of whom 2 million are under fourteen years. The Brazilian Institute of Geography and Statistics reports that child workers between eleven and fourteen years make up approximately 11.6 percent of the total labor force. Of all child workers, 3.5 million children are under fourteen years. Given the varying numbers, there is little doubt as to the prevalence of child labor in Brazil. As with all statistics reporting on child labor, numbers are underestimated due to the difficulty in obtaining accurate counts of exploitation.

In rural areas, many children are forced to work with their parents in cane fields, cutting hemp, or feeding wood into charcoal ovens. Family survival requires children's work. However, accidents and unhealthy working conditions are common. Other industries where child labor is used include leather processing, gold and tin mining, distilleries, plastics, handicrafts, electronics, and on tea plantations.

Brazil struggles with all the worst forms of child labor: child slavery, child trafficking, child prostitution and pornography, child crime, child domestic servants, and other hazardous forms. Of these forms, Brazil has one of the worst child prostitution problems in the world and is a favored destination for pedophile sex tourists from Europe and the U.S. In the charcoal industry, children are victims of forced labor and debt-bonded labor. In commercial agriculture, sugarcane growers illegally use children ranging from seven to seventeen years of age to cut cane with machetes. Cultivators of hemp in the northeast and orange growers depend upon illegal child labor. Children also are found in the mining and logging industries in the Amazon region. Children still work in the shoe industry despite government and industry efforts to eliminate child labor.

Poverty, experienced by more than 40 million needy or abandoned Brazilian children and adolescents, increases the potential for sexual exploitation of children. According to the government's Institute for Applied Economic Research, in 1998 approximately 800,000 girls between the ages of ten and seventeen years worked as domestic servants. While there are no reliable figures on the number of street children and child beggars nationwide, estimates put the numbers at 30,000 in Rio de Janeiro, 16,000 in Salvador, and 12,000 in Sao Paulo. Increasingly, children pick through urban trash dumps to generate income for their families. UNICEF estimates the number to be 50,000.

Vignette

Mariângela and her family live near the dump located on the periphery of the city. They are among the hundreds of people who live around and work on the dump. Men, women, children, and adolescents share the workspace with animals (oxen, cows, pigs, and black vultures) in a cruel and insane dispute for survival. Mariângela and her family are among those who are considered by Brazilian society to be at the bottom rungs of the social hierarchy. She has never known a permanent home in spite of government efforts to relocate the dump's shanties.

Mariângela, her brother Félix, and her parents earn less than twenty reals (R$20.00, about US$7.00) each week. Her family competes with the other dump-pickers for the most highly valued types of garbage, which are perishable items or food. Competition is fierce for these items. Although they are learning quickly, ten-year-old Mariângela and nine-year-old Félix find it difficult to compete with older, more experienced children and adolescents. Usually they have to settle for less valuable garbage such as paper, cardboard, metal, glass, rubber, and wood. The children use pitchforks to dig through the dumps and uncover items to sell. Mariângela's nasty scar running the length of her left arm reminds her of a painful fight with other dump-pickers over one bag of food. She has learned to let the older and stronger children have their way—until she is older.

As difficult as the work is, her family prefers working the dump to other options because it gives them a sense of independence. Although, like other children her age, she dreams of having a job in an office when she grows up, since neither Mariângela or Félix are able to attend school, this remains more a dream than a reality.

Mariângela's parents hearts break as they watch their children pick through the dump day after day. Sometimes they wish they were never born. Struggling to hold onto a fragile dignity of performing honest work, the parents dream of a life for their children that is far removed from their present reality.

HISTORY OF CHILD LABOR

In Brazil, the forms of child labor in industrial sectors commonly associated with Dickens' England began at the turn of the nineteenth century and continued through to the 1930s (Alvim, 2000). Throughout the country, conditions emerged under which children were turned into premature adults, into "free" workers. During that period, "underage workers" became a legal category structured through various bills presented before the Chamber of Deputies. Characteristic of these bills was the assumption of work as a panacea for poor children and adolescents struggling to escape crime and marginality. The factory's superior environment over the disorganized and lawless world of the streets held many benefits for the newly identified social misfits called "street children." These environments helped poor children increase their family's income and acted as schools for labor.

A succession of such bills during the 1910s and 1920s culminated in the drafting of the labor-specific section of the 1927 Minors' Code. This act established minors as a legally recognized group and allowed legal action to be brought on behalf of children and adolescents in "irregular situations." Specifically, the Minors' Code (Decree 1794; 12 October 1927) set a minimum age of fourteen years for work in factories, shipyards, mines or any other underground activities, quarries, workshops, and their outbuildings. However, conflicts arose between employers and judges over how "irregular situations" were defined or, more specifically, how child labor was defined. This code struggled to support what appeared to be opposing values: the cultural value of children's needs to be given protection at work, and the value of work as a lesser evil than the danger of delinquency.

From 1930–43, the judges' interpretations of the code resulted in the criminalization of poor children. Between 1943–60, the code was used mainly for cases of delinquency. It was the peak period for institutional homes. At this time, criticisms of the system began to arise. From 1964–90 the institutional homes were faced with mounting criticism from advocates of the rights of poor children. Government struggled to address the welfare of poor children under national security laws that treated destitution with detention.

"Street children" were recognized as a social category in the late 1980s by representatives from UNICEF and the Social Services Bureau of the Department of Health. They had been previously referred to as *menores*, but that legal term held derogatory meanings left over from the 1950s. To Brazilians the word *menor* meant poverty and above all delinquency, a false meaning reinforced by the press. As a result, these representatives attempted to change society's negative views of street children. Social workers from government and nongovernmental organizations collaborated to develop new initiatives and approaches in opposition to the traditional approaches of internment, which used state homes for both protection and punishment of street children.

The Children and Adolescents Act of 1990 was the outcome of a major social movement to redemocratize the country. The general underlying principles of the act—based on the U.N. tenet of full protection—were defined when Brazil's constitution was reformed in 1988. With the emergence of activists and educators working with the movements for the protection of children and adolescents within new institutions, child labor has emerged as a social problem in the Brazilian social consciousness.

CHILD LABOR TODAY

Within Brazilian society, the social problems of marginalized families and child labor surface in the violation of human rights, especially of the violation of the human rights of children. This picture of social exclusion emerges within the context of abject poverty, which in Brazil is growing and acquiring greater visibility. These excluded ones are at the focal point of socioeconomic questions that emphasize, construct, and marginalize whole groups of people. Too many families are excluded from the normal world of work. These families do not possess the skills required by the new demands of the market and have become economically inessential.

Millions of children in Brazil continue to suffer as the immediate consequence of their families' poverty. Children must work to survive and therefore fail to get an education. Brazil has free and compulsory education for children between the ages of seven and fourteen years. Education is available in all parts of the country, although not all children attend school regularly. In spite of increasing enrollment, 1.1 million children between seven and fourteen years do not attend school (U.S. Department of State, 2002).

Brazilian law prohibits racial discrimination. However, Afro-Brazilians frequently encounter discrimination. The Institute of Applied Statistics (IPEA) reports that citizens of African descent make up 60 percent of the poorest segment of society and receive 7 percent of the national income. Studies also have shown that Afro-Brazilians are grossly overrepresented in rates of police torture, child labor, and illiteracy.

In Brazil, child labor refers to any work, paid or unpaid, for at least one hour per week, and any type of labor is illegal for children under fourteen. Current information on child labor in Brazil comes from the 1996 Brazilian national household surveys, called *Pesquisa Nacional por Amostragem a Domicilio (PNAD)*, which are conducted by Instituto Brasileiro de Geografia e Estatística (IBGE), the Brazilian census bureau. It is an annual labor force survey similar to the current population survey in the United States. In 1996, *PNAD* estimated that 2.6 million children between ten and fourteen, or 15 percent of the population in this age group, work at least an hour a day.

More boys than girls work in Brazil, especially in rural areas and in the agricultural sector. Many children both work and attend school. Girls attain higher levels of education than boys on average. Exceptions are found in the eleven-to-fourteen-year-old age category. Studies show that the earlier a child begins to work, the lower the earnings. Girls are more adversely affected by early labor force entry than boys; with the gender difference increasing the earlier a child begins to work (Gustafsson-Wright and Pyne, 2003).

Key activities identified as the priority forms of child labor are best understood by urban or rural residence. In urban areas children may be involved in illicit activities (drug trafficking, prostitution, etc.), scavenging dumps, or street vending (newspapers or other products). In rural areas activities may include the collection or production of charcoal, agave, cotton, vegetable products, sugarcane, tobacco, horticultural products, citrus, salt, flour, fish, wood, textiles, tiles or ceramics, and work related to the extraction of stones and gems—that is, mining.

In Brazil the agricultural sector is the main source of labor for both female and male children, particularly in rural areas (Fassa et al., 2000). It is also consistently ranked as one of the most hazardous industries, characterized by injury from farm machinery, strenuous labor, exposure to chemicals and pollutants, adverse weather, poor field sanitation, and lack of potable water for drinking.

Children working in the streets, particularly those making a home in the street, face the most severe working conditions. These children are exposed to drugs and violence as well as traffic accidents, extreme weather, poor sanitation, and psychological distress from ostracization and discrimination.

One of the most harmful activities for Brazilian children on the street is prostitution. Girls are most often the target of recruitment and coercion into the sex industry. The Brazilian Center for Childhood and Adolescence of the Ministry of Social Services estimated that about half a million Brazilian girls are engaged in prostitution in large cities or in the migrant mining settlements in Amazonia. Although fewer in numbers, boys are also involved but are more invisible due to the stigma attached to male prostitution. The plight of children involved in prostitution and other street work—vulnerability to violence, substance abuse, and HIV infection—is well documented (Green, 1998).

Child soldiers are not a widespread phenomenon in Brazil. However, even though the minimum age for conscription is nineteen years, there are indications of youth under eighteen in the government armed forces. How is this possible? The minimum age of voluntary recruitment in Brazil is seventeen.

POLITICAL VIEWS AND PUBLIC POLICIES

In Brazil, organizations such as workers' unions, churches, and nongovernmental organizations (NGOs) have been critical in lobbying for governmental programs to address child labor and street children. As a result, the Brazilian government has made issues related to children a policy priority. In 1988 the federal constitution of Brazil identified children and adolescents to be an "absolute priority": Article 227 states that "It is the duty of the society and the state to ensure that children and adolescents are an absolute priority—and that they have the right to life, health, food, education, leisure, training, culture, dignity, respect, familial and community relations—as well as to ensure that they are not subject to any form of negligence, discrimination, exploitation, violence, cruelty, or oppression." The government also supported the prohibition of nocturnal, dangerous, or unhealthy labor for children under eighteen years of age and any type of labor for children under fourteen except in situations of learning or professional training. In 1990, Law 8.069 (the Statute of Children and Adolescents, or ECA), Article 60, prohibited labor for children under the age of fourteen because of the harm to their physical, psychological, and moral development. It also established the regulations of apprenticeships, compulsory education, activities compatible with an adolescent's development, and a reduced workday.

In 2000 the government ratified both ILO Convention 138 (January), which addresses minimum ages for employment, and Convention 182 (September), which addresses the abolition of the worst forms of child labor. The government has committed itself to eradicate the worst forms of child labor by the year 2000 (Gustafsson-Wright and Pyne, 2002). In its policy on the protection of children, the government supports programs and projects that stimulate equality in conditions of access and return to schooling as well as increasing socioeducational activities, sports, and leisure before and after the normal school day.

SOCIAL VIEWS, CUSTOMS, AND PRACTICES

Children work for a variety of reasons, though it is widely believed that one of the main reasons is poverty. Poor families are forced to send their children to work to contribute to family income. Many families do not see themselves as having an alternative, as children's earnings may be necessary for family survival. Other factors influencing the decisions about child labor include work opportunities for adults; social norms that encourage children to work; inability to pay school fees, supplies, or uniforms; inability to access schools due to distance/transportation difficulties; and poor quality of schools and teachers. Child labor becomes part of family labor, which is particularly true in rural areas (Gustafsson-Wright and Pyne, 2002).

Another critical factor is the social norm that values child labor as an integral and positive part of a child's development. A working child is perceived as receiving discipline and training for their future entry into the labor market as an adult. Furthermore, working occupies time that might otherwise be spent "getting into mischief" (Gustafsson-Wright and Pyne, 2002).

The decision to send children to work is most likely made not by children themselves but by households out of dire need (Basu, 1999). If it is the head of the household making the child labor decision, then there is the possibility of intergenerational patterns in child labor. Recent studies provide evidence for the potential for intergenerational child labor traps (Baland and Robinson, 2000; Emerson and Souza, 2003). These studies also provide strong evidence that children who did not work as child laborers earned higher salaries later in life, suggesting that schooling versus apprenticeship increases children's opportunities and life chances.

It is important to note that the need for children to work does not mean that parents are not concerned about their children's welfare or that the consequences of all child labor are negative. Child labor and child schooling may not be mutually exclusive. Many working children also attend school, particularly in rural areas (Gustafsson-Wright and Pyne, 2002).

THE FUTURE OF CHILD LABOR

The social issues impacting child labor at the end of the twentieth century and beginning of the twenty-first century are set in the context of confrontation with globalization face-to-face with the disappearance of employment and the establishment of instability. The social exclusion of youth and families has been redefined. Within this context, children and adolescents are denied their infancy. Social injustices are reflected in the day-to-day life of marginalized segments of the population. Children, youth, and families are forced to live their lives while at the very same time their lives are robbed from them by the unhealthy and degrading work.

Proposed Solutions and Strategies

The federal government administers thirty-three programs under five separate ministries for eradicating child labor. The Brazilian government has concentrated much of its efforts on providing conditional cash grants with the objective of increasing education and discouraging child labor. Acknowledging poverty as the primary cause of child labor, these programs compensate families for a child's earnings and focus on factors that lead families to poverty. As far as children working on the streets, government programs have focused on urban areas.

Programs to eradicate harmful forms of child labor in Brazil include the National Forum for the Eradication and Prevention of Child Labor (1994), which is linked to the Ministry of Labor. This forum receives technical and financial support from the ILO and UNICEF and concentrates on the critical industries using child labor, such as sugarcane, sisal mate, and charcoal production.

The Federal Program for the Eradication of Child Labor (PETI) provides cash stipends of R$25 per month to poor families who keep their children in school and out of work. PETI also offers after-school activities such as sports and cultural activities to keep children away from work. Initiated in 1996 in rural areas of Brazil, by 1999, PETI had managed to reach 166 municipalities in eight states and 131,000 working children. To be eligible, all school-age children in the family must attend school, participate in after-school activities, and agree not to work.

Other programs include: the *Bolsa Escola* programs, which are minimum income guarantee programs administered in metropolitan school systems. As a preventive rather than remedial program, *Bolsa Escola* aims to eliminate poverty in the short run, reduce long-term poverty through increased educational attainment, and reduce child labor. The program provides cash grants to all school-age children in poor families on the condition that children have 90 percent school attendance. Since the program's first implementation in 1995 in Campinas and Brasilia, it has expanded to include around fifty-eight municipalities and four states.

The Minimum Income Assurance Program *(Funda Garantia de Renda Minima*, or *FGRM)* was established by the Ministry of Education to provide financial aid and technical support to municipalities with revenues less than the state average. Having since merged with other programs, the *FGRM* originally offered incentives for children to attend school by increasing the income of their families. Estimates from the Ministry of Education report that the *FGRM* has benefited 1 million children and more than 500,000 families. In 2001 the funding was increased to US$850 million to benefit almost 11 million children. In September 2000, *FGRM, Bolsa Escola*, and PETI were merged under the umbrella *Alvorada Program.*

Additionally, a new program, *Sentinela* was established under *Alvorada* to reduce child prostitution. This program, meant to be both preventive and combative, targets at-risk children ages seven through fourteen years from families with per capita less than half of minimum wage. By providing US$20 to each child and US$12 per child per month for the *Jornada Ampliada* (PETI's after-school activity programs), the government proposed to reach 8,500 children working in the sex industry. The preventive measures included a national campaign to raise awareness and increased workshops for service providers regarding the severity of the problem of prostitution. The combative measures included coordinating plans with councils, facilitating access to social services, and guaranteeing interaction between families, schools, and communities. In addition, these combative measures are proposed to improve the social and cultural environment of the targeted children, increase educational opportunities, and establish training for the purpose of income generation.

It is seen that programs intervening with street children need to consider: a) the type of activities in which boys and girls are engaged; b) the risks and hazards boys and girls face (physical and psychological), either through the activities or working and living conditions; and c) the different reasons that boys and girls work in the street. The government could subsidize policies to eliminate dumps.

More resources are needed to extract families from the child labor trap. Studies demonstrate that even though the poor rely on child labor only to assure survival, given a choice they would always opt for educating their children. Children are more likely to be child laborers if their parents were as well. Children are less likely to be child laborers the more educated their parents are. Policies that break the cycle family by family are potentially the most effective instruments to reduce the incidence of child labor (Emerson and Souza, 2003).

BIBLIOGRAPHY

Alvim, R. (2000) Debates on poor children in Brazil: Between marginalization and premature labour. In Schlemmer, B., ed. *The exploited child*, 160–175, New York: Zed Books.

Baland, J., and J. A. Robinson. (2000) Is child labor inefficient? *Journal of Political Economy* 108(4): 663–79.

Basu, K. (1999) Child labor: Cause, consequence, and cure. *Journal of Economic Literature* 37(3): 1083–1119.

Bellamy, C. (1997) *The state of the world's children 1997*. Oxford: Oxford University Press.

Buckley, S. (2000) The littlest laborers; In a wealthier world, children still hard at work. *The Washington Post*, Washington, D.C. Mar. 16, 2000, pg. A01.

Emerson, P. M., and A. P. Souza. (2003) Is there a child labor trap? Intergenerational persistence of child labor in Brazil. *Economic Development and Cultural Change* 51(2): 375–98.

Fassa, A., L. A. Facchini, M. M. Dall'Agnol, and D. Christiani. (2000) Child labor and health: Problems and perspectives. *International Journal of Occupational and Environmental Health* 6(1): 55–62.

Fukui, L. (2000) Why is child labour tolerated? The case of Brazil. In Schlemmer, B., ed. *The exploited child*, 118–34. New York: Zed Books.

Green, D. (1998) *Hidden lives: Voices of children in Latin America and the Caribbean*. London: Save the Children.

Gustafsson-Wright, E., and H. H. Pyne. (2002) Gender dimensions of child labor and street children in Brazil. World Bank Policy Research Working Paper 2897, October 2002. Retrieved June 24, 2003, from http://econ.worldbanki. org/files/19189_2897.pdf.

ILO. (1999) *Convention No. 182 concerning the prohibition and immediate action for the elimination of the worst forms of child labour*. Geneva.

———. (1996) Child labour today: Facts and figures. *World of Work* 16: 12–17.

ILO-IPEC. (1996) Children wage war on child labour. *Children and Work* 2: 10.

Jeter, J. (2003) Brazil pays its poor to send kids to school; Officials say program cuts truancy, hunger. *The Washington Post*, Washington, D.C. Jun. 1, 2003, pg. A07.

Schlemmer, B., ed. (2000) *The exploited child*. New York: Zed Books.

United Nations. (1996) *Report of the Committee on the Rights of the Child*. General Assembly, Official Records, Fifty-first Session, Supplement No. 41 (A/51/41). New York.

U.S. Department of State. (1999) *Country Reports on Human Rights Practices*. (2000, February 25). Bureau of Democracy, Human Rights, and Labor. U.S. Government, Washington, DC.

———. (2002) *Brazil: Country reports on human rights practices*. U.S. Government, Washington, DC.

———. (2003) Bureau of Democracy, Human Rights, and Labor. Retrieved June 24, 2003, from http://www.state.gov.g.drl.rls.hrrpt/2001/wha/8305pf.htm. Also see www.globalmarch.org/worstformsreport/world/brazil.html, retrieved June 25, 2003, and http://www.cia.gov/cia/publications/factbook/geos/br. html, retrieved June 25, 2003.

Vawda, A. (n.d.) *Brazil: Stipends to increase school enrollment and decrease child labor*. Human Development Network, World Bank. Retrieved June 24, 2003, from http://ifc.org/edinvest/brazil.htm.

3

CHINA

Xiaojun Tong and Shizhen Lu

PROFILE OF CHINA

The People's Republic of China is the world's third-largest country by area and the largest by population. According to the most recent census, done in 2000, China has an estimated population of 1.3 billion, excluding Taiwan, Hong Kong, and Macao, which together include another 30 million people. The majority of China's population lives in the eastern part of the country near the eastern seaboard, while the mountainous regions of the inland are sparsely populated. The eastern portion of China is rapidly becoming a world-class industrial and commercial center while China's inland remains quite rural and agrarian. Though concepts of modernization and economic reform seem common worldwide, many parts of central China have only the bare infrastructure seen in many poor countries.

Administratively there are four municipalities (Beijing, Tianjing, Shanghai, and Chongqing), twenty-three provinces, five autonomous regions (Inner Mongolia, Xinjiang Uygur, Ningxia Hui, Guangxi Zhuang, and Tibet) and two special one-country, two-system areas (Hong Kong and Macao). Hong Kong and Macao were previously colonies of Britain and Portugal and were returned to China on July 1997 and October 1999 respectively. Taiwan Province is separated by the Taiwan Strait from mainland China and has been ruled by Kuomintang and Minjintung administrations successively since 1949. Mainland China includes all the above except the two special administrative districts and Taiwan Province. This chapter is limited to discussing the child labor issue on mainland China.

China is a multiethnic country with fifty-six recognized ethnic nationalities. The Han people account for about 92 percent of the total population while the other fifty-five nationalities comprise the remaining 8 percent. Most of these minority groups are distinguished from the Han population by language or religion rather than by physical characteristics. Most individuals in the minority groups live in the five autonomous regions.

China is one of the world's earliest civilizations. Its recorded history dates back some five thousand years. China has been a powerful nation in East Asia and the world throughout most of history. Emperors ruled the nation using Confucianism, based on the thoughts of a Chinese philosopher named Confucius. Confucianism dominated Chinese society for centuries, influencing every aspect of people's lives until recently. During the Opium War from 1840–42, imperialist countries such as Britain, France, and Germany ended China's isolation with guns and warships. They divided the important commercial port cities. As result, China became a politically and economically weak nation. The Qing dynasty, the last dynasty in Chinese history, ended in 1911. The People's Republic of China was established in 1949 after brief periods of rule under the precommunist nationalist government.

Economically, China adopted a central planning economic system. Everything was determined by the central government. People enjoyed a cradle-to-grave welfare network until 1978. Before 1978, China had a one-party central government. The party led a series of socialist movements to rid China of anything bourgeois or feudalist. Among the most influential movements were the Hundred-Flower Movement and the Anti-Rightist Campaign (1957), the Great Leap Forward (1957–61), and the Great Cultural Revolution (1966–76). These movements promoted socialist ideology among citizens but did not help with economic development. During the ten-year Cultural Revolution, almost all national resources were devoted to the class struggle, which led to a near collapse of the national economy. By the end of the revolution, China was one of the poorest countries in the world. Diplomatically, the government had a closed-door policy. This isolation ended in 1978.

The new government led by Deng Xiaoping launched economic reforms and opened the door to the outside world in 1978. China now has a market economy and has experienced an average national increase of 7–8 percent since 1978. In 2000, with its almost 1.3 billion people and a GDP of $3,600 per capita, China stood as the second-largest economy in the world after the United States. People have benefited from the economic prosperity. The government now plays an active role in international affairs. Along with the rapid economic growth, China is experiencing increasing social problems, including increasing unemployment and a growing gap between the poor and the rich.

OVERVIEW OF CHILD LABOR

Child labor has existed in China since the beginning of its history. It was not framed as a social evil in the eyes of the Chinese until the early twentieth century. This was almost half a century after its industrialization, which began with the introduction of Western machinery in the mid-nineteenth century. In 1923 the first law referring to child labor was passed. The provisions under this and subsequent laws were not enforced until the Chinese Communist Party (CCP) came to power in 1949. Child labor disappeared under the strict control of socialist ideology and did not reappear until the political changes brought about by Deng Xiaoping's government. From this growing concern over child labor, the government and society created relevant laws and regulations to protect young children from exploitation and harm. Chinese people believe that children are the future of the country and that both the government and society are responsible for creating an environment for their healthy growth.

Systematic statistics on child labor in China are not available. Approximate estimations for different historic periods have been made based on the numbers of school dropouts at those times. While there has been no systematic collection of statistics on child labor in China, some data is available from the larger municipalities.

According to census data, in 1997 there were 160,000 children under fifteen years of age among the shifting population in Beijing; 66,392 were school-age children between the ages of six to fifteen. Of these children, 13.9% were not going to school. It was also reported that 1.8% of children ten to fourteen years old were employed in factories or ran businesses. Of all the children who were part of this census, 32.1% indicated that they worked in a factory, ran a business, or were temporarily out of job (Duan, 2001). Extrapolating these figures across the population, there are approximately 924,000 children fifteen years of age or younger working in mainland China. These estimates are probably understated. Many children work in agricultural and family businesses in their native villages and towns. In addition, gang-controlled child slaves and other highly illegal forms of child labor and abuse are always kept secret. Finally, children in very remote rural areas are typically left out during the national population census.

According to a report carried out by the China Civil Education 2000 Supervisory Group and jointly issued by the United Nations Educational, Scientific and Cultural Organization (UNESCO) and China's Ministry of Education, in December 1999, 98.9% of school-age children were attending primary schools, an increase from 97% in 1990. This report found a 94.3% progression rate to junior secondary school. This report provides evidence of substantial progress toward adhering to the Compulsory Education Law of 1986.

It appears that, particularly in rural parts of China, girls are more likely to be engaged in child labor than boys. A survey conducted of school-age children in villages in five major provinces showed that, for workers under the age of fifteen years, girls represented 73.5% of the total child laborers in those villages. Most of those children were also illiterate and school dropouts (Gong, 1997). School dropout statistics are also not available. Different sources seem to point to high dropout rates stemming from high levels of poverty. Children work to help their families survive.

Vignette

Mei Li, a bright and compassionate fourteen-year-old girl, works for a factory in Pingyang County, Zhejiang Province. Day in and day out, week in and week out, month in and month out, she and her twelve-year-old sister Chai Mi work for greedy contractors sewing plastic bags. Abusive conditions, including a twenty-hour workday, are driving Mei Li to despair. Along with over a dozen young workers who are also from poor countryside areas, Mei Li and her sister begin work at 5:00 A.M. every morning. They do not leave the factory until their work has ended, usually at midnight or sometimes much later, when orders are urgently due. Struggling to survive together in cramped quarters without air-conditioning or ventilation, Mei Li lets her sister sleep close to the open door of this thirty-square-foot cubicle next to the factory.

Wei Sheng, struggling to complete his work quota, strips down to just his pants in order to survive the factory's sweltering heat. He notices that Mei Li and her sister found old, dirty towels to drape around their necks to wipe off their sweat. Wei Sheng sighs and wonders when the boss will allow them to have their five-minute toilet break. It has already been three hours since their fifteen-minute lunch break.

Chai Mi gazes down at the piece of plastic tightly formed into a geometric envelope. Her eyes raise to see the row upon row of all the plastic bags sewn by the children that day. Yet the contractors tell them that today they must work beyond the normal midnight hour because of a large rush order they suddenly received. The contractor considers this a very important order. Chai Mi does what she always does to escape the pain from her fingers. She learned quickly to continue working even when she was injured. She begins to count in her mind what her earnings for her work will be (0.008 yuan or U.S.$.001 per bag) never realizing that the contractor receives 0.025 yuan (U.S.$.003) per bag (14-year-old, 1999). As she counts, Chai Mi dreams of a better life for her and her older sister.

Mei Li's desperation grew with the deception of the contractor who had lured her and Chai Mi away from the cotton mill to his factory. Hoping to escape an exploitative workday starting at 4:00 A.M. and ending at 10:00 P.M., Mei Li found conditions at the factory even worse. Keenly observing everyone and everything in the factory, Mei Li discovered that the local government inspectors did nothing to change the children's conditions. The money from the contractor was powerful persuasion to turn a blind eye toward the factory. After a recent fire injured her sister, Mei Li tried to ask for fire extinguishers in the factory. She was immediately forced into silence. When word came around of government officials from the state inspecting the fire, the contractor immediately closed operations during the day while forcing the children to work through the night.

Standing in the opening of the second-floor window of the only bathroom, Mei Li closes her eyes and takes a deep breath of the sticky, hot, polluted air. As the only means of escape from the squalor and abuse of conditions in the factory, Mei Li wonders if she will find death or freedom after her fall.

HISTORY OF CHILD LABOR

The history of child labor in China parallels the development of the public education system. That development is examined here by dividing the history into four phases: (1) before the Opium War (1840–42); (2) after the Opium War (1843–1949); (3) during the Communist central planning economy (1949–1978); and (4) in the socialist market economy after 1978.

Child Labor before the Opium War (1840–1942)

Before the Opium War, China was a traditional agricultural country. The family was the basic unit of productivity. Everybody, including children, played a role in productivity. Children in a typical agricultural family worked alongside their parents. Girls were involved in domestic work such as taking care of younger ones, cooking meals, and washing clothes for the family. Boys were involved in lighter regular adult work in the fields. Children also worked in family businesses such as tea shops, wood shops, and drugstores. Children and adults in these situations might work long hours. At this time children were not seen as being exploited by their parents but rather as contributing to the family's survival. The involvement of children in agricultural productivity was an inseparable part of survival for the family and society. Public schools did not exist at that time. Education before the Opium Wars was a luxury for only the wealthy families and those in the official classes of privilege.

Identifiable groups of children were clearly being exploited in traditional Chinese society. These included bonded and enslaved children from poor families. Some girls, called *tong yang xi* (child wife), were sold or occasionally sent to wealthy families to be the future wife of one of the male members in the family. Often this was the only way parents of girls could ensure their daughters' survival. Before the marriage, a young girl in this situation was usually treated as a free maid. Many female children were sold by their parents or immediate relatives to wealthy families as domestic maids.

Another group of bonded children were apprentices in the handicrafts such as silk-weaving, furniture-making, fabric-dying, and brick-making. Once sold, children became slaves to wealthy families or the masters of the mills. The parents most often signed a contract and received a onetime payment. Usually the child would receive only housing and food, and be forbidden to leave until the contract ended. The worst of the bonded children were those sold to *Qing Lou*—brothels that forced children into prostitution. Their fate was totally at the mercy of their masters. There were no laws to either protect the children or eliminate exploitative practices before the Opium War.

Child Labor in Nationalist Revolutionary China (1843–1949)

After the Opium War, Chinese nationalists devoted themselves to finding a way for the nation to become strong and independent. Turmoil among factions brought multiple changes in the government and leadership. A period of political instability ensued. Young children continued to help with the vast agricultural productivity, and the practice of *tong yang xi* and sale of female children persisted.

During this period, foreign influence precipitated significant social changes that profoundly impacted the life of children in China. The Western educational system influenced the curriculum and the structure of education. The concept of a unified public education system, which enabled the children from working families to attend school, was introduced. The curriculum expanded dramatically with the addition of subjects such as mathematics, physics, chemistry, and nature. One of the most significant changes was the extension of public education to girls, who were not allowed to go to school until 1907 when the national system of women's education was approved. By 1919, 20 percent of the total school-age children were enrolled in primary schools. Male enrollment outnumbered female enrollment seven to one. Although 80 percent of the population was rural, the availability of public education was primarily urban.

Another significant change during this period of history was the industrialization of China. Foreign machinery was imported and small factories were established in the 1880s and 1890s. The Nationalist Ministry of Industry estimated that 75 to 85 percent of the total national labor force was involved in industrial labor by 1930. Children from poor families joined the workforce. Many female children worked for the textile industry, including in cotton mills and silk factories, and for match producers and cigarette and tobacco factories. They also worked in the laundry trade or domestic services. Typically children began work at a young age; some as young as five.

While no national statistics are available before 1949, data from Shanghai, the most industrialized city, estimates the rate of adult females to children as 2:1 (Anderson, 1928; Foreign Office, 1927; Ebrey, 1996; Shen, 1927).

Young children were hired for long hours and low wages; their small fingers were good for tending the spinning machines. Almost all the workers in match factories in Shanghai were women and their young children. Workers in match factories ran the dangerous risk of phosphorus poisoning. Another norm of the time was for young male children to work as apprentices in the building trades, engineering, shipbuilding, and printing (Anderson, 1928). In addition, young children were observed working in sugar refineries and flour mills.

The sanitary conditions in industries where children worked were poor—if they even existed. In the silk factories, windows and doors were kept closed, which exposed workers to dust and airborne pathogens. Often the child laborers worked, ate, and slept in the same quarters. From the cinnabar mines of Hunan it was reported that whole villages, including women and children, worked at the mines. They worked about fourteen or fifteen hours a day, seven days a week. No sanitary or protective measures were taken, and consequently the whole village was slowly poisoned (Foreign Office, 1927).

During this period, laws were passed based on recommendations from both foreign and Sino-joint organizations. The most prominent of these were the Child Labor Commission in Shanghai and the international child labor standards developed at that time. These laws were designed to give China the appearance of having an enlightened labor policy, but in reality they existed only on paper. There were many barriers to enforcing these laws: poverty; lack of birth records making it difficult to establish age; lack of national educational organization; and inadequate sanitary conditions in the average household, which decreased the demand for better conditions in factories. Most important, the government was dependent on the support of industrialists and financiers.

By the end of this period, child labor began to receive more earnest attention. Child workers began advocating the protection of young child workers. As Shen Dan-Ni points out in her 1927 book on child labor in China, Chinese society during that period believed that compulsory education would be an effective way to deal with the issue of child labor. Advocates encouraged officials to embrace the international labor standards and the government to protect the welfare of workers.

Child Labor Elimination in Communist China (1949–1978)

The Communist regime was a one-party government. The Chinese Communist Party (CCP) instituted economic reform and expanded mass public education. Through its socialist movement and strict social control, child labor was eliminated. The practice of selling girls for prostitution, apprenticeships, and *tong yang xi* were regarded as forms of class exploitation and oppression. Hence they were eradicated in this new social system. The practice of having domestic maids at home was also eliminated. Former prostitutes, apprentices, and domestic maids as well as their employers were sent home and educated with communist/socialist ideology.

All factories and enterprises, including schools and universities, became state-owned. A highly centralized economic planning system was organized. The central government decided what and how much to produce, how to produce it, and how to distribute the products. Everyone in the cities belonged to a work unit or neighborhood committee through which they were assigned employment and received welfare such as food coupons, free housing, and health care. When people applied for employment, their age, family background, education, and criminal record were checked. It was impossible for a young child to get employment.

In rural areas, land was confiscated and redistributed to those in poverty based on the number of people in a household. At first the family made the decisions on the use of the land. Children were often involved in the productivity, sharing some light work. In the mid-1950s, mutual aid groups were organized and later, cooperatives. Eventually the land became state-owned with the central committee of the group making decisions. Young children were not assigned any work.

The CCP government took immediate action to develop the public education system in both urban and rural areas. There was an urgent need for a skilled and educated labor force. Even though during this period child labor was eliminated, successful participation in education was slow. In 1952, only 49.2 percent of school-age children were enrolled in school. Almost all the school-age children who lived in cities attended school, while only a small percentage of children in rural areas were enrolled. In rural areas, facilities were limited, parents could not afford the tuition and fees, children could not meet initial entrance requirements, and children, particularly girls, were needed for household chores.

Enrollment rose sharply beginning in 1957 with the introduction of the half-study, half-work schools in rural areas. These schools were self-supporting and also trained children for work. By 1965, primary school enrollment had risen to 84.7 percent of all school-age children (Dreyer, 1996). These schools expanded to urban areas, where children assisted in half-time work in agricultural fields or factories. During the busy agricultural seasons, children in many schools in rural areas spent all their time helping in the fields. Children in some urban schools also spent one or two weeks helping in the fields. By 1975 the primary school enrollment rate was 96.8 percent. The majority of those not enrolled in school were still in rural areas.

Child Labor after 1978

The Great Cultural Revolution ended in 1976. Economic reform began and China opened its doors to the world in 1978. With the switch from a centrally planned economy to a free market economy, farmers were now allowed to have their own land, individuals to own their own businesses, and foreign investors to invest in certain types of business. Individual wealth has grown since 1978, and average living conditions are rising dramatically. Child labor, however, has reappeared with this economic development.

Within the free market economy, factory owners and managers favor the labor of children because they are paid less than adults. In addition, they are frequently more docile workers and unaware of their rights. Some local government officials ignore child labor in factories as long as the business taxes are paid. Businesses and small factories owned by subcontractors often do not have business licenses, and enforcement is typically weak in this informal sector. In order to escape notice, some reverse their work hours. Another technique used by some factories in remote areas is to move frequently. Conditions in these businesses are extremely hazardous—no fire equipment and no fans for ventilation.

CHILD LABOR TODAY

Children work in construction, electronics, the apparel industry, and other industrial and commercial enterprises. In the 1990s, of 10 million construction workers in China from rural areas, one-quarter of them were male child laborers. As part of its drive for economic growth, the government has set up Special Economic Zones in the southern part of China. Policies favor both domestic and foreign investors in these zones. Evidence indicates that the exploitation of children is rampant in these zones. Epstein (1993) described one factory in which workers hand-painted dolls without wearing masks to protect them from the toxic fumes. In another factory, female workers, some as young as twelve years old, slept in dark and damp dormitories, two or three to a bed.

In its 1994 international report, the U.S. Department of Labor's Bureau of International Labor Affairs reported on underage garment workers in Asian countries such as China, India, Indonesia, the Philippines, and Thailand, where garments were made for export to the U.S. In those factories, children were likely to work in small subcontracting shops or in work-at-home situations. Children performed tasks such as sewing on buttons, cutting and trimming threads, folding, and moving and packing garments. In some cases children worked long hours six or seven days a week. Some children received less than minimum wage and were not paid for overtime work (Gay, 1998).

Children are also employed as domestic maids. Girls from economically poor areas crowd into the large cities to work to build their dowry. It is estimated that there are ten thousand babysitters or housekeepers in the city of Beijing, one-third of whom are school-age children from outside the city (Gong, 1997). Some are sent by their parents to distant relatives or friends of distant relatives in the city. The rest come to make money for their dowry in order to get married back in their hometown. They usually come with someone who has experience and are either introduced to master families or go to the babysitter market and wait to be selected. These young children are under the control of their masters and vulnerable to psychological and sexual abuse. Because of the Chinese tradition of saving face as well as lack of communication with family and friends, babysitters who have been assaulted frequently choose to keep silent.

There are reports of young children in cities who are being controlled by gang members and forced into slave labor. They do not have housing or a steady source of meals and are often kept locked in one room in a suburban area during the day. At night they are sent to work at jobs such as prostitution or selling flowers in busy downtown areas.

Organized student labor constitutes another form of child labor. Nonhazardous and healthy light work is allowed on campus. Any hazardous or unhealthy work that interferes with normal school life is forbidden by law. Some schools, however, become subcontractors, organizing students to work a couple of hours or even longer to make money outside the government funding system.

POLITICAL VIEWS AND PUBLIC POLICIES

Since the economic reform, the Chinese central government has been committed to addressing the problem of child labor. Child labor is regarded as a serious social problem. New laws have been passed to strengthen old laws. Among the relevant laws are the Constitution, the Compulsory Education Law, the Marriage Law, the Labor Law, the Protection Law for Underage Adults (ages sixteen through eighteen), and the Regulations on Prohibiting the Use of Child Labor. Some local governments have also passed their own laws and regulations to protect children. Furthermore, China is an active supporter of the international fight against child labor launched by the United Nations. After signing the U.N. Conventions on the Rights of the Child and the Government Action Plan, China signed the International Labour Organisation's Minimum Age Convention in 1999.

The Compulsory Education Law was first issued and came into force in 1986. There are seven clauses relevant to child labor. These clauses support equitable access to nine years of compulsory education for all children. One clause in this law specifies the consequences for those who employ school-age children. Anyone caught violating the law will have their name published.

The Labor Law contains six clauses that specifically address child labor. One clause prohibits employment of children under age sixteen. The Labor Law specifies regulations for work, including laws that limit a worker's average work week to no more than forty-four hours.

In 1988 the Department of Labor along with five other relevant offices of the central government issued an announcement prohibiting the use of Child Labor through various strategies. Background checks are required for contractors and subcontractors. A fine from 3,000 to 5,000 yuan (US$360.00 to $600.00) per child is levied against any work unit, enterprise, or individual who employs young children. The parents and legal guardians of child laborers are provided education about the issues and the children sent back to school.

The 1994 Regulations on Prohibiting the Use of Child Labor distinguishes illegal child labor from the use of children under sixteen in non-hazardous ancillary labor. This work category includes tasks necessary to family productivity and work organized by schools and approved by the government. This law also prohibits government offices, social groups, enterprises, or individuals—including private business owners, farmers, and urban citizens—from introducing children under sixteen to any employment opportunity. Also, business licenses may not be issued to children. The regulations set specific fines to be levied against any work units, individuals, or parents/legal guardians violating the law.

SOCIAL VIEWS, CUSTOMS AND PRACTICES

Chinese labor law prohibits the employment of any child under 16. Evidence exists, however, that suggests that violations occur and that employers who violate these laws do not face heavy penalties. When child labor is discovered, nothing is changed to protect children. The exploitation of children as laborers is strongly associated with poverty. Both poverty and parental illiteracy contribute to attitudinal factors that support child labor over education. Lack of awareness regarding the importance of education and tolerance for illiteracy contribute to parents permitting their children to work rather than attend school. This is especially true for girls.

In economically poor, remote rural areas, work is a matter of survival for children and their families. Fifty million residents still live below the national poverty line—8.24 yuan (US$1.00) per capita per day. For areas that are remote, less accessible, and very resource poor, the potential for increasing agricultural production is limited. In the face of very low standards of living, child labor provides income critical to the daily survival of the family.

Additionally, poor families cannot afford the expenses related to education. According to a 1986 law, education from first to ninth grade is universal and free in mainland China. Even with free education, many families cannot afford their children's education. With the privatization of education, some schools charge fees, which force children from poor families to drop out. The International Labour Organisation (ILO) estimates that the cost of sending one child to primary school may exceed one-third of the family's income in poor families. These estimates support other research showing that poverty is a major reason why parents keep children out of school. The semester's fees and expenses for one primary school student were about 180 yuan (US$21.60) and for one secondary school student about 280 yuan (US$33.60). These fees would come from an average total household yearly income of about 400 yuan (US$48.00) (Li, 2002).

Poverty is not the sole factor in child labor in China today. Current business strategies allow child labor to continue hidden away from authorities. The contract system of employment is prevalent in joint adventures between foreign and private enterprises. It is a system open to grave abuse. The contractor supplies the labor and is paid based on production. Frequently the contractor obtains young children from poor rural areas. These children work long hours for low wages. Too often they are housed and fed under the miserable conditions. The deplorable conditions of child labor have been documented in many reports (Gong, 1997; 14-year-old, 1999; Xia, 1996; Zhang, 1998). Some state-owned enterprises employ contract employees without background checks. These child workers are frequently untrained and vulnerable to the dangers on the job site. There is little in the form of an occupational safety infrastructure, and child workers are most vulnerable to existing dangers. Although child labor is illegal in China, many employers are adept at covering their abuses. Among the worst forms of child labor are prostitution and slavery.

In rural areas, some parents continue to rely on their young children as helpers around the home and farm or include them as helpers in their businesses. In these remote areas, the situation is similar to the conditions in ancient history. This practice is widely accepted throughout the whole country (Tang, 2001).

THE FUTURE OF CHILD LABOR

It is not the lack of laws that contributes to child labor in China. It is the lack of effective enforcement. The central government recognizes the problem and has passed relevant laws. Society as a whole, however, does not agree that child labor is a problem.

The Chinese government has made great efforts to enforce its child labor laws. The Labor Department holds the responsibility for monitoring and investigating child labor. Other government institutes such as the women's federation, education committee, work union, and youth federation are collaborative organizations that work in conjunction with the Labor Department. The most recent and largest-scale action was a collaborative venture by the nine government departments in September 2001—the Labor and Security Department, the Legal Justice Office of National Internal Affairs, the Economy and Trade Department, the Public Security Department, the Industry and Commercial Management Bureau, the Education Ministry, the All China Workers Union, the All China Youth Federation, and the All China Women's Federation. This collaboration examined records, met with local people, and performed on-the-spot investigations.

While government investigations are effective with licensed enterprises, there are difficulties with the informal business sector. Unlicensed businesses can hide their activities. In these cases the government relies on ordinary citizens to report. The media plays an important role as well. They not only help with investigating abuses, but also help educate the public about the issues.

The compulsory education system plays a major role in the reduction and elimination of child labor. The Education Committee, the All China Youth Federation, and All China Women's Federation are active in the enforcement of the Compulsory Education Law. They educate parents, legal guardians, and society as a whole on the rights of children and the importance of education. They have worked to reduce the number of children dropping out of school. Since 2000, collaborative efforts have been responsible for reducing the dropout rates in secondary high schools. These rates have dropped from 6.07% to 2.65% in one province (Dong, 2001).

A series of semiprivate initiatives, including Project Hope, are designed to promote educational development in the poor areas in China. The China Youth Development Foundation has helped gather resources. By the end of 1998, Project Hope had received enough donations to help more than 2 million dropouts return to school. They were also able to build 7,111 Hope primary schools. Another initiative, Project Spring Bud, formerly the School Girl Grant Fund, was founded by several government organizations to help female dropouts return to school. By the middle of 1995, Project Spring Bud had helped 61,000 girls to return to school. This project has made a significant difference in female education, especially in impoverished and minority areas (Mackerras, 2001).

CONCLUSION

Child labor has yet to be eliminated in China. Many children under the age of sixteen are still being hired to work long hours for low wages. To effectively eradicate child labor, some see that China's next steps could include analyzing the issue of poverty and creating situations in which families do not need their children's income. China could also strengthen its nine-year universal education programs. Supporting children's successful completion in school reduces the likelihood that they will be exploited for their labor. This requires human and financial resources. Projects like Hope and Spring Bud are examples of nongovernmental organizations (NGOs) effectively addressing China's child labor problem. However, the government can play a much more active role in this battle.

At the beginning of the twenty-first century, China ranks low among its neighbors such as India, Japan, Malaysia, Singapore, Cambodia, South Korea, and Thailand in the proportion of its gross national product (GNP) (2.3%) spent on education. It is thought that if the government of China can increase its commitment to education to include even the poorest children, then child labor may be reduced.

BIBLIOGRAPHY

Anderson, A. M. (1928) *Humanity and labor in China: An industrial visit and its sequel (1923–1926)*. Russell Square, London: Student Christian Movement.

Barendsen, R. D. (1964) Half-work half-study schools in communist China: Recent experiments with self-supporting educational institutions. Washington, DC: U.S. Government Printing Office.

Chaffee, F. H., G. E. Aurell, H. A. Barth, J. H. Dombrowski, N. A. Walpole, and J. O. Weaver. (1967) *Area study for Communist China*. Washington, DC: U.S. Government Printing Office.

Dong, Z. (2001) "Parents will be sued if not sending their young children to school" (Bunengran haizi shang "xuetang" jiuran fumu shang "gong tang.") *Hebei Education* 2: 24.

Dreyer, J. T. (1996) *China's political system: Modernization and tradition*. Boston: Allyn & Bacon.

Duan, C. (2001) Analysis on the young children in the shifting population in Beijing. *Population and Economy (Renkou Yu Jinji)* 1: 5–10.

Ebrey, P. B. (1996) *Cambridge illustrated history of China*. London: Cambridge University Press.

Epstein, I. (1993) Child labor and basic education provision in China. *International Journal of Educational Development* 23: 227–38.

Foreign Office. (1927) *Memorandum on labor condition in China No. 2*. London: His Majesty's Stationery Office.

14-year-old jumping from upper floor to escape heavy job volume. (1999) *Journal of Laodong yu Jiankang* 1: 37.

Gay, K. (1998) *Child labor: a global crisis*. Brookfield, CT: Millbrook Press.

Gong, W. (1997) Sobbing "little suns": An analysis on child labor. *Hunan Jinji* 1: 56–57.

Han, D. (2000) *The unknown cultural revolution: Educational reforms and their impact on China's rural development*. New York: Garland Publishing.

Hobbs, S., J. Mckechnie, and M. Lavalette. (1999) Child labor: A world history companion. Santa Barbara, CA: ABC-CLIO.

Li, Q. (2002) Analysis of the survey on the universal education in Zhuangzhu Minority Areas. *Basic Education Research* 1–2: 16–18.

Mackerras, C. (2001) The new Cambridge handbook of contemporary China. Cambridge, UK: Cambridge University Press.

Montaperto, R. N. (1979) China's Education in Perspective. In Montaperto, R., and J. Henderson, eds. *China's schools in flux: Report by the state education leaders delegation, National Committee on United States–China Relations.* White Plains, NY: M. E. Sharpe.

Mountain Fort: The Factory to Produce Quilts with "Black" Cotton. (2001, September 26 & 27) *Guangzhou Daily.*

Nyberg, A., and S. Rozelle. (1994) *Accelerating China's rural transformation.* Washington, DC: World Bank.

Peng, X. (2000) Introduction. In Peng X., and Z. Guo, eds. *The changing population in China.* Malden, MA: Blackwell Publishers.

Primary Education. (1999) In *China education yearbook (Zhongguo Jiaoyu Nianjian),* p. 166.

Shen, D. (1927) *Child Labor (Tong Gong).* Shanghai: World Publishers.

Tan, Z. (2000) Hiring child labor—Illegal! *Guang Cai,* 3.

Tang, M. (2001) A discussion on the modernization of the population: A case study of Zhejiang Province. North-West Population (Xibei Renkou), Vol. 3, pp. 11–15.

Wang, L., and S. MacPherson, eds. (1995) Social change and social policy in contemporary China. Avebury, Brookfield, VT: Ashgate Publishing.

Xia, A. (1996) Dropouts, not only because of poverty (Shixue, bu jinjin yinwei pinkun). *Journal of China Youth College for Political Sciences* 2: 20–25.

Zhang, Y. (1998) Enterprise should take sole responsibility for its child workers (Qiye Shiyong Tonggong Ying Chengdan Quanbu Zeren). Work Protection (Laodong Baohu), Vol. 8.

4

THE DOMINICAN REPUBLIC

B. J. Bryson and Tina Bryson

PROFILE OF THE DOMINICAN REPUBLIC

The Dominican Republic is located in the Caribbean region and occupies two-thirds of the island of Hispaniola along with the country of Haiti. It is approximately the size of Vermont and New Hampshire combined. Mountains, fertile lands, and coastal areas compose the topography of the country. A tropical climate with seasons determined primarily by rainfall, the rainy season runs from May through November in most of the country.

The vast majority (64%) of its 8,721,594 people live in urban settings (CIA, 2002; Dominican Republic, n.d.). Of the population, 73% identify ethnically/racially as mulatto (mixed), with 16% white and 11% black (Dominican Republic, n.d.). Ninety percent of the population identify as Roman Catholic. Dominican Republic history illustrates the intersection of diverse people that have contributed to its unique culture.

In efforts to sail to "the Indies," Christopher Columbus arrived on an island he called "La Isla Espanola" in 1492. Friendly Taino Indians (Arawaks) adorned with gold welcomed the crew. These voyagers bartered the Indians for the gold and later extracted the gold deposits directly from the island. The first attempted Spanish settlement was located where Santo Domingo now sits, which is currently the capital of the country. Spanish was established as the official language, but English is spoken in most tourist areas.

The country's rule and leadership has changed many times between Spanish, French, and Haitian authority. Juan Pablo Duarte is considered the father of the Dominican Republic. February 27 is Dominican Independence Day. Its current form of government, as provided by the Dominican Republic's Constitution, is a democracy with a presidency, a bicameral National Congress, and a legal system based on French civil codes. There are multiple political parties that influence popular elections.

Efforts are underway to improve the economic outlook for the Dominican Republic. Diversification has resulted in an increase in tourism, telecommunications, and industry in the free trade zones while reliance on sugar and other agricultural exports decreases (Bureau of Democracy, Human Rights, & Labor, 1998). President Fernandez attempted to infuse the economy with an economic stimulation package in 1996, including income tax cuts, reduced import tariffs, and increased gasoline prices. Many of these efforts stalled in the legislative process (Geofacts, 2002–3). Tourism and telecommunications are industries that continue to grow.

The labor force is 50% agricultural, 32% services and government, and 18% industry. Agricultural products include sugarcane, coffee, cotton, cocoa, tobacco, rice, beans, cattle, pigs and dairy products. The major industries include tourism, sugar process, ferronickel and gold mining, textiles, cement, and tobacco. The electrical power industry experiences many problems, contributing to the slow development of electricity-dependent industries. Privatization of the electrical industry has met delays but shows movement. Power outages continue to exist. If the Dominican Republic is to improve its economy, the development of electricity-dependent industry is necessary.

The Dominican Republic is considered one of the poorest countries in the Caribbean with 25% of the population living below the poverty line (CIA, 2002). Sixteen percent of the population lives on less than two dollars per day (EngenderHealth, 2003). A 1997 estimate found the unemployment rate was around 16%, and this remains consistent. The unemployment rate does not include those potential workers who have ceased to look for employment. Income is highly skewed, and more than half the population lives in poverty (Geofacts, 2002–3). Poverty affects 60% of the population. Nearly 20% of the population survives on less than one dollar a day, as extreme poverty continues to exist. In 1997, 64 percent of rural families could not cover their basic needs (Inter-American Commission on Human Rights, 1999).

The high poverty rate contributes to a willingness of some Dominicans to support themselves by a variety of other industries. For example, an illicit drug industry exists, as the Dominican Republic is the transshipment point for South American drugs destined for the United States and Europe, and the transshipment location of the drug ecstasy from the Netherlands and Belgium destined for Canada and the U.S. Substantial money-laundering activity has emerged, with Colombian narcotics traffickers favoring the country.

The status of Dominican women is especially fragile as they face additional burdens due to the cultural mores of the population, which are based in traditional Roman Catholic ideology. According to an international women's health group, women marry young and have children quickly (Engender-Health, 2003). While 59 percent of Dominican women use modern contraception methods when available, sterilization is the most popular method. Abortion is illegal but widely used. The fertility rate is approximately three children per woman (CIA, 2002). The maternal mortality rate is 220 per 100,000 live births (EngenderHealth, 2003). The disparity in women's treatment is often related to the concept of *machismo*, a version of male dominance and privilege in many Latin, South and Central American, and Caribbean countries. Domestic violence and sexual harassment are widespread (Bureau of Democracy, Human Rights, & Labor, 1998).

Hurricane George

The most recent natural disaster was Hurricane George, hitting on September 22, 1998, with winds of approximately 120 miles per hour. According to the USAID (2000) it affected every region of the country, with at least 280 people killed, 300,000 left homeless, and a total direct cost in losses estimated at $1.96 billion. The agricultural industry was considered the worst hit. Sixty percent of all bridges and 25 percent of the transportation infrastructure suffered severe damage. Housing, hospitals, schools, airports, sanitation facilities, and irrigation systems were all damaged. This contributed to the widespread contamination of water and food, the prime source for higher rates of diseases.

Over $50.3 million in assistance funneled through nongovernmental organizations (NGOs) came from the U.S., which is ranked as the Dominican Republic's fifth-largest donor following the Inter-American Development Bank, the World Bank, the European Union, and Japan (USAID, 2000). Aid supported many areas including health, community development, energy, irrigation, water/sanitation, and natural resources/agriculture. Currently the agricultural industry and the electrical power network have recovered. The transportation infrastructure is lagging behind as roads in some remote regions of the country have had only minimal repairs completed.

OVERVIEW OF CHILD LABOR

The examination of child labor in the Dominican Republic is multidimensional, consisting of formal, as viewed by the government, and informal structures, those related to practice and normative behavior. Widely recognized aspects include bonded labor, child prostitution, and disproportionate unacknowledged work by female children in homes. Children work in the fields, homes, and industry at young ages and with differing responsibility to their families, employers, and communities. Much of children's labor has minimal to no compensation and is often accompanied by deplorable working conditions and expectations. Child labor in the Dominican Republic encompasses the legal status of children as reported by the government, the commercial sex industry, and the work of female and Haitian children.

The Secretaria de Estado de Trabajo (n.d.) estimates that 20.3 percent of boys, girls, and adolescents (*niños, niñas, y adolescentes*) do unpaid family work. The vast majority of minors (68 percent) attend school, work outside the home, and work where they reside. Males are the largest proportion of minor workers who work outside the home. The inference then is that girls work inside the home. Data are not available on the work of female children's in the home. Societal behavior norms and values buffer and cloud the picture.

Dominican Children

The status of children as reported by the Secretaria de Estado de Trabajo (n.d.) is presented to provide a context for understanding child labor. It is estimated that there are 2,422,489 *niños, niñas, y adolescentes* between the ages of five and seventeen in the Dominican Republic. Three out of four (74.1%) are less than fourteen years old. Children are equally distributed by gender; 50.3% males and 49.7% females. The majority of children reside with both parents (62.7%) or with the mother only (16.3%). Nearly 12% of children reside with neither of their parents (11.8%). School attendance is considered high (92.6% for males and 93% for females) and reflects a cultural value for education. The majority of children in attendance are between the ages of seven and twelve (96.9%). Attendance diminishes with age, with the lowest school attendance rates for those fifteen through seventeen (79.5%). This is reflective of a legal employment age of sixteen. The highest rate of school attendance (94.2%) is in the urban zone known as the National District.

According to a recent study conducted by the Secretaria de Estado de Trabajo (n.d.), in which nearly 8,000 households and over 9,000 *niños, niñas, y adolescentes* ages five through seventeen participated, children working is a reality. While the government seeks to protect the rights of children, this study indicates that child labor is predominately masculine, with 74.5% of the males known to seek employment. As females age, employment-seeking increases for them. Employment-seeking occurs outside the home. The greatest numbers of children who work are under the age of fourteen (56.2%). Child labor is slightly higher in the rural zone (19.9%) compared with the urban regions (16.4%).

Niños, niñas, y adolescentes work in personal service, commercial work, sales, factories, and agriculture (Secretaria de Estado de Trabajo, n.d.). Forty percent of these workers provide services, like personal and social services; 21.5% work in restaurants and hotels; and 17% are in agriculture. More than half (51.3%) are salaried workers or apprentices. Fifty-one percent of *niños, niñas, y adolescentes* work permanently, 26% work occasionally, and 23% work temporarily. Thirty-two percent of minors who work also go to school.

Conditions for agricultural workers are worst in the sugar industry. Workers of all ages are paid by weight rather than the hour. This is often sabotaged by companies that allow the cane to dry on the side of the main road before it is picked up. By doing this, they reduce the pay because the cane is lighter when dry (Bureau of Democracy, Human Rights, & Labor, 1998). Villages for workers resemble those of the early American coal industry. They have poor facilities, unsanitary conditions, and lack schools for children, who are most often expected to work beside their parents. Children and their mothers frequently go without pay. Their work is considered under any payment to the male providers. Workers are paid with vouchers usable only at the company store. Any actual wages are kept low while the cost of goods is inflated. Few families escape this cycle of exploitation (Bureau of Democracy, Human Rights, & Labor, 1998; Lopez-Calva, 2001).

Haitian Children in the Dominican Republic

The story of Haitian children in the Dominican Republic is tied to the historical connections between the two countries and associated with oppression toward the Haitian population. Both countries experience high levels of poverty, but the situation in Haiti is much more desperate. Haitian labor is considered cheap, therefore one of the ways Haitian children come into the Dominican Republic is to work, most often for the sugar harvest (Inter-American Commission on Human Rights, 1999). A 2002 UNICEF report reveals that "2,500 Haitian children are smuggled illegally into the Dominican Republic annually to work as manual laborers" (as cited by Dominican Republic, n.d., History, paragraph 9).

On June 11, 1991, the nongovernmental organization Americas Watch denounced to the House of Representatives of the United States of America the human rights violations affecting Haitian cane cutters employed in the Dominican Republic, noting in particular, what it considered to be a forced labor regime affecting Haitian children on the plantations of the State Sugar Council (Bureau of Democracy, Human Rights, & Labor, 1998).

Commercial Sex Industry

Some aspects of child labor, by virtue of their form, are not well documented. This is the case of the commercial sex industry, which exploits children through pornography, prostitution, sex tourism, and trafficking (Sullivan, n.d.). Sexual abuse of children entails economic, social, and political aspects. There are documented cases of child exploitation with boys and girls as young as six years of age in various aspects of the sex trades.

According to the Secretaria de Estado de Trabajo's (n.d.) large study of child labor, 6% of children involved in the sex industry are ten through twelve years old, 24% are thirteen through fifteen, and 70% are sixteen and seventeen. An estimated 39% of these children are not schooled and considered illiterate. Men are the primary aggressor of male and female children, approximately 78%. Among adolescents, 89% of all clients were male. Nearly 60% reported having their first paid sexual encounter without the services of an intermediary; 25% were introduced by a friend. One-third of those children engaged in prostitution are male. Prostitution itself is not illegal in the Dominican Republic; however, law does prohibit the corruption of persons less than eighteen years of age. UNICEF (n.d.a) estimates there are 25,455 minors employed as prostitutes.

One aspect of the commercial sex industry is child sex tourism. International travel excursions are planned for the explicit purpose of tourists engaging in sex with minors (ECPAT-USA, n.d.). Estimates are that every sixth person employed globally somehow depends on or relates to travel, making it the biggest employer globally. It is estimated that 25 percent of international sex tourists are Americans. The Dominican Republic is one country where continued poverty helps maintain an active industry for the sexual exploitation of children. Countries with weak economies rely on tourism, and while sex tourism is unwanted, it is often tolerated in pursuit of economic gains.

Vignette

Fernando is twelve years old and lives with his parents, two brothers, and one sister in Santo Domingo. Their house is small and they share bedrooms. With little money for the family, its members have the basics of food and shelter only. Extra clothing is not available. Francisco goes to school every day with his brothers. His sister stays home, as she is younger. Francisco works with his father and fifteen-year-old brother at a small fireworks factory after school. It is very hot, with no breeze or fresh air, and the bathroom is a pot in the corner, used by males and females alike. There is only one door in and all other doors are locked. They work until dark. Francisco has a place on his hands where he was burned when he started working. His father told him to be very careful handling the gunpowder and reminded his son of the children who had died there a few years ago. When Francisco goes home, he must do his schoolwork by candlelight as the electricity is often out. He makes very little money, but it helps his family. Together they make just enough to live on, about 1,555 pesos (US$111) a month.

HISTORY OF CHILD LABOR

The Dominican Republic's history of child maltreatment was initiated during early colonialization. Current relationships are in part a result of the historical relationships among its people, including the indigenous people of the Dominican Republic and those who sought to dominate. From the days when Columbus served as royal governor for Spain up to 1499, the Taino Indians were maltreated and denied basic freedoms. The women and children were physically abused and used for labor. They were thought of, believed to be, and therefore treated as less than others.

The Spaniards established the *repartimiento* system, which allowed Spaniards to settle large portions of land, including lands occupied and considered home by the Indians. These settlers were "awarded" land with the "required" native labor of the Taino Indians (Library of Congress, 1989). By 1503 this became the *encomienda* system that made all land, in theory, the property of the royal crown, thus making the indigenous Taino Indians tenants. By this time the Taino labor force of men, women, and children had dwindled from an estimated population of 1 million in 1492 to approximately 500. The children lost their potential to grow up in the Taino traditions and became workers for households or fields.

By 1520 a new labor force was brought to La Isla Española from Africa. Bitter battles between the French and Spanish who occupied different sides of the island resulted in Spain's disengagement from its colony. The French had displaced over a million Africans as slaves to work on the plantations to create goods for export to France. The French and the freedmen (those Africans who came to the Dominican Republic as free people, or those who had purchased or were granted their freedom) ran these plantations and were highly successful at this enterprise. The history of Haiti is tied to that of the Dominican Republic and reflects the French and African influences of the Haitian people and to a lesser extent that of the Dominican Republic. Many individuals along the Haiti–Dominican Republic border speak Spanish, French, and Creole (a mixture of these languages and African dialects). While the French tried to occupy the entire island, Pierre Toussaint L'Ouverture, a French-trained Haitian, helped the country of Haiti gain its freedom (Dominican Republic, n.d.). One central issue is that the French and Spanish, and later the Haitians and Dominicans, had culturally different worldviews that contributed to the clash of these cultures as ruling efforts shifted multiple times. In this battle for the land, children were always the victims of violence and forced to work in some capacity for those who exploited their presence. Children's work in the sugar fields and as personal servants continues out of this history.

Dominicans and Haitians have shared the island of Hispaniola for decades with the rule transitioning repeatedly between governments. There has been a natural migration of Haitians to areas of the Dominican Republic. Here they are most often considered unwanted based on responses to racial and cultural differences. Haitians who came to cut cane with legal documents are now engaging in other types of work in urban areas, including tourism, construction, and domestic service. It is more often the case that Haitians live in the Dominican Republic for twenty, thirty, or more years without any documentation, being subject to harsh treatment. They live in a state of "permanent illegality" that is passed to their children, as these are born in the Dominican Republic (Inter-American Commission on Human Rights, 1999).

CHILD LABOR TODAY

As a result of the ongoing poverty, families live in marginal conditions. Societal poverty is the greatest underpinning factor related to the work status of children and affects every aspect of their lives. Parents are unable to provide for themselves or their children, resulting in extreme difficulty in areas of health, housing, and education. The poverty situation of families contributes to children entering and remaining in the workforce. As Ryan (2002) indicates, child labor is a product of oppression of the weakest members of a society whose general life existence is steeped in poverty.

A related contributor to children's work in the Dominican Republic is the lack of work for their parents. The continued problematic economic situation in the country forces parents to take any action that contributes to maintaining the basics such as food and shelter for the family. They are often willing to risk health and physical integrity. Desperation can even incline good parents and their children to engage in "delinquent acts" as a survival effort (Inter-American Commission on Human Rights, 1999). Parents send their children to work to assist in the survival of the family and hope their children will endure the situations they face. This obligation to family is a cultural value to be upheld by each impoverished generation. *Niños, niñas, y adolescentes* most often work in personal service (28.2 percent). They shine shoes and work in domestic service and as maids. Many children, once they leave their families, lose those connections and any level of protection.

The risks for agricultural workers are physical and financial. Children are at risk of injury in performing work in the fields. Cutting sugarcane requires the ability to handle a machete, and then the children must drag the cane to the main road while avoiding snakes and other poisonous vermin. The burning of sugarcane presents other hazards. The process of harvesting creates harsh air pollutants that the children breathe. There is also the potential of being caught behind the fire wall. Haitian children, as migrant laborers, are at the highest risk. They experience abusive labor practices as well as forced labor by the police and military who support the powerful sugar industry. Benefits are awarded to adult males, although women and children in a family may also work in the fields. If something happens to the male provider, the women and their children, regardless of the work they have performed, are left uncompensated for any of the family's work.

Cultural behavioral standards related to female children as well as Haitian children in the country are long-standing. They have developed over time and serve the interests of those privileged in the culture. Global human rights and social justice standards suggest changes should occur to benefit all members of Dominican Republic society. International groups monitor the country's practices in relationship to the intersection of culture and work.

Children within the commercial sex industry face many hardships. Research illustrates that they experience physical and mental abuse as well as financial exploitation. Intermediaries and clients withhold money for services delivered. The effects of these experiences are long term (Voss, 1999). Girls' physically undeveloped bodies experience lifelong reproductive problems, and HIV/AIDS is widely seen among prostituted children of both genders. The average price for each sexual encounter is $22 for boys and $35–thirty-five for girls. These earnings are shared with parents, intermediaries, or others involved in service delivery. Those interviewed reported high levels of daily alcohol consumption (50%) along with cocaine use (10%) and un-specified marijuana usage (Secretaria de Estado de Trabajo, n.d.).

A central question is, How do these children enter the sex industry? Some are given the opportunity to work for the family's benefit. Parents are told that for a small monetary transfer, their children will enter the service in-dustry. Poor families, desperate to survive, frequently interpret this as some form of housework. This is not an unrealistic assumption by families, as the majority of children work in the service industry, as reported by the Secretaria de Estado de Trabajo (n.d.). Other children enter the sex industry as their only mode of survival. These children come from the nearly 12 percent of abandoned children living without parents. Their daily survival depends on their actions alone as few services exist to assist them. A significant number of "street children" survive by begging, one-third participate in robbery or sell drugs, and one-fifth of these children engage in prostitution (Inter-American Commission on Human Rights, 1999).

POLITICAL VIEWS AND PUBLIC POLICIES

Children's Labor in General

"The Labor Code of the Dominican Republic, at Title II, prohibits children under 14 years from working and establishes, at Articles 244 to 254, the conditions in which work must be performed" (Inter-American Commission on Human Rights, 1999). Contained in the overall country labor code that is a part of the Constitution is the Code of the Minor, which provides specifics about working and protections provided for children in the Dominican Republic. With the permission of a parent, a minor may begin to work at age fourteen. When children work, they have the same rights as adults. Other stipulations on children's work include prohibitions against working more than twelve consecutive hours per day and against working in unhealthy environments as established by the Dominican secretary of state.

Several formal structures are in place to prevent the abuse of children through work. The Consejo Directivo Nacional (National Directive of Advice) meets bimonthly to review and monitor the status of child labor in the country. Encuesta Nacional de Trabajo Infantil is a committee that collects data on children ages five through seventeen. The Prevención del Trabajo Infantil Labores Agrícoles de Alto Riesgo in cooperation with twenty-seven community organizations, removes children from agricultural jobs, assists with education, and raises public awareness about the issue (Secretaria de Estado de Trabajo, n.d.).

The labor code prohibits the employment of children under fourteen and provides restrictions regarding hours worked each day, level of environmental danger, and the serving of alcohol (Bureau of Democracy, Human Rights, & Labor, 1998). The law also prohibits bonded or forced labor of minors. The International Labour Organisation (ILO) estimated that in August 1997 approximately 169,000 children ages seven through fourteen held jobs (Bureau of Democracy, Human Rights, & Labor), but no sanctions were placed on their families due to high levels of unemployment. The Dominican Social Security Institute addresses workplace health and safety conditions, but it is hampered by a small workforce and political patronage. Therefore, while children's work is in theory prohibited for those under age sixteen years and protected for minors over sixteen, little is done to address violations.

The 1994 Minors Code also contains provisions regarding child labor, sexual exploitation, and child abuse, and it provides for the removal of mistreated children (Bureau of Democracy, Human Rights, & Labor, 1998). These forms, like other forms of child abuse, are underreported according to local monitors due to cultural mores and traditional beliefs regarding the sanctity of the family. Under this code, little governmental protection is offered to those children involved in the tourist sex industry, even when children attempt to escape. Minimal recent efforts have been directed at arrest, jail, and deportation for foreigners involved in child prostitution. But the government, with a minimal enforcement team, often looks the other way given the need for tourist dollars in a country suffering high rates of poverty.

Dominico-Haitian Children

Following repeated publicity of abuses to Haitian children less than sixteen years of age and to Haitians over sixty years of age, the Dominican government began the repatriation of Haitians to Haiti (Human Rights Watch, 2002). This included those who were considered Haitian even if they were born in the Dominican Republic. The primary issue became one of legal documents in a country that refused to accept documents from the country of Haiti. After abusive experiences on the sugar plantations and within the community, Haitians were expelled without warning. This often affected Haitian women who had lost their husbands due to work-related deaths or injuries and their children.

Without documents it is difficult to determine a positive course of action. Dominican Republic officials repeatedly removed children by force when parents or fathers were working in the fields. This forced separation was detrimental to families and especially to children. The location of some of these children became unknown. Haitian children and women have no legal status in the Dominican Republic and are subject to abuses. Women and children were placed in cells with neither beds nor space to sleep on the floor. Also, limited food rations meant that adults often shared their rations with the children.

THE FUTURE OF CHILD LABOR

Behavioral and attitudinal changes in the Dominican Republic in relationship to the conditions that foster child labor are slow. Cultural attitudes toward gender roles are entrenched. Male dominance and patriarchy continue. Attitudes about female roles in society are steeped in traditional Roman Catholic ideology with its deep roots in this country, which has little diversity in belief systems. The impact of racism and racial exploitation also continue for Dominico-Haitian children trapped in the political debate over their legal status and the lack of a motivation to provide for children born and raised in the Dominican Republic.

The infrastructure needed to alter the widespread poverty is now a political debate. A diversified economic base is needed to reduce poverty rates, shift the social structure toward child education rather than labor, and assist the families in decreasing the need for children to work. In the end, children of the Dominican Republic survive with few resources or outlets to assist them. And, while the increases in the tourism industry have some positive economic impacts, it contributes to an increase in children's participation and exploitation in the commercial sex industry, including sex tourism. Despite efforts at coordination among the various governmental entities, little political change is suggested due to scarce government resources directed at the problem. The inability and unwillingness of the government to foster a true response to the plight of its children is a sad dilemma.

The Dominican Republic faces many hurdles in alleviating the social problems that contribute to the need for child labor. Ryan (2000) makes two points about the nature of child labor; it is rooted in poverty, and no clear strategy has emerged on how to best attack this issue. Recommended remediation includes:

1. Economic growth strategies designed to reduce unemployment and provide improved opportunities for adult employment;
2. Promotion of a tourist industry developed strategically to survive the industries' current volatility related to global terrorism while also eliminating the risk for children within the sex tourism industry;
3. Legitimizing Dominico-Haitian children to reduce their exploitation and current deportation experiences;
4. Increasing resources for the government institutions responsible for the welfare of children;
5. Using education and the media to change the attitudes of the Dominican people regarding child labor, education, and gender issues in employment, education, and service in the home.

The lack of resources leaves private social and religious institutions to carry the principal burden without government compensation (Bureau of Democracy, Human Rights, & Labor, 1998). As a result, the response is minimal and piecemeal. No single strategy will alter the change in child labor in the Dominican Republic. It will take a comprehensive holistic strategy that utilizes the assistance of international, national, and family systems.

CONCLUSION

Child labor is a complicated issue related to global and national social, economic, and political systems. These systems impact the socioeconomic status of families in the Dominican Republic. The country's current economic deficits make child labor an unfortunate viable alternative for families trying to simply survive. Children are able to gain employment when parents are not. While government entities seek to protect children, low budgetary priories foster a low-impact method of addressing an entrenched behavior pattern. Promotion of children's rights seems philosophical when juxtaposed against the harsh realities of children's experiences.

BIBLIOGRAPHY

Bureau of Democracy, Human Rights, and Labor (January 30, 1998) *Dominican Republic Country Report on Human Rights Practices for 1997*. Retrieved March 26, 2003, from the U.S. Department of State: http://www.state.gov/www/global/human_rights/1997_hrp_report/domrepub.html.
CIA (2002) *The World Factbook 2002: Dominican Republic*. Retrieved March 26, 2003, from http://www.odci.gov/cia/publications/factbook/geos/dr.html.
Dominican Republic (n.d.). Retrieved March 26, 2003, from http://www.infoplease.com/ipa/A0107475.html.

ECPAT-USA (n.d.). *Child Sex Tourism*. Retrieved April 27, 2003, from http://www.ecpatusa.org/travel_tourism.html.

EngenderHealth (2003) *Country by Country: Dominican Republic*. Retrieved March 26, 2003, from http://www.engenderhealth.org/ia/cbc/dr.html.

Geofacts (2002–3) *Dominican Republic*. Retrieved March 26, 2003, from http://www.indbazaar.com/country/conpage.asp?cat=Government&id=69.

Human Rights Watch (2002) Illegal people: Haitians and Dominico-Haitians in the Dominican Republic. Retrieved March 26, 2003, from http://hrw.org/reports/world/dr-pubs.php.

Inter-American Commission on Human Rights, Organization of American States (1999). Chapter XI: *Situation of Minors in the Dominican Republic*. Retrieved April 27, 2003, from http://www.cidh.org/countryrep/DominicanRep99/Chapter11.htm.

Library of Congress Country Studies (1989) *Dominican Republic: The First Colony*. Retrieved March 21, 2003, from http://lcweb2.loc.gov/cgi-bin/query/r?frd/cstdy:@field(DOCOD+do0013).

Lopez-Calva, L. (2001) Child labor: Myths, theories and facts. *Journal of International Affairs* 55(1).

Ryan, M. (2000) Child labor as an issue comes of age. *National Journal* 32(18).

Scanlon, T., V. Prior, M. Lamarao, M. Lynch, and F. Scanlon. (2002) Child labour. *BMJ: British Medical Journal* (August 24): 325(7361).

Secretaria de Estado de Trabajo (n.d.) *Trabajo Infintal*. Retrieved April 4, 2003, from http://www.set.gov.do/submenu/trabajoinf/index.htm.

Sullivan, S. (n.d.). How UNICEF is working to curb the sexual exploitation of children. Retrieved April 27, 2003, from http://www.unicef.org/sexual-expolitation/.

UNICEF (n.d.a) *Second World Congress against Commercial Sexual Exploitation of Children: Report Draft*. Retrieved April 27, 2003, from http://www.unief.org/events/yokohama/regional-montevideo.html.

———. (n.d.b) Child Work. Retrieved April 27, 2003, from http://www.childinfo.org/eddb/work/index.htm.

USAID (2000) Congressional Presentation fy2000: Dominican Republic. Retrieved March 26, 2003, from http://www.usaid.gov/pubs/cp2000/lac/domrep.html.

Voss, M. (1999) *The Commercial Sexual Exploitation of Children: An Overview*. Retrieved April 4, 2003, from ECPAT-USA, http://www.ecpatusa.org/background.html.

5

GEORGIA

Nona Tsotseria

PROFILE OF GEORGIA

The Republic of Georgia, on the south slope of the Caucasus Mountains, is nestled on the shore of the Black Sea. It is a beautiful country encompassing 27,000 square miles (70,000 square kilometers). Even though it is small, there is great climatic diversity with glaciers, deserts, and subtropical gardens. For the most part Georgia is mild climatically, with fertile soil. Georgians call the country "Sakartvelo."

Tbilisi is the capital, with a population of 1 million. It is the cultural, political, educational, and economic center of the country and is noted for its beauty. The capital is overcrowded with a population that has been increasing since 1990. This is in part a result of the phenomenon of internally displaced persons (IDPs). IDPs are refugees from the Abkhazia and South Ossetia regions of Georgia, where war and ethnic cleansing occurred a decade ago. People from other parts of Georgia are also moving to Tbilisi for economic reasons.

The Georgian population is a proud one with a rich history and language. It is a history marked by dramatic changes. Agricultural settlement dates back to the seventh to fourth millenniam B.C. In the eleventh century B.C., according to the Assyrians, Georgian tribes inhabited the territory, and the Greeks had contact with Georgian tribes during the eighth century B.C. In addition, the recent archaeological find of Homo erectus identifies the presence of the earliest human beings in Georgia, approximately 1.6 million years ago.

In spite of numerous incursions, in large part due to the geopolitical importance of the region, the people of Georgia have maintained their distinct identity, language, and literature. The Georgian language with its unique alphabet is one of the oldest still in use. It dates back to the third century B.C. The many invaders and conquerors have also left their mark on the language and culture. Among the populations Georgians have had to defend against are the Romans, Greeks, Persians, Arabs, Ottomans, and Russians. Today ethnic Georgians still comprise approximately 70% of total population of 5 million (see Table 5.1). Other ethnic groups represented are the Russians (6.3%), Armenians (8.1%), Azeris (5.7%), Ossetians (3%), Abkhazs (1.8%), and others (5%) (United Nations Development Programme, 2002b; Table 5.1).

In 2000, two significant anniversaries were celebrated—the 3000th year of statehood and 2000th year of Christianity. The most widespread religion is Georgian Orthodox (65%) with another 10% of the population identifying as Russian Orthodox. The capital is also home to Catholic and Protestant churches as well as mosques and synagogues. Eleven percent of the population identifies as Muslim and 11% as Armenian Apostolic. Religion was suppressed from 1921–91 under Soviet rule. Families, however, maintained their faith and traditions (United Nations Development Programme, 2002c).

Three powerful countries—Russia, Turkey, and Iran—controlled Georgia politically for three centuries. Wars against Turkey and Iran during the eighteenth century depleted the country's energy. Assistance was requested from Russia, and in the Treaty of 1783 responsibility was given to Russia to protect eastern Georgia from Turkish and Iranian invaders. This treaty, however, was violated, and Russia annexed the territory of Georgia as one of its provinces in 1801. Georgia was independent again from 1918–21 but became a part of the Soviet Union as the Georgian Soviet Socialist Republic. Georgia declared its independence in 1991 after the Soviet Union collapsed.

There has been conflict between Georgian political groups since independence. The civil war of 1991–92 resulted in political instability and economic uncertainty and the corruption of Georgian government officials. Today the Abkhazia and South Ossetia territories belong to Georgia but are really ruled by Russia. Russia was not pleased with Georgian independence, and many ethnic Georgians, who were in the majority in these regions, were killed or forced to leave.

As a part of the Soviet Union, Georgians lost their independence, which was difficult. On the other hand, during this time those in poverty experienced increased well-being. There was a commitment to the children. Literacy was at almost 100 percent, and many of Georgia's people had an advanced education. Approximately 30 percent of adults had higher education degrees and technical qualifications, and child protection was a high priority for the country. The government provided, by constitution, education and health care, and child labor was not an issue. Independence has witnessed a decreased

Table 5.1
Basic Data on the Republic of Georgia

Population	5 million
Government	Presidential Republic
Capital	Tbilisi
Legal system	Civil law
Voting rights	18 years, universal
Ethnic diversity	Georgians (70.1%), Armenians (8.1%), Russians (6.3%), Azeri (5.7%), Ossetian (3%), Abkhaz (1.8%)
Religion	Georgian Christian Orthodox (65%), Russian Christian Orthodox (10%), Armenian Apostolic (8%), Muslim (11%)
Natural Resources	Timber, hydropower, manganese, iron ore, copper, some coal and oil
Languages	Georgian, Russian, Armenian, Azeri, Abkhaz, Ossetian, Greek
Literacy	99%
Life expectancy	64.5 (USA, 77.2 years)
GDP, per capita	$4,600 (USA, $36,200)

Source:
American Councils for International Education, 2002.

level of well-being. Increasingly, problems that threaten the quality of life for children are surfacing—poverty, lack of health care, political and economic instability, and the reemergence of child labor.

The last ten years have been devastating for the former Soviet Republics, including Georgia. Established economic ties were destroyed before new ones were developed. The global economic crisis that began in 1997 interacted with this transition, increasing the negative impact. Even people who have a higher education and better employment can end up living in poverty. Now 20% of the urban population is unemployed and 70% of the population lives at or below the subsistence level ($51 per month); 59% live below the poverty line. Because salaries are so low in the public sector, $20 per month for teachers and physicians, people still live in poverty. It can be worse in rural areas, where there is practically no employment. Subsistence farming is the core economic activity.

OVERVIEW OF CHILD LABOR

While the issue of child labor has historical roots, it was not an issue during the Soviet era. The reemergence of child labor as a problem in Georgia parallels the political and economic shifts following the collapse in 1991 of the Soviet Union. While enormous energy has been paid to child well-being historically, now, due to declining economic conditions, the well-being of children is being challenged in Georgia. The intensity and severity of the social problems emerging over the last decade overshadow the issue of child labor, keeping it hidden. Child labor is a social issue that needs attention. According to information from international and national organizations, child labor is not an alarming issue in Georgia today, but it is an emerging trend that deserves attention.

Data from the Multiple Indicator Survey (MIS) provides information on the magnitude of the problem (UNICEF, 2000). Almost a third (30%) of children in Georgia are engaged in paid and unpaid work, including housework. For paid work, overall the rate was 3.5% to 4.8% for boys and 2.2% for girls. Few gender difference surfaced; age differences did. More likely to work were children ages ten through fourteen (39%); among children five through nine years old, only 19% worked. Regional differences also exist. The percentage of children who work in the capital is only 18%; in parts of the western region of Georgia the rate rises to 39%. Similarly the rate in urban areas is 21%, but it rises to 40% in rural areas. Paid work was more available in urban areas, with the highest rates (5%) located in the Tbilisi, Kakheti, and Samegrelo regions.

Vignettes

Georgi is a twelve-year-old boy living in a village near Tbilisi (the capital of Georgia). His parents are young and his father has a higher education. As a result of the high unemployment rate, they survive by farming. His grandmother takes dairy products (milk, yogurt, and cheese) to Tbilisi to sell twice a week. Georgi misses school to accompany his grandmother. He watches the large bags while she goes door to door, knocking to sell her goods. His oldest brother Kakha, age fourteen, helps his grandfather collect wood in the forest. The majority of houses in Georgia have wood heating, since electricity, oil, and gas are less available and more expensive. Many boys who live in rural areas collect (cut) wood in the forests to sell in the market.

Lela is fifteen years old. She lives in a rural area near the Turkish border. The best student in her school, she also keeps house and helps her grandmother because her mother goes to Turkey to work in merchandising. While she denies being hampered by her responsibilities, there is a sadness that appears when she talks about her mother, whom she misses. Her younger brother helps with the farming. Three generations living together is traditional in Georgia. This is helpful to families. Grandparents can fill the gaps when the parents are away at work. It is also helpful economically because it increases the affordability of housing.

Nodar is only twelve years old. A refugee from Abkhazia, he looks older than his years and feels responsible for his family. He is already selling newspapers in an underground train station in the capital. His family became IDPs during the armed conflict in the region. His father was killed and he now lives with mother and younger brother in one room of a former hotel. The housing is provided by the government. He dreams of returning home in Abkhazia.

HISTORY OF CHILD LABOR

Before the Soviet era, children were forced to work at an early age to help support the family. They were mainly involved in agricultural work and had little chance to receive an education. In fact, many families could not afford to educate their children. This shifted during the Soviet era. Education became mandatory, and no parent was allowed to prevent the education of their children. If parents had problems that prevented them from caring for their children, the government took responsibility. Children in rural areas were involved in family farming, but their health, education, and rights were protected. Sometimes schools helped farmers with harvesting. Age and conditions of employment for minors were defined in the Labor Code of Georgia. At the age of sixteen, young people were allowed to work. They worked a shorter day until the age of eighteen years.

The transition period since independence has had a negative impact on the children of IDP families and other families struggling with poverty. Children who are orphaned or disabled have felt the destructive impact. New categories of children in need have emerged—including street and working children, child prostitutes, and a growing number of young delinquents. The phenomenon of "street children" is so new in Georgia that it catches eyes. In Georgia, when child labor is spoken about, it is mainly street children who are considered. Currently it is estimated that Georgia has over twenty-five hundred street children, with an average age of thirteen years; most no longer attend school and lack basic life skills (UNICEF, 2000). The 1996 *Street Children Survey*, financed by UNICEF, found that about one-fifth of street children work in either the formal or informal economy.

They sell ice cream and newspapers, work in gas stations and cafés, and unload railway carriages. The average age of this group was thirteen. No recent data is available on street children, but one can observe that the number of those begging and working on the street is rising.

CHILD LABOR TODAY

The frequency of child labor is higher in rural areas, where the work of children is primarily unpaid. If they are paid, they receive less than their counterparts in urban areas. Further, because children in rural areas are primarily involved in either family businesses or housekeeping, their labor goes largely unrecognized. This work is encouraged because it is believed to provide children with training, which prepares them for the future. Involvement in family businesses, however, can have negative consequences if a child's health and education rights are not protected. If they are denied an education, they can be disadvantaged in future potential and their health can be compromised. Although the government has established departments and committees to oversee the rights, health, and safety issues for women and children, they are underfunded.

POLITICAL VIEWS AND PUBLIC POLICIES

Georgia is considered the most democratic country among the former Soviet republics. Despite the economic hardships it is experiencing today, there are instruments in place to protect human rights. Child labor, almost nonexistent in Soviet times, is not yet a major issue on the national agenda of Georgian public policy. There are, however, laws and policies in place to help protect the rights of children. The rights of working minors are protected by articles of the Georgian Labor Legislation Code. Additionally, the Constitutional Institute of the Public Defender has a commissioner for the rights of women and children who examines complaints. And, the national ombudsman's office has been working since 1996 to ensure that human rights and freedoms are protected. More recently, a Children's and Youth Parliament of Georgia was elected to examine children's issues and make recommendations to the National Parliament. This mechanism is an attempt to provide children a voice in the policy process (UNICEF, 2000).

The government of Georgia has also ratified major international human rights acts. In April 1994, Georgia acceded to the international Convention on the Rights of the Child (UNICEF, 2000). Among other human rights acts passed are Civil and Political Rights (United Nations, 1966); Economic, Social and Cultural Rights (United Nations, 1966); Minimum Age for Admission to Employment (International Labour Organisation, 1973); and Vocational Guidance and Vocational Training: Human Resources Development (Human Resources Development Corporation, 1975).

SOCIAL VIEWS, CUSTOMS, AND PRACTICES

The major child labor concerns expressed by Georgians are in regard to street children and prostitutes. The children of the streets lack care and attention. Many are involved in crime, prostitution, and/or trafficking. Unfortunately, statistics on them are not reliable. The other concern, often overlapping, is the rise in prostitution. This rise parallels changes in sexual behavior and the increase in economic hardship. A threefold increase occurred between 1995 and 1996. Although reliable statistics do not exist regarding child and adolescent prostitution, it is estimated to be half of the total. Boys and girls are both represented, and these youths are usually the only support for their families (UNICEF, 2000).

Some in the refugee population have joined the informal economy of buying and selling. Both adult and child workers are a part of this informal selling economy in the metro, bus, and railway stations as well as on the streets. They sell newspapers, ice cream, and miscellaneous items; they beg, dance, or pick pockets. Some of them are the only breadwinners in their families. Some adults organize children as workers in the informal economy, giving them protection from other groups while receiving part of their earnings.

Financial difficulties leave state-owned orphanages and children's shelters unable to fulfill all their objectives (UNICEF, 2000). Private organizations have responded to the crisis by developing centers that offer food and shelter for street children. The Peristvaleba nunnery opened the Dzegvi Children's Home near Tbilisi in 1995 after observing the conditions of the street children. Initially children were served in the monastery. The orphanage was opened when the demand became too great. Other refuges were developed in response to children thrown into the streets by families no longer able to care for them. There are stories of children turned out when family homes are sold, and of families attempting to arrange marriages for daughters in exchange for cash.

The Georgian government has been unable to adequately respond to the needs of children without the assistance of international organizations. The increasing global awareness of the emerging social problems connected to child labor in Georgia has drawn the attention of multiple international nongovernmental organizations and institutions. A coordinating council of nongovernmental organizations (NGOs), involving up to thirty-five organizations, is now active in working on the issues. Others involved include Save the Children, World Vision, Oxfam International, Johns Hopkins University, and the United States Centers for Disease Control (UNICEF, 2000). The lack of reliable statistical data about the economic activities of children has hampered the response. Therefore the United Nations Development Program launched a program in 1999 aimed at gathering reliable data. The goal of this project was to support the development of effective intervention in the child labor arena.

THE FUTURE OF CHILD LABOR

Despite the fact that the issue of child labor is hidden behind other socioeconomic problems in Georgia, governmental and societal awareness of child labor is rising. International organizations operating in Georgia are providing financial support and expertise to local institutions trying to handle the issues. Efforts of the national government along with those of nongovernmental and international organizations are interfacing to work toward a solution to child labor problems. The ongoing Labor Force Survey (United Nations Development Programme, 2001/2002a) is compiling statistical data as a basis for developing effective interventions.

Efforts are under way to increase awareness, provide basic services, and address the economic difficulties that contribute to the need for child labor. Newspapers and television are providing insight but need support to expand their educational role regarding child labor. Also, within the changing political and social context, NGOs are increasingly able to present their observations, advocate, and lobby for the children they work with and for. Of greatest concern are the street children. UNICEF (2000) recommends making support services and basic resources available for street children, including clothes, food, housing, health care, and rehabilitation services. Services need to be available for children abused physically and sexually, and for recovery from substance abuse.

One of the many strategic and tactical steps in the process is the major focus on the economic development of Georgia. These efforts support the move toward permanent change. The economic development of Georgia includes the creation of jobs for adults, poverty eradication, support for families with children, and assistance to public and private institutions that aim to help children. Several United Nations–supported projects have the potential to assist in ending the forms of child labor that interfere with the development of children. The Anti-Poverty Programme of Georgia (United Nations Development Programme, 2001/2002e) addresses the issues that force poor families to depend on child labor for family survival. It is designed to address the structural issues of poverty, improve education and health, and provide assistance. Unfortunately, the program is underfunded. There is also a Women in Development project (United Nations Development Programme, 2001/2002d), which is committed to creating gender equality. Improving the conditions for women improves the condition for children.

Poverty in Georgia is partially a result of the globalization process. Developed countries gain wealth while less developed countries grow poorer. The issues therefore are global. The large developed countries, which dominate the world economy, have a major role in the resolution of the problems.

BIBLIOGRAPHY

Chilashvili, L., and N. Lomour. (1999) A brief history of Georgia: The eternal crossroads. In O. Soltes, ed., *National treasures of Georgia*, pp. 30–38. London: Philip Wilson Publishers.

Gogishvili, T. (2001) *Trends of child and family well-being in Georgia*. Background paper prepared for the Regional Monitoring Report No 8: A Decade of Transition. Florence: UNICEF Innocenti Research Centre. Retreived June 4, 2003, from www.unicef-icdc.org/research/ESP/CountryReports2000_01/ Georgia00fam.pdf.

Human Resources Development Corporation. (1975) Retrieved July 1, 2003, from http://ilolex.ilo.ch:1567/cgi-lex/convde.pl?C142.

Human Rights Internet. (1998) *Initial Report of the Republic of Georgia*. For the Record 1997: The Human Rights System. Retrieved October 9, 2002, from http://www.hri.ca/fortherecord1997/.

International Labour Organisation. (1973) *Recommendation concerning minimum age for admission to employment* (Recommendation No. 146). Appendix B. In E. Mandelievich, ed., *Children at work*, pp. 155–58. Geneva: International Labour Organisation.

Soltes, O. (1999) The eternal crossroads. In O. Soltes, ed., *National treasures of Georgia*, pp. 18–29. London: Philip Wilson Publishers.

UNICEF. (2000) *National Report on Follow-up to the World Summit for Children: Georgia, December 2000*. New York: UNICEF.

United Nations. (1966) *The United Nations Human Rights Protection System*. Retrieved July 1, 2003, from http://www.droitshumains.org/uni/Formation/ Images/spdh_a.pdf.

———. (1997) Conventions on the Rights of the Child. *Initial reports of states: Addendum, Georgia*. Retrieved June 29, 2003, from http://www.hri.ca/ forthrecord1997/documentation/tbodies/crc-c-41-add4.htm.

———. (1997) *Promotion and protection of the rights of children*. Retrieved June 29, 2003, from http://www.hri.ca/forthrecord1997/documentation/genassembly/ a-52-482.htm.

United Nations Development Programme. (2001/2002a) *Child Labor Survey Module in Georgia*. Retrieved October 9, 2002, from http://www.undp. org.ge/Projects/childlabor.html.

———. (2001/2002b) *Child Labor Survey Module in Georgia*. Retrieved July 1, 2003, from http://www.undp.org.ge/Projects/gender.html.

———. (2001/2002c) *Facts about Georgia*. Retrieved July 1, 2003, from http: //www.undp.org.ge/Projects/georgiabrief.html.

———. (2001/2002d) *Gender in Development*. Retrieved July 1, 2003, from http: //www.undp.org.ge/Projects/gender.html.

———. (2001/2002e) *Improving targeting of poor and extremely poor families in the anti-poverty programme of Georgia*. Retrieved July 1, 2003, from http: //www.undp.org.ge/Projects/poorfam.html.

6

GUATEMALA

David Keys and Adam DeFayette

PROFILE OF GUATEMALA

Life in the republic of Guatemala, where over 8.5 million of the nation's 11.4 million people live below the poverty line, is a matter of chance. The average income is the equivalent of US$1,711 per year. Although the government set the legal minimum wage for agricultural workers at the equivalent of $2.25 per day, rarely do employers comply. Consequently, those in extreme poverty in urban areas number 36%, while in rural areas 73% of the population is caught in the grip of absolute poverty (Interamerican Development Bank, 2001). One writer, in his recent writing on Guatemala, says, "Guatemala is a patently unhealthy place" (Barry, 1992, p.169). He goes on to comment that conditions throughout the country are "appalling."

Alarming health care disparities exist between *indigenas* (native indigenous peoples) and *mestizos*, who are largely of mixed european and indigenous ancestry. Life expectancy for *ladino* men and women is 64 and 65 years respectively. Indigenous, or Indian, men live on average only 48 years, and indigenous women have even shorter lives at just under 47 years. Part of this difference can be traced to the location of the nation's physicians, 80 percent of whom practice in the Guatemala City area. In contrast, rural areas, where most of the indigenous populations live, have only 1.1 doctors per 10,000 people. These statistics are part of a larger picture of neglect that is an element of government policy. Since 1980, Guatemala has cut its national health budget by nearly 70%. It went from being 1.9% of the gross domestic product (GDP) in 1980 to just under 1% in 1990 and to 0.6% in 2000 (Interamerican Development Bank, 2001). Cuts have been deep in rural areas. Of the present health care budget, 67% has been spent in the Guatemala City area, primarily to maintain the city's hospitals (United Nations Children's Fund, 1992). Hardest hit are the native Maya people, with 80% of their child mortality being due to preventable diseases such as diarrhea, measles, and prenatal problems. By removing doctors from the countryside and concentrating funds and hospitals in areas that are primarily *ladino*, Guatemala's recent governments have succeeded in creating the worst environment in Central America in regard to health for its native people and their children. Despite the appalling conditions, children have some value as laborers and commodities in Guatemala; as sexual objects, combatants, agricultural labor, factory help, or as trade goods in the international black market of adoptions.

OVERVIEW OF CHILD LABOR

The economic base of Guatemala is focused on agriculture and livestock, two industries that have traditionally used children in large numbers. Of the labor force in Guatemala, 58% is employed on the nation's agricultural land, while 14% work in service and 13% are employed in manufacturing. Crops such coffee, bananas, and sugarcane require considerable hand labor. Growers frequently use children. Livestock, approximately 2.5 million cattle, along with 109,000 goats and 600,000 sheep, require tending, tasks that even very young children can perform.

The small industrial base in the country produces raw rubber and textiles, products that also make use of children as a major labor source (*New York Times*, 2000, 2001). Since Guatemala has been burdened with a large population of poor for most of the last five hundred years, there has always been a willing workforce of children. This workforce now numbers about 1.4 million children, or approximately 38% of those ages seven through fourteen years (International Labour Organisation [ILO], 2001). The ILO figures differ substantially from those published by the Guatemalan government in the national commercial census, which puts the child labor force at 152,000. That is about 4.1% of 3.7 million children ages seven through fourteen years in the country (La Comisión de Trabajo, 1998). Whatever their numbers, the sight of children as permanent members of the labor force is not one that distresses many *ladino* Guatemalans, who regard it as a function of class status. Only the children of middle-class professionals (doctors, lawyers, civil servants) and *los ricos* (the rich) are exempt. In view of the nature of Guatemala's economy, with agriculture, light industry, and tourism as important elements, it is clear that children may always occupy an important niche in the labor market unless policy changes are made.

Many children in Guatemala labor in textile mills, agriculture, and domestic work, even though the law in Guatemala states that children under age fifteen may not be employed. Sex workers and soldiers are normally thought to be adults, but there is a disturbing trend in developing countries experiencing political upheaval that forces children to do the worst and most dangerous jobs. Owners of the *fincas* pay children on average about eighty cents a day to cultivate and harvest coffee beans, and they use private security forces to keep workers of all ages on the land and away from union organizers.

According to Father Jimenez-Garcia many of these private security forces are in fact demobilized national guards and regular army troops who left government service after the 1996 treaty. They now function as vigilantes in the pay of *finca* owners.

Many of the same people who intimidated and murdered *campesinos* [peasants] during the civil war are back among us in the pay of the *jefes* [plantation bosses]. A man who supervised the murder of an entire village now is the chief of security for a banana grower a few kilometers from here. The provincial authorities got him his job. (personal communication, March 22, 2002)

Amnesty International estimates that over three hundred thousand children—some as young as ten years old—are fighting in various armed conflicts throughout the world (Fishman, 2002). This is clearly a different kind of child *labor*, and, along with prostitution, it is probably the most dangerous kind of labor that exists.

Vignettes

Felipe Cuevas-Flores (personal communication, November 19, 1982) was eleven years old and shouldering a rifle and squatting in the jungle of the Zacara Highlands of eastern Guatemala in the fall of 1982. He was a member of a guerrilla band organized by former *campesinos* who had become rebel fighters. The country had recently endured its worst months of government-sponsored death squads, ordered by then President Rios Montt. Felipe's family had been killed in the village of San Luis in the province of Petén only weeks before, and the guerrilla band had picked Felipe up on the road. He said that when the band found him, he had not eaten for four days. He had no family, which in Guatemala was a virtual death sentence for a child.

The guerrilla headman was man of thirty years named Gonzalo, who had once been a coffee plantation laborer. Gonzalo took Felipe into the band, gave him a meal of beans and some dried goat meat, and told him he was a soldier now. Felipe's first duties were to stay absolutely still when he was ordered, to bring water to the other men when they were on guard duty, and to drive a dilapidated jeep. "It took a few hours to learn the shifting of the gears," but, Felipe said, "I was a good driver by the end of the first morning with the band." On the third day the band attacked a government supply station. There were shots and the blasts of grenades over the hill, out of Felipe's vision, until two of the group brought another man to the jeep. It was Alejandro, a thin sixteen-year-old who had a large, bloody hole in his chest, plugged with a rag. Felipe parked the jeep under some trees and tried to give him water. "Alejandro was bleeding from his mouth and could not drink. He died thirty minutes later." That afternoon Gonzalo took Alejandro's rifle, gave it to Felipe, and said, "You will take his place now."

In the weeks following Alejandro's death, the band had picked up seven new recruits, all under twelve years of age. There were four boys, Miguel, Ernesto, and two Maya who spoke no Spanish; and three girls, Maria, Juana, and Christia, all orphaned by the death squads and without families. Felipe became the senior of the child's group. He fought with the older men and provided some meager food for the other children. During the next sixty days, two of the children were killed and another was severely hurt. Maria stepped on a land mine and was mortally wounded. One of the Maya boys escaped the band one night and was later found at the side of dirt road, apparently crushed to death. Villagers said that government paramilitaries had run him down with a pickup truck. Juana, who was ten years old at the time, blew off four fingers on her right hand while capping a stick of dynamite. These tragedies were accepted in turn as "the realities of the times" ("*las realidades de las veces*"). In all, Felipe lived and fought with several rebel bands for twelve years, surviving the realities.

In 1996 the Guatemalan government signed a peace treaty, and Felipe, then twenty-three, returned to his village in Petén. Any relatives no longer lived there, and only a few of the original families were still alive. He now farms a small common plot of land, growing coffee.

Alicia was fourteen years old in 1998, when her mother died of a ruptured appendix. Some neighbors took their house in Guatemala City, and the police did nothing when Alicia went to the station to complain. Her only choice was to follow other orphans to the city dumps and rummage for food and anything of value. With a boy and girl, Mario and his sister Elena, Alicia built a small shelter near the dump and for weeks survived there. Periodically, priests and aid workers would come and try to get the children to come to an orphanage. Elena warned Alicia not to believe the workers. Alicia finally agreed to go with them, and she was taken to a house on the western edge of the city. There were no priests or nuns there, only women, who gave her a hot meal, some clean clothes, and trimmed her hair. The next day she was taken to a nightclub near downtown and told to do whatever the customers asked her to do. "I had to do what they told me. I discovered I was a prostitute." Alicia also found out that almost all of the girls, ages thirteen through twenty years, had been orphaned or lost their parents, ending up as sex workers. Some of the girls had AIDS, and two died just a few months after Alicia was brought to the club, while other girls had babies who were sold as black market adoptions. All lived together in rooms above the night-club. They were watched closely by the bosses and could not leave without permission. After a year and a half working in the club, a client helped Alicia escape, giving her thirty-five American dollars to buy a bus ticket to Belize City. Alicia now is attending college in Canyon, Texas, studying mathe-matics. She wants to teach high school math when she gets her teaching certificate.

HISTORY OF CHILD LABOR

The history of child exploitation in Guatemala is linked to the changing idea of childhood in Western cultures. For much of Guatemala's recent history (since 1500) there has not been a clear idea of those periods of life known to us as "childhood" and "adolescence." There was a clear idea of one being a "baby," an infant dependent on a mother or a caretaker, but this period ended when a child could do some simple jobs, follow directions, and be trained for more complex tasks. In the Americas, including the United States, child labor has been common for the poor since before 1900, and in the case of Guatemala it has been considered necessary for survival in most indigenous communities to the present day. Having a childhood was con-sidered something a privileged young person experienced, in part because time was taken up with education and social events. These things cost more money than most poor Guatemalans could ever afford. Members of the family, by ages seven or eight years, were expected to contribute to the family income. In the United States, increasing income levels and the decline in numbers of the very poor has reduced the need for child labor, and over a period of years (1900–1920) the states and federal government passed child labor laws. Guatemala did not have the economic prosperity realized in the U.S. during the twentieth century and consequently did not change its attitude on the working poor child. These ideas have combined with the almost constant social and political struggles in the country. As a conse-quence, the exploitation of young children as labor commodities has been a constant since 1940.

CHILD LABOR TODAY

The Changing Problem of Child Exploitation

While the labor of children in factories and on farms are common images of exploitation in developing countries like Guatemala, the mistreatment of the young has invaded institutions such as adoption, tourism, and political liberation movements. Legitimate industries, which have been economically and socially beneficial to Guatemala in the past, have developed serious problems in their exploitation of children.

Ofelia Calcetta Santos, Special Rapporteur to the United Nations, in 1997 found that the sale of children under the auspices of adoption as well as child prostitution and child pornography were serious human rights problems in Guatemala (Casa Alianza, 1999; United Nations Committee on Human Rights, 1997). Again, in August 1999, acting on reports of violations of human rights, the United Nations dispatched a second Special Rapporteur, Param Cumarasway, to Guatemala. Cumarasway's mission was to investigate the shooting of "street children" by paramilitary police in and around Guatemala City. There were also reports of abuses by persons connected to the Guatemalan military, who continue to threaten watchdogs such as Amnesty International, the United Nations Mission to Guatemala (MINUGUA), and the Roman Catholic Church. Cumarasway's report to the United Nations Committee on Human Rights detailed a litany of abuses. This included the murders of orphans in the capital and death threats against human rights workers who reported the killings (United Nations Committee on Human Rights, 1999a).

The incidents of child maltreatment have been documented in a number of settings, the worst being a total devaluation of children, as in "Guatemala's Laboring Children: Police Abuses in Detention" (Human Rights Watch, 1999). Human Rights Watch found that juvenile correctional centers routinely released children held in custody to factory owners and farmers to become unpaid labor. Documented cases implicating officials at the Gaviotas Detention Center (for boys) and Gorriones Detention Center (for girls), both located in Guatemala City, commonly "loaned" juvenile inmates to local businessmen and *finca* owners. This is a common practice. Children from another detention center on the outskirts of San José were also released to become illegal laborers. The Office of Teatment and Guidance for Children, or TOM *(Tratamiento y Orientación de Menores)*, the government agency that administers juvenile detention and protection services, is the manager for all juvenile facilities. To date no acknowledgment of these cases of mistreatment has been made by the government. No actions have been taken to remedy the abuses.

However, detention and forced labor seem to be the least of the country's problems when the fate of children orphaned or unwanted live on the streets of Guatemala, where they routinely experience beatings, thefts, and sexual assaults. It is unfortunate that members of the National Police and private security guards are often the perpetrators of these crimes. There has been a decrease over the past decade in the serious crimes committed against street children, including murder and torture. In April 1996, two Guatemala City National Police officers raped a sixteen-year-old girl. A third officer kept watch. Then a drunk Treasury police officer killed a sixteen-year-old youth, Ronald Raúl Ramos, in September 1996. More than ten other street children were murdered. Also in 1996, there were at least ten children of the street suspiciously murdered. None of the offenders has been captured (Human Rights Watch, 1999).

United Nations Special Rapporteur, Param Coomarasway of Sri Lanka, investigating the trafficking of minor children for sexual exploitation, went to Guatemala in 1999. Her investigation found that indeed Guatemala was one of several countries in Central America that acted as a transit point for the trafficking of children in illegal adoptions as well as for the growing industries of "sexual tourism," child pornography, and slavery (United Nations Committee on Human Rights, 1999b).

Legitimate and Illegitimate Business Side by Side

One common feature in all United Nations Special Reports on the abuse of children in Guatemala over the past five years has been the parallel growth of child exploitation alongside legitimate activities. A small tourist industry, focusing at first on Mayan archaeology and culture, has also developed a seedy side in which foreign businessmen travel to Guatemala, gain access to child prostitutes, and purchase unrestricted child pornography. This is known as "sexual tourism." While legitimate tourism is a significant asset to Guatemala, marketing the bodies of children, either on film or in the flesh, represents quick and sure profit.

The bodies of children have become profitable in a number of ways. While in most cases poor children on the street are viewed as a social burden and a nuisance, in recent years a trade in illegal adoptions has emerged, with nearly 80 percent of the children going to the United States (Chapman, 1999). The number of legal adoptions in Guatemala ranges from 1000 to 1500 a year, mostly children of young girls between the ages of 15 and 19 years, whose fertility rate is six times that of any other age group in the country (United Nations Economic Commission, 2001). In the years since 1996, international adoptions make up 95% of all adoptions in Guatemala and generate in excess of $20 million dollars annually. Most of the revenue goes to lawyers who handle the paperwork, guide the process through the government bureaucracy, and solicit American and European couples. The tremendous demand for infant children and the large profits in adoptions have created a child market, which reduces babies to merchandise. By all reports this trade is growing every year while homeless, abandoned, and orphaned children numbering 5000 at any given time in Guatemala City are ignored according to Casa Alianza, a branch of New York City's Covenant House.

Guatemala is the leader in Central America, sending more illegal babies to the international black market that any other nation in the region (Chapman, 1999). Between 1000 and 1500 illegal adoptions occur that involve children born to Guatemalan mothers, the average payment for a child to its mother being about $100. The Guatemalan attorney handling the sale charges on average about $15,000 (*Boston Globe*, 1997). In many cases the children are born to prostitutes who are held against their wills (*Houston Chronicle*, 1997) and their babies are taken away and profitably sold. The fallout from the illegal baby trade also has created a growing number of throw-away children who have not been adopted, know as "expired" or "useless." Many end up in orphanages enduring terrible conditions. In the case of one institution, dozens of children were kept in corrals (*La Jornada*, 1997). It is clear that children in a very real sense have become commodities to be bought and sold, stored and priced, as well as wasted and disposed of. As of this writing, the trade remains a major source of income for persons in the Guatemalan government and lawyers arranging illegal adoptions. This has prompted a United Nations' Human Right investigation, which found that babies have been reduced to "objects of trade and commerce" (*Miami Herald* 2000, p. 1; United Nations' Human Rights Commission Report, 1997).

POLITICAL VIEWS AND PUBLIC POLICIES

The situation in Guatemala is complicated by a civil war that officially ended in 1996 without a clear political resolution. The legacy of the civil war is everywhere in Guatemala, and the reality of child exploitation and abuse seems to some in the Guatemalan government a small problem, one that outsiders worry about. For outside investors seeking to capitalize on the cheap child labor created by poverty-ridden conditions, war has a threefold purpose: war keeps the country poor (as money is allocated for weapons rather than food, housing, and education); war places a low value on human life (which translates to low wages for the easily disposable laborer); and last, war delivers precious economic resources to the winners.

Claiming a shortage of funds and political obstruction from opposition parties, the Guatemalan government has not implemented the Child and Adolescent Code passed by the Guatemalan Congress in 1996. This would specifically outlaw the exploitation, mistreatment, or incarceration of minors. In March 2000 the Guatemalan Congress, led by former dictator Gen. Rios Montt, "suspended indefinitely" the Child and Adolescent Code, claiming that it was "not among the immediate priorities of the nation" (La Prensa, 2000, p. 6). Opposition groups in the Congress, who were military opponents of General Montt during the recent war, say, "Protecting children is seen by the entrenched powers as helping the Left, and Montt wants no part of that" (La Prensa, 2000, p. 6). The United Nations Special Rapporteur, Coomaraswamy, reported that the suspension of the Child and Adolescent Code is a major problem, and that resistance to it primarily comes from interests (lawyers and American adoptive parents) in the commercial adoption market (United Nations Committee on Human Rights, 1999b). Human rights organizations such Casa Alianza have filed complaints in Guatemalan courts on behalf of nearly four hundred child victims of abuse, but justice is slow and unsure in the country. Roughly 5 percent of these have resulted in convictions, with remainder being dismissed (United Nations Committee on Human Rights, 1999b).

Father I. Jimenez-Garcia (personal communication, March 22, 2002) observes that most of the peasants wish to forget the thirty years of brutal civil war. It was one that pitted indigenous peoples, Marxists, and social democrats against what the American press called the "most oppressive and ruthless military in Central America" (Corporation for Public Broadcasting, 1985). "The poor are frightened and exhausted by the war and will sacrifice their children to a life of toil if they think they must. Families here have immediate concerns of food and life. Social reform in the long term is too remote an idea" (Jimenez-Garcia, 2002).

THE FUTURE OF CHILD LABOR

As the economic base of the country gradually changes from export agri-culture to more service-oriented businesses, the exploitation of children is changing. The image of children working on coffee *fincas* and in factories continues to be a reality, in part because of the poverty and the social structure. Children have also emerged as a resource in the service economy that is developing in Guatemala. The changing role of children in the un-derground economy of Guatemala is matter for serious consideration. Children are forced into this work because of economic circumstances. Ex-treme poverty enlarges the scope and forms of child labor. As the majority of Guatemalans continue to be steeped in poverty, children will be found employed in all imaginable forms of labor—as combatants fighting in wars, as sex workers, and as commodities for sale. The solutions to these problems are rooted in the economy of Guatemala.

Because the current government is at best indifferent to the plight of children, these abuses are growing. If careful regulation either by Guatemala or the international authorities is not carried out, children will remain a target for baby brokers, child pornographers, and unscrupulous businesses. In order for abusive child labor to disappear, the overall economic circumstances of Guatemala must be improved.

Education, particularly for young girls, has been found to be a factor in reducing birthrates and child labor in many developing countries. It is known that introducing low-cost education for poor children assists in the elimi-nation of unwanted pregnancies, reducing the number of adoptions, and empowering young people so they can avoid exploitation. Greater attention by the United Nations to the plight of the least powerful members of a given society as well as pressure to enforce their national laws protecting the young will help ensure a diminishing of exploitative and abusive practices.

Poverty in Guatemala is, on the surface, the reason why many children find it necessary to work. It is also the excuse made by many adults in their use of children in legal as well as illegal occupations. However, after one scratches the surface, it becomes clear that the racial divisions (between the indigenous peoples and the *ladinos*) and the lack of a real democratic system representing all ethnic peoples in Guatemala are the conditions that underlie both poverty and the exploitation of children. Institutionalized racism and military rule stand as the major obstacles in the paths of reform.

BIBLIOGRAPHY

Barry, T. (1992) *Inside Guatemala.* Albuquerque, NM: Inter-Hemispheric Education Resource Center.

Boston Globe. (1997) Exposé on child trafficking. 14 September, A17.

Casa Alianza. (1999) High hopes for visit by UN special rapporteur to guatemala. Casa alianza last minute news, 16 July, 1.

Chapman, M. (1999) Buy Buy Baby. *The Guardian (London)*, 27 August, a3.

Corporation for Public Broadcasting (PBS) (1985) Revolution in Central America: Part #3—Revolution in Nicaragua—The fall of Anastasio Somoza-Debayle.

Fishman, T. (2002) Making a killing: The myth of capital's good intentions. *Harper's Magazine* 305, 33–41.

Houston Chronicle. (1997) Guatemalan prostitutes tell bitter tales of bondage and baby trade. 1 November, 2.

Human Rights Watch. (1999) Guatemala's laboring children: Police abuses in detention. Washington, DC: Human Rights Watch Pamphlets.

Interamerican Development Bank. (2000) *IDB Country Economic Assessment.* Washington, DC: IDB Publications.

———. (2001) *Annual Economic Report.* Washington, DC: IDB Publications.

International Labour Organisation. (2001) *Global Labor Statistics.* Geneva, Switzerland: ILO Publications.

La Comisión de Trabajo. (1998) "El censo de Trabajo." Congreso de Republic.

La Jornada. (1997) In Quezaltenango, 29 children seen as "expired" or useless products. 24 September, 3.

La Prensa. (2000) Los pueblos y los ninos (Managua, Nicaragua). 9 Noviembre.

Lopez, O. (2002) Los ninos y los trabajadores. *Prensa Libre*, 12 Marzo (Ciudad Guatemala).

Miami Herald. (2000) Baby-selling a major business in Guatemala. 5 June, 1.

Reuters New Service. (2001) Guatemala: Child labor on the rise, ILO says. 11 December.

United Nations Children's Fund. (1992) Report on health and demographic change: Latin America. M. Cuevas (Spain), Rapporteur.

United Nations Committee on Human Rights. (1997) Report on sale of children, child prostitution and child pornography. O. Santos (Philippines), Special Rapporteur. Geneva, Switzerland.

———. (1999a) Report on the application of justice. P. Cumarasway (Malaysia), Special Rapporteur. Geneva, Switzerland.

———. (1999b) Report on violence against women. R. Coomaraswamy (Sri Lanka), Special Rapporteur. Geneva, Switzerland.

United Nations Economic Commission on Latin America and Caribbean (ECLAC). (2002) Report to the General Assembly. M. Barrientos (Peru), Special Rapporteur.

Wallis, D. (2002) Give them the business. Interview with Ralph Nader. *New York Times Magazine*, 16 June, 13.

7

HONDURAS

Raul Zelaya and Desi Larson

PROFILE OF HONDURAS

Honduras is a Central American country bordered by Guatemala, El Salvador, and Nicaragua. Slightly larger than the state of Tennessee, Honduras features a mostly mountainous interior and narrow coastal plains flanked by the Caribbean Sea and the Pacific Ocean. Natural resources include timber, gold, silver, copper, lead, zinc, iron ore, antimony, coal, and fish.

Its climate is subtropical in the lowlands and temperate in the mountains. The Honduran environment is marked by susceptibility to hurricanes and floods along the Caribbean coast. In 1998, Hurricane Mitch devastated much of the countryside, which was already marred by erosion due to deforestation, slash-and-burn, and other unsustainable agricultural practices. Hurricane Mitch was responsible for the deaths of about fifty-six hundred people and caused an estimated $1 billion in damage. In addition to the environmental havoc wreaked by deforestation, mining activities have polluted the country's most significant source of freshwater, Lago de Yojoa, as well as several rivers and streams, with heavy metals. It has caused over $3 billion in destruction, seriously damaged the road network, virtually wiped out the banana crop, and deprived tens of thousands of their livelihoods. Massive international humanitarian assistance—led by the U.S.—has saved many lives, provided for basic needs, and temporarily reopened the road network. Honduras now relies heavily on substantial international aid to help rebuild its infrastructure and productive economic capacity.

Honduras, historically part of Spain's empire, became an independent nation in 1821. Its history includes two and one-half decades of military rule during the mid-twentieth century followed by the election of a civilian government in 1982. In 1999 the population of Honduras was 6,560,608. Ninety percent of Hondurans are *mestizo* (mixed Amerindian and European), 7% are Amerindian, 2% are black, and the remaining 1 percent are white. Approximately 74% of the population is literate.

One of the poorest countries in the Western Hemisphere, Honduras is marked by an extraordinarily unequal distribution of income. Economic growth depends to a large degree on the economy of the United States, its major trading partner. Recently, Honduras has also seen a dramatic rise in crime.

OVERVIEW OF CHILD LABOR

Table 1 presents a cursory overview of Hondurans distributed by age. Over half (53%) of Honduras's people live below the poverty line. In 2002 the unemployment rate was reported as 28% of a labor force of 2.3 million.

Table 7.1
Population Distribution in Honduras

Age	Total Population (%)	Distribution
0–14 years	41.8	Male 1,400,778; Female 1,340,834
15–64 years	54.6	Male 1,774,619; Female 1,806,568
65 years and over	3.6	Male 112,100; Female 125,709

Source:
CIA, 2003.

Hondurans work in the agricultural (34%), industry (21%), and service (45%) sectors. Agriculture, the most important sector of the economy, employs nearly two-thirds of the labor force and produces two-thirds of exports. Manufacturing, still in its early stages, employs about 9% of the labor force, and generates 20% of exports. Labor force statistics are based on the "working" population, from the ages of fifteen through sixty-four. However, there are also immigrant *(remesa)* working populations and child populations that are not included in employment statistics. *Remesas* (remittances from immigrant workers in other countries) accounted for 7.5% of Honduras's GDP in 2001.

Honduras's economy faces a multitude of challenges including high unemployment rates, inflation, a lack of basic services, rapid population growth, and a strong dependence on coffee and bananas in the export sector. These crops are subject to sharp price fluctuations.

To exacerbate these conditions, Honduras's highly polarized society positions a small percentage of the population in control of 95 percent of the country's scarce resources. This leaves very few resources for the general population. Up to 35 percent of the nation's households are headed by women, who are forced to work to sustain their families.

Currently 50 percent of the Honduran population lives in the countryside. Large landowners have been instrumental in pushing the small farmer, or *campesino*, from the good agricultural lands to the hillsides, where they live in a typical nuclear family with four to five children. It is not uncommon for families to have as many as ten children. As it has been for centuries, it is very common for children to work on the farms, carrying water, caring for the garden and livestock, and gathering firewood.

It was estimated in 1998 that 241,000 Honduran children ages eleven through seventeen were working. In Honduras, children can be found working at building sites, in dairy plant refrigerators, in food processing factories, and in textile factories *(maquilas)*. Child labor can account for up to 50 percent of intensive labor activities, like coffee harvesting. With the fall of coffee prices worldwide, this phenomenon has increased because companies cut costs to maintain profits. In addition, these industries benefit from the lack of control of child labor in the country.

As early as fourteen or fifteen years of age, Honduran females start to procreate; as many as 35 percent of them will take care of this new family by themselves because the men move away and migrate to larger cities like Tegucigalpa and San Pedro Sula and to the U.S. (New York, Los Angeles, Texas, Louisiana, Florida). This perpetuates and amplifies the poverty cycle, by creating more and younger families who have fewer and fewer resources. Children and youth in the Honduran countryside live a life bereft of a childhood, where education and play is as scarce as the food on their plates.

For those children who migrate to the cities (mainly Tegucigalpa and San Pedro Sula), the situation is worse. *Maquilas* and other factories attract young women (sixteen years old and up) who last an average of one to two years on the job because of the high turnover in the factories. Later they end up as maids or even worse, as prostitutes.

Boys migrate into urban areas to work as bricklayers and in similar jobs. Honduran law allows youths sixteen years old and older to work under special schedules and circumstances with their parent's permission. This opens up the opportunity to illegally hire underage youth as unskilled labor for less pay. It is common to see underage children working at construction sites. To make things worse, many boys and girls end up in gangs *(maras)* and become involved with drugs and crime.

For younger children the situation is similar. The corner streets of the major cities in Honduras are filled with children as young as five years of age begging for food and money. Some are part of organized rings of adults who exploit them. Slightly older kids, ten to fourteen years old, drug themselves with glue vapors as their starting point in a life full of drugs and dangers.

Many children become part of the informal economy: reselling candies, combs, and pens, earning just enough each day for a small bite to eat. These street vendors live a dangerous life far from the safety of home, running around moving cars and sleeping on the cold sidewalks of the "big" city, where their parents once came to look for a better life. For them, the little farm in the countryside has been lost and forgotten; now they dream of surviving in a society and with a government that cares less about their dreams and their rights.

Vignette

Lita, eleven years old, spends her days working with her mother and two younger siblings at a busy intersection in Tegucigalpa selling vegetables. She has an older sister, Helena, a fourteen-year-old *maquiladora* who works in a *maquila*. Here textiles are manufactured for companies like Disney, Gap, Nike, and Eddie Bauer. Helena sometimes leaves for work at 7:00 A.M. and does not come back to their small rented room until early the following morning. She knows if she becomes pregnant, her pay will be docked to pay for an abortion injection. Helena has heard of girls in other *maquilas* who are forced to take birth control pills daily. These girls are not allowed to leave each day until they fill a production quota.

The plights of Lita and Helena are not uncommon. More and more young children are fending for their existence on the streets and in the *maquilas* of Honduras. Their parents grew up on a small farm in the hills in central Honduras, but as large agricultural corporations took over more of the arable land, they found themselves forced to farm on steep hills. A severe storm would lead to landslides and eliminate months of labor and fragile sustenance crops in a matter of hours. When their father fell into deep despair, unable to provide for his family, their mother took the girls to the city in hope of a better life. Now the family is caught in a trap, with all of their energy going to earning enough money to stay fed. Little energy or resources are left for pursuing an education or finding alternative ways to make a living.

HISTORY OF CHILD LABOR

The history of child labor in Honduras starts with the settlement of indigenous cultures in the region, centuries ago. As is the case with many agricultural societies, children have long worked side by side with their parents on farms and in households in Honduras. From a very early age, children have worked. Young girls six to seven years old have traditionally been responsible for fetching water from wells and creeks many miles from their homes. Young girls have always helped in the kitchen and with the care of the vegetable garden and small livestock. Boys traditionally gather firewood and help in the larger agricultural activities, usually related to the production of basic grains, like corn and beans.

The work of children underwent a significant change along with the changing economy that forced more farmers to eke out a living from the hills or to migrate to cities in hopes of making a better living in industry. With several political reforms in the mid-eighties, many laws were enacted to reduce child exploitation. In practice, however, the laws had little impact on reducing child labor.

Even though primary education is compulsory, children in rural areas rarely attend beyond fifth grade. Farm duties claim their presence at home, schools are usually one or two walking hours distant from home, and teachers attend their schools an average of 2.5 days per week.

CHILD LABOR TODAY

By 2002, government and human rights groups estimated that 350,000 children were working illegally in Honduras. There were credible allegations of compulsory overtime at plants in export processing zones, in particular for women, who constitute an estimated 80 percent of the workforce in the *maquiladora* sector. Clearly there have been initiatives aimed at improving the child labor situation in Honduras. Although Honduras has been blessed with abundant natural resources, mismanagement and unsustainable practices have left it one of the poorest countries in the hemisphere. It has been argued that growth of the *maquila* industry constituted an economic success story for Honduras in the 1990s. The industry grew from its inception in the early 1990s with virtually no income to generating over $300 million in foreign exchange and employment for one hundred thousand workers in 1998. However, as we have seen, the abuse of these employees has caused considerable concern.

Honduran law allows sixteen-year-old kids and older to work with the permission of their parents. Because of economic need, this has become the rule instead of the exception. Furthermore, because the government has little control over this, younger kids are hired to do the most repetitive tasks. One of the newest child labor trends in Honduras is reported by the U.S. Department of Labor, referring to prostitution:

Children are involved in prostitution, in many cases as part of sex tourism. Government estimates show that nearly 40 percent of street children regularly engage in prostitution. Honduran girls from Tegucigalpa, San Pedro Sula, and El Progreso have been found working in brothels in nearby Central American countries and in Mexico. Some of these minors have been victims of trafficking. Children have also been used to peddle drugs. A recent report indicates that 200 Honduran children between the ages of 10 and 13 were involved in selling cocaine in Canadian cities. (U.S. Department of Labor, 2003, paragraph 4)

According to a study undertaken by the Ministry of Labor and Social Security in association with the United Nations Children's Fund (UNICEF) and the Honduran Institute for Childhood and the Family (IHNFA), approximately 97,000 children from the ages of ten through fourteen, and another 260,000 adolescents from fifteen through eighteen, have left school to work. The study found that nearly one-half of all working children are employed in agriculture, cattle farming, or fishing, representing nearly 6.5% of the country's agricultural workforce. About 20% of children work in the manufacturing, mining, electricity, gas, and construction sectors, constituting close to 3.5% of these sectors' labor force. The remaining 30% of children work in commerce, transportation, finance, or service industries, accounting for 3.5% of the industry's workforce. Nearly two-thirds of working children work on family farms or for small family businesses and receive no compensation for their labor. Children ages ten through fourteen who receive remuneration for their work earn on average between 100 and 500 Honduran lempiras (US$6.75 and $33.78) per month (U.S. Department of Labor, 2003).

Children in Honduras work as hired hands on small family farms, as street vendors, and in small workshops. They work in food processing factories, where they may work with industrial knives and slicing machines. Children work on coffee and tobacco plantations, and on melon farms. They manufacture fireworks and are involved in lime production, mining, and domestic service. Children also work at building sites, pushing wheelbarrows and operating power saws. In the *maquila* sector over the past few years, there have been few reports of child labor. Children found working were using false work permits to bypass age regulations in the sector.

The issue of child labor abuses in garment factories was brought to national attention in a stark way. In 1995, child labor in Honduras came to global attention with cry of outrage raised in response to the dismal conditions of teenage girls working in the Global Fashion plant making Kathie Lee Fashions garments for Wal-Mart stores in the U.S. Charles Kernaghan of the National Labor Committee testified to the U.S. Congress in the spring of 1996 that "13-year-old girls were being forced to work 13-hour shifts, under armed guard, for 31 cents an hour sewing pants for Kathie Lee Gifford and Wal-Mart" (National Labor Committee, 2002, paragraph 10). Later that year, Kathie Lee Gifford met with fifteen-year-old Honduran *maquila* worker Wendy Diaz in the Manhattan residence of Archbishop Cardinal O'Connor along with leaders of religious, human rights, and labor organizations directly involved in ending sweatshop abuses. After their meeting, this group agreed that different sectors (government, the apparel industry, unions, citizens) had diverse responsibilities. They also agreed that Kathie Lee Gifford had met her responsibilities regarding labor abuse by acknowledging the reality of child labor and speaking out against it.

In 1998, Honduras launched a plan to take nearly a quarter million children out of building sites and factories and put them back in school. According to the International Labour Organisation's (2002) International Programme on the Elimination of Child Labour, some 241,000 Honduran children from eleven through seventeen years old were working in 1998, mainly because they come from poor families. Many other programs have been developed in response to the problem of child labor in Honduras, for example, Casa Alianza/Covenant House (Casa Alianza, 2000). This nonprofit organization provides support and education for street children in Honduras (as well as Mexico, Guatemala, and Nicaragua) at crisis centers that operate in direct support of the United National Convention on the Rights of the Child (CRC). Honduras is one of the countries that ratified the CRC and so, at least in theory, supports what the CRC espouses: namely children's political, economic, and civil rights. In addition to providing immediate assistance to children and their families, Casa Alianza also plays an advocate role in legal battles on behalf of exploited child workers (Casa Alianza, 2000).

POLITICAL VIEWS AND PUBLIC POLICIES

Honduran law prohibits forced or compulsory labor. According to Honduran labor laws, workers have the right to form and join labor unions. Unions are free to participate in public rallies and often make use of the news media to make their issues known. The Honduran Constitution also provides for the right to strike, although government workers are denied this right according to the civil service code. The law also protects the rights of workers to organize and bargain collectively. In addition, forced or compulsory labor is outlawed in Honduras. There are also laws to enforce acceptable work conditions, such as minimum wage and vacation laws. However, these regulations are frequently ignored as a result of high unemployment and underemployment, and the lack of enforcement by the Ministry of Labor (Campaign for the Abolition of Sweatshops and Child Labor, 2002).

The Honduran Constitution and Labor Code specifically prohibit the employment of minors under the age of sixteen. There is an exception for children under the age of fifteen who may work with the permission of parents and the Ministry of Labor. According to Honduran law, individuals who allow children to work illegally can face prison sentences of up to five years. However, Ministry of Labor authorities are ineffective in enforcing these laws, except to some degree in the *maquiladora* sector. Another government response was creation of the National Commission for the Gradual and Progressive Eradication of Child Labor in 1998 (Bureau of International Labor Affairs, 2003), although it is not yet possible to measure the impact or efficacy of this commission.

CONCLUSION

The future of child labor in Honduras appears bleak given the context of widespread and abject poverty. However, a number of agencies and sectors have responded to the situation and are making progress toward righting some of the wrong inflicted by both poverty and abusive child labor. This complex and multifaceted issue depends on the response of different key players: industry, education, and governmental and nongovernmental sectors.

International alliances and coalitions have been formed to support the lawful and ethical development of the *maquila* industry. In November 2002, in San Pedro Sula, Honduras, the Conference of the Central American Regional Coordinating Body of Maquila Unions developed an alliance document in support of a solidarity effort including student, union, religious, and community representatives. At their meeting, this group agreed that they would encourage the permanency of *maquila* companies that respect rights of workers and comply with international labor rights norms (Campaign for the Abolition of Sweatshops and Child Labor, 2002).

Some programs are using education as their primary weapon in the war against abusive child labor. Programs like the Basic Education and Policy Support (BEPS) Education to Combat Abusive Child Labor hold much potential, and pilot projects are under way in many countries, including Honduras (BEPS, 2003).

BIBLIOGRAPHY

Basic Education and Policy Support (BEPS). (2003) Providing education to Honduran child laborers and their families. *Education to Combat Abusive Child Labor*. Retrieved June 30, 2003, from http://www.beps.net/child_labor/labor_honduras2.htm.

Bureau of International Labor Affairs. (2003) *Economic Policy Report on Honduras.* U.S. Department of Labor, Washington, DC. Retrieved June 30, 2003, from http://www.dol.gov/ILAB/media/reports/iclp/Advancing1/html/honduras.htm.

Campaign for the Abolition of Sweatshops and Child Labor. (2002) *No More Sweatshops! Conclusions of the Conference of the Central American Regional Coordinating Body of Maquila Unions and No More Sweatshops: The Coalition for the Abolition of Sweatshops and Child Labor.* Retrieved June 30, 2003, from http://www.abolishsweatshops.org/agreement.html.

Casa Alianza. (2000) *Tenth Anniversary of the United Nations Convention on the Rights of the Child: Special Reports & Coverages.* Retrieved June 30, 2003, from http://www.casaalianza.org/EN/newstuff/crc/latinlabor.shtml.

Central Intelligence Agency. (2003) *Honduras: The World Factbook.* Retrieved June 30, 2003, from http://www.cia.gov/cia/publications/factbook/geos/ho.html.

International Labour Organisation. (2002) International Programme on the Elimination of Child Labour. Retrieved June 30, 2003, from http://www.ilo.org/public/english/standards/ipec/partners/index.htm.

National Labor Committee. (2002) Home page of the National Labor Committee for Worker and Human Rights. Retrieved May 7, 2003, from http://www.nlcnet.org/nlc/BIOS/Charlie.shtml.

Orozco, M. (2001) Statement to Oversight Hearing on "Accounting and Investor Protection Issues Raised by Enron and Other Public Companies." U.S. Senate Committee on Banking, Housing and Urban Affairs. Retrieved February 7, 2003, from http://banking.senate.gov/02_02hrg/022802/orozco.htm.

U.S. Department of Labor. (1996) Bureau of International Labor Affairs. Retrieved June 30, 2003, from http://www.hartford-hwp.com/archives/28/049.html.

———. (2003) *Child Labor in Honduras.* Bureau of International Labor Affairs. Retrieved June 30, 2003, from http://www.dol.gov/ILAB/media/reports/iclp/Advancing1/html/honduras.htm.

U.S. Department of State. (1998) *Country Report on Economic Policy and Trade Practices: Honduras.* Washington, DC. See http://www.state.gov/www/issues/economic/trade_reports/wha98/honduras98.html.

U.S. Government. (1997) *The Apparel Industry and Codes of Conduct: A Solution To the International Child Labor Problem?* Congressional Record. Retrieved June 30, 2003, from http://www.house.gov/bernie/town_meeting/1997/maryann_schrupp.html.

———. *Labor Law in Honduras.* See http://www.sweatshopsretail.org/NRF%20Website/honduras.htm.

8

INDIA

Desi Larson

PROFILE OF INDIA

Large and diverse ethnically and geographically, India was home to the Indus Valley civilization, one of the oldest in the world, which is traced back at least five thousand years. India gained her independence from Britain in 1947 under the leadership of Jawaharlal Nehru. Independence was possible in large part due to the nonviolent resistance to colonialism led by Mohandas Gandhi. Independence ushered in the end of centuries of external rule, which included Arab incursions in the eighth century followed by Turkish rule in the twelfth and British occupation in the nineteenth. Hindoostan, as the British called the subcontinent, was made up of many kingdoms and ethnicities. These diverse groups played a major part in the political, ethnic, and economic strife that has resulted since India's independence, when the subcontinent was divided into India and Pakistan. A civil war between Urdu-speaking West Pakistan and Bangla-speaking East Pakistan resulted in East Pakistan becoming a separate nation, Bangladesh, in 1971. India continues to have disputes at her borders, particularly with China and Pakistan. The capital of India is New Delhi. Other major cities include Chennai (Madras), Kolkata (Calcutta), and Mumbai (Bombay).

About one-third the size of the U.S., India is bordered by the Arabian Sea on the west and south and the Bay of Bengal to the east. The landscape includes the Himalayan Mountains to the north, the Deccan Plateau in the south, a flat to rolling plain along the Ganges, and deserts in the west. The climate ranges from temperate in the north to tropical in the south.

Bangladesh, Bhutan, Myanmar (Burma), China, Nepal, and Pakistan all share borders with India. Rich with natural resources, about 54 percent of its land is arable. India's resources include its people, coal, minerals, natural gas, diamonds, petroleum, and limestone. However, India's large and growing population puts a tremendous strain on natural resources. In addition, environmental calamities such as deforestation, overgrazing, desertification, and pollution threaten environmental sustainability.

India is home to over a billion people, and nearly a third of those are under fourteen years of age. Table 8.1 gives an overview of the distribution of the population of India by age and gender. A majority of its citizens are Hindu (81.3%) with a substantial Muslim population (12%). Other religious groups include Christian, Sikh, Buddhist, Jain, and Parsi. Hindi is the national language and the first language for 30% of Indians. While it is not official, English is widely used in commerce, business, entertainment, and political sectors. Among the 325 languages spoken in India, 14 additional official languages (after Hindi and English) include: Assamese, Bengali, Gujarati, Kannada, Kashmiri, Malayalam, Marathi, Oriya, Punjabi, Sindhi, Sanskrit, Telugu, Tamil, and Urdu.

Up to 40% of the population (almost half a billion people) live below the poverty line (ILO, 1995). During the 1990s the economy grew at an

Table 8.1
Population Distribution

Age	Male	Female	Total
Less than 14 years	175,858,386	165,724,901	32.7%
15–64 years	338,957,463	316,063,497	62.6%
65 years and over	24,975,465	24,265,514	4.7%

Source:
CIA, 2002.

average rate of 6%, which reduced poverty by about 10%. Over 52% of adults (age fifteen and over) can read and write. It is estimated that of those who are literate, 66% are men and 33% are women (CIA, 2002).

India's economy includes traditional farming, modern agriculture, handicrafts, industries, and service enterprises. India's response to the information technology age has been an enthusiastic one, and India is now a major exporter of software services and software workers. In 1999, India's labor force was estimated to include 406 million people (CIA, 2002), with most (60%) engaged in agriculture. The remaining people worked either in services (23%) or industry (17%).

Extreme overpopulation, massive poverty, environmental degradation, ethnic strife, and religious conflicts mark India on the one hand. On the other, it is a country with a rich and diverse culture that has made major contributions to the world. The overpopulation, poverty, and visages of a caste system have contributed to a growing problem of child labor.

OVERVIEW OF CHILD LABOR

More children work in India than anywhere else in the world (Human Rights Watch, 1996). In fact, 100 to 150 million children ages five through fourteen years are estimated to be working, and nearly half of those children (at least 44 million) are engaged in hazardous work. A significant number of these children, somewhere between 15 and 25 million, are in bonded labor. Bonded child labor is a form of work in which children find themselves in servitude, working to pay off a debt. Bonded labor is a particularly compelling problem in India.

In the late 1980s the government of India reported approximately 20 million child laborers. However, this estimate may be conservative given that some nongovernmental organizations estimated the number of child laborers in India to be closer to 50 million. India's 1981 census organized child labor into nine categories (as cited in Nangia, 1987). Table 8.2 shows the percentage distribution of child workers by these categories. From this table it is evident that most rural child workers (84%) were employed in cultivation and agricultural labor. Urban child laborers were distributed differently, with 39% of them involved in manufacturing, processing, servicing, and repairs (Nangia, 1987). Although historically more children have been involved in agriculturally related work, human rights organizations focus on the manufacturing types of child labor because most children in these situations are bonded laborers. Bonded labor "refers to the phenomenon of children working in conditions of servitude in order to pay off a debt" (Human Rights Watch, 1996, p. 2). In the early 1990s, it was estimated that close to 1 million children were working as bonded child laborers in India (ILO, 1992).

Table 8.2
Percentage Distribution of Child Workers by Industrial Divisions,
Census of India, 1981

Type of Worker	Industrial Divisions								
	Cultivation	Agricultural Labor	Livestock, Forestry, Fishing	Mining and Quarrying	Manufacturing, Processing, Servicing	Construction	Trade and Commerce	Transport, Storage	Other Services
Urban	5.32	14.73	3.07	0.20	39.16	3.27	15.03	2.45	16.77
Rural	38.87	45.42	6.61	0.25	5.72	0.47	0.96	0.10	1.60
Total	35.93	42.74	6.30	0.24	8.65	0.72	2.19	0.30	2.93

Source:

Nangia, 1987, p. 72.

Most prevalent in the northern part of the country, child labor is a grave and extensive problem in India. Children under the age of fourteen are forced to work in hazardous industries such as glass-blowing and fireworks. Underage children have commonly been found in carpet-making factories. Factory owners find children attractive employees; they work for wages far below what adults would work for and can be trained to labor under hazardous and unhygienic conditions. Many of the children working in factories are migrant workers from northern India, earning money that their families depend upon.

The situation of children working in bonded labor in India is desperate. Most children work twelve-hour days, seven days a week, with barely a break for meals. Ill nourished and underfed, children in bonded labor often reach maturity physically exhausted and sometimes terminally ill or deformed (Human Rights Watch, 1996).

Vignette

Mina, who lives in Bengal, is one of the millions of children working in bonded labor in India. Her family is among the 75 percent of India's poverty-stricken population living in rural areas. For many rural families, children are viewed as a form of economic security. The work of these children is necessary to help supplement their families' income. However, bonded labor most often comes about as a response to a parent or guardian incurring debt.

Mina's story is typical. Just ten years old, Mina works in bonded labor rolling cigarettes *(beedi)* with her brother Ram. Ram, eight years old, just started working a few years ago, but Mina has been working in a small *beedi* factory for almost five years now, since she was barely six years old. Even if the economic situation were to improve for their family, these children are caught in the web of bonded labor that is difficult, sometimes impossible, from which to be extracted.

Mina's mother died of cholera not long after the birth of her brother. Her father had been barely making ends meet working in brickyard when he had an accident and broke his leg. The break was severe and he needed 600 rupees (approximately US$17) for medical expenses. Desperate, Mina's father accepted a loan from a bonded labor employer, who agreed to employ Mina, then barely six years old, to roll *beedi* until the debt was paid off. It is highly likely that she will work until she has matured. She may then be released from bondage to allow for younger, cheaper labor. It is also likely that she will pass this debt back to her father, to other family members, or even to her own children.

Mina has worked twelve hours a day, seven days a week, for nearly five years, but the debt is not paid off. Her employer charges her for food and other expenses. The low wages she is paid cannot begin to make a dent in the immensely high rates of interest charged on her parent's loan. Even with her brother working, they have made little progress toward repaying the loan.

Mina's fingers are almost literally worn to the bone from thousands upon thousands of hours of repetitious cigarette rolling. She works sitting on the floor of a dark and musty hut with a basket of tobacco on her left and a slowly growing mound of tiny *beedis* in a basket on her right. Sometimes she glimpses children running by on the street, through a crack in the door. Mostly numb now to life outside of her work, sometimes something small flutters deep in her chest when she hears the sound of children playing. She might have been one of those children; if only her father hadn't broken his leg, if only her mother hadn't died.

HISTORY OF CHILD LABOR

As in most countries down through history, children have worked along-side their adult family members farming, fishing, or in trades. Historically, child labor in India has been an accepted practice, particularly for the very poor and working-class children, which have made up the majority of the population for thousands of years. In India in particular, manufacturing has involved highly specialized labor since medieval times. India has long had a large pool of relatively cheap labor from which to draw and train in the many specialized tasks of manufacturing (particularly, for example, in silk sari-making, carpet-making, and other similar industries).

The caste system, which is connected with the hereditary professions, has long played a significant role in the work of children in India. For thousands of years children of artists and other professionals were trained by adult family members in vocations such as weaving, farming, painting, and carpentry. Children were expected to work with their elders in these home industries, and they continue to do this sort of work today. Poor children in India have a long history of working as domestic servants in the households of higher caste and wealthier people.

CHILD LABOR TODAY

Extreme poverty plays a critical role in child labor. For many families in India the income children bring in is vital to their survival. One study indicates that child labor provides 34% to 37% of household income for poor families in India (Mehra-Kerpelman, 1996). Over the past forty-five years the war against poverty in India has had very uneven outcomes. Trend rates of poverty reduction have differed considerably between states (World Bank, 2002). According to a UNICEF report, every third house in India has a child working as a domestic, and every fourth child works to earn wages that are the sole income of the entire family (UNICEF, 1997).

It has been estimated that 15 to 25 million children living in India are working in bonded labor situations (Human Rights Watch, 1996). As in Mina's situation, children in bondage typically work twelve-hour days, seven days a week, with perhaps two days off each month. They work these hours until they are released from bondage, which can be many years. Because of the high interest rates and low wages, some children never work themselves out of bondage and raise their own children in bondage. In addition to rolling *beedi*, child laborers also work as domestic servants, in factories, in sari production, in the leather industry, in prostitution, and in tea shops. International attention was brought to bonded child labor in the handwoven carpet industry by the case of Iqbal Masih. From Pakistan, Iqbal was a twelve-year-old who had escaped his bondage in the carpet industry and was sharing his experiences in the international arena when he was murdered. Iqbal's case raised awareness of bondage and led to the formation of organizations such as Kids Can Free the Children.

POLITICAL VIEWS AND PUBLIC POLICIES

Child labor is illegal in India and school attendance is "free and compulsory" until age fourteen. Child bondage and servitude have been illegal since the 1893 Children (Pledging of Labour) Act was enacted under British rule. Since its independence, India has enacted an abundance of laws governing child labor. For example, in 1989, India invoked a law making the employment of children under fourteen illegal, except in family-owned factories. India enacted the Bonded Labour System (Abolition) Act outlawing all forms of debt in 1976. Nevertheless, these laws are rarely complied with or enforced. Human Rights Watch argues, "In truth, the Indian government has failed to protect its most vulnerable children" (1996, p. 5). The issue of bonded child labor is particularly challenging because it primarily affects the poorest and most destitute children in India. It also necessitates collusion on the part of authorities, politicians, and policy officers, who too often look the other way. Of the many and complex types of child labor in India, one of the most abhorrent forms is bonded child labor.

SOCIAL VIEWS, CUSTOMS, AND PRACTICES

Poor people in India have very few options when it comes to obtaining loans or other forms of credit. The local moneylender, working for one of the industries that exploit child bonded labor, offers a family a loan in exchange for their child's labor. Since the earnings of bonded child laborers are less than the interest on the loans, these children are forced to work in servitude while interest on their parents' loan accumulates at mercurial rates (Badiwalla, 1998). According to Human Rights Watch, a bonded child can be released only after the parents make a lump sum payment, which is extremely difficult for families in poverty (Human Rights Watch, 1996, p. 17). Even if bonded child laborers are released, "the same conditions of poverty that caused the initial debt can cause people to slip back into bondage" (International Labour Organisation, 1993, p. 12).

Also contributing to the issue of bonded labor is India's social structure. India's complex social caste system contributes to the entrenchment of child bonded labor. In addition to the four categories of people described earlier, the term "caste" is also used in reference to India's 660 kinship groups, which include 405 scheduled castes and 255 scheduled tribes (Elder, 2003). Bonded labor is integrated tightly in the social fabric of India:

Bonded child labor is convenient, cheap, compliant, and dependable. It depresses wages. It is easily replenishable. Bonded labor among both adults and children is not a new phenomenon in India. It is an old arrangement, and a convenient one for the lucky top layers of privilege. Those who have the power to change this arrangement are, by all measures, uninterested in doing so. (Human Rights Watch, 1996, p. 5)

It is the poorest children and their families, those in the least protected castes, who are most likely to be prey to bonded labor. Given the pivotal role of the caste system in Indian culture, a brief description of the caste system is included here.

Caste System

Caste plays an important role in many aspects of life in India. It is a complex concept that can mean different things and is sometimes difficult for people from Western cultures to grasp. One reason for this is that the term "caste" is applied to different social phenomena (Elder, 2003). According to Elder (2003), the term "caste" comes from the Portuguese *casta*. This term was used by the Portuguese to describe groups that had different proportions of *"racial purity"* as they mated with indigenous peoples and African slaves in their colonies, such as Brazil. The Portuguese inappropriately used the term *casta*, which has racial overtones, to what they observed about the social groups in India. The British changed the word to "caste" and incorporated it into their legal documents, where it continues to be used by the independent government of India.

The social distinctions marked by caste in India today have roots that go back thousands of years. The Hindu creation story has four categories of humans emerging from different parts of the first man, Parusa, when he sacrificed himself at the beginning of creation. In Sanskrit, these different categories are called *varna*. The four categories were the *Brahman varna* (from Parusa's mouth), the *vaisya varna* (from Parusa's thighs), *ksastrya varna* (from Parusa's arms), and the *sudra varna* (from Parusa's feet). Eventually in Indian society, rules for each of the four categories were developed, for example, the Laws of Manu. The Laws of Manu require that men and women marry within their category *(varna)* and perform occupations assigned to their category *(varna)*. Thus *Brahmans* should be priests, *ksastryas* should be warriors, *vaisyas* should produce wealth, and *sudras* should serve the other groups. There is a fifth "mixed" *varna*, the *candalas*. *Candalas* were, according to myth, the offspring of *Brahman* women impregnated by *sudra* men in gross violation of the rules, which prohibited inter-*varna* sexual relations.

According to the Laws of Manu, *candalas* were to be dealt with as social pariahs. They were excluded from sacred places and events and required to perform the least pleasant tasks of society, including removing human feces and disposing of the carcasses of dead animals. The mythical *candalas* may have provided the basis for the more recent identification and segregation of India's "untouchables" (Buhler, 1969; Elder, 2003).

THE FUTURE OF CHILD LABOR

Child labor in India persists as a result of cultural beliefs and traditions, social and economic factors, weak enforcement of existing laws prohibiting child labor, and the lack of a compulsory education policy (USAID, 2002). Even when legal action is taken against child labor, there are few implications for the perpetrators. Laws cannot overcome the necessity of income from child labor and the bondage of poor families. Effectively eliminating child labor in India would require an extensive reform process that includes battling poverty. Key to the success of any program that tackles the issue of child labor is access to education for the working or "out of school" child (USAID, 2002). Establishing schools and eliminating the rampant illiteracy that plagues the country would preserve structural changes. These changes cannot be accomplished immediately or in isolation. Support from the international community, especially the United States government, seems critical to facilitating change in India (U.S. House of Representatives, 1995).

Many believe that any lasting solution to tackling the child labor problem would include education for working children. Pilot activities in India, funded through a $2.1 million small grants program, are demonstrating that improved access to quality education can help reduce child labor (USAID, 2002). Examples include the "School Works Initiative," which is managed through the United Nations Development Program (UNDP) and Catholic Relief Services (CRS). Initiatives of these sort support nongovernmental organizations (NGOs) that integrate child labor concerns with education efforts in local communities. The "School Works Initiative" is targeting nearly sixty-nine thousand out-of-school children who have been working in such industries as brick kilning, leather tanning, and glass bangle making. Nonformal education centers and early child care programs supported under the grants are providing these children with a full-time education (USAID, 2002).

In another example of an effort to combat child labor, the United States Agency for International Development (USAID) obligated $1 million to support the work of small NGOs in getting out-of-school children in the six-through-fourteen-year age group employed in agriculture, industry, or back into school. Activities in this program focused particularly on female children, children of migrant laborers working in the brick kilns, and street children living on railway platforms, in squatter colonies, or in red-light districts. USAID also supported a Catholic Relief Services (CRS) project that targets schoolchildren in the six-through-fourteen-year age group. Special focus is being placed on girls from traditional sex-worker villages and children engaged in industries such as bulb-making, shoe-making, agriculture, and household chores (USAID, 2002). Table 8.3 provides an overview of NGO partners involved in projects with USAID to combat child labor. Also listed in this table are the number of children reached by these projects in 2002.

Table 8.3
Overview of USAID Projects Combating Child Bonded Labor

NGO Partner	Location	Grant Manager	Grant Amount	Number of Children Reached
Child in Need Institute (CINI)	W. Bengal	United Nations Development Program (UNDP)	$300,000	4,890
Vidhayak Sansad	Andhra Pradesh	UNDP	$300,000	3,500
Dr. Reddy's Foundation	Andhra Pradesh	UNDP	$100,000	750
Centre for Rural Education and Development Action, Mirzapur (CREDA)	Uttar Pradesh	UNDP	$300,000	5,250
M Venkatarangaiya Foundation (MVA)	Andhra Pradesh	Catholic Relief Services (CRS)	$511,860	52,000
Gramodaya Sansthan	Uttar Pradesh	CRS	$159,805	3,320
R.C. Diocesan	Rajasthan	CRS	$38,281	930

Source:

USAID, 2002.

The Convention on the Rights of the Child recognizes that the "inherent dignity and the equal and inalienable rights of all members of the human family is the foundation of freedom, justice and peace in the world" (UNICEF, 1989, preamble, paragraph 1). Further, it states that children have the right to be "protected from economic exploitation and from performing any work that is likely to be hazardous or to interfere with the child's education, or to be harmful to the child's health or physical, mental, spiritual, moral or social development" (Article 32, paragraph 1). Eradicating bonded child labor will be a significant step toward respecting the rights of India's poorest and most vulnerable children.

BIBLIOGRAPHY

Badiwalla, M. (1998) *Child labour in India: Causes, governmental policies and the role of education.* Retrieved June 29, 2003, from http://www.geocities.com/ CollegePark/Library/9175/inquiry1.htm.

Buhler, G., trans. (1969) *The Laws of Manu*. Vol. 25. Sacred Books of the East. New York: Dover.

Burton, D. (1995) *The exploitation of child labor in India*. U.S. House of Representatives, July 25, 1995 [Congressional Record, page E1507]. Retrieved June 30, 2003, from http://www.dalitstan.org/journal/rights/104/250595.html.

Central Intelligence Agency. (2002) *India: The World Factbook*. Retrieved June 30, 2003, from http://www.cia.gov/cia/publications/factbook/geos/bg.html.

Elder, J. (2003) *Enduring Stereotypes about Asia: India's Caste System*. The Dalit Solidarity Forum in the USA. Retrieved June 21, 2003, from http://www.dalitusa.org/es.html.

Human Rights Watch. (1996) *The Small Hands of Slavery: Bonded Child Labor in India*. New York: Human Rights Watch.

International Labour Organisation. (1992) *World Labour Report*. Geneva: International Labour Organisation.

Kids Can Free the Children home page. (n.d.) Retrieved June 29, 2003, from http://www.freethechildren.org/.

Mehra-Kerpelman, K. (1996) Children at work: How many and where? *World of Work*, 15: 8–9.

Nangia, P. (1987) *Child labour: Cause-effect syndrome*. New Delhi: Janak Publishers.

UNICEF (1989) *Convention on the Rights of the Child*. Retrieved June 29, 2003, from http://www.unicef.org/crc/crc.htm.

———. (1997) *The State of the World's Children 1997 (Focus on Child Labor)*. Retrieved June 29, 2003, from http://www.unicef.org/sowc97/report/summary.htm.

USAID (2002) *Combating child labor in India*. South Asia Regional Initiative (SARI) Women's and Children's Equity. Retrieved November 12, 2003, from http://www.usaid.gov/in/aboutusaid/projects/childlabor.htm.

U.S. Department of Labor. (1996) *The Apparel Industry and Codes of Conduct: A Solution To the International Child Labor Problem?* U.S. Department of Labor, Bureau of International Labor Affairs, Washington, DC. Retrieved June 30, 2003, from http://www.hartfordhwp.com/archives/28/049.html.

———. *Child Labor in India*. Retrieved June 30, 2003, from http://www.dol.gov/ilab/media/reports/iclp/Advancing1/html/india.htm.

U.S. House of Representatives. (1995) *The Exploitation of Child Labor in India*. Congressional Record. Retrieved June 15, 2003, from http://pangaea.org/street_children/asia/carpet.htm.

World Bank. (2002) *The India Poverty Project: Poverty and Growth in India, 1951–94*. Poverty Net. The World Bank Group. Retrieved June 29, 2003, from http://www.worldbank.org/poverty/data/indiapaper.htm.

9

IRAN

Reza Jalali

PROFILE OF IRAN

Iran is the largest country in the Middle East. It has a population of 67 million; youth make up more than 45% of the total population. Based on the 1991 census, there were 24,723,875 children under fourteen years of age in Iran. According to the 1996 census, 61% of the population lives in urban areas and 38% in rural areas (United Nations, n.d.).

Iranians are not Arabs but Persians. They claim to be the descendants of the early group of Aryans who settled in the region more than three thousand years ago. The early Persians were the founders of the Persian empire, the home of early civilization. This period ended with the defeat of the Persians by the Muslim Arabs, who brought the religion of Islam to Iran. Today's modern Iran is what remains of the ancient Persian empire that once ruled the mass of lands from India to North Africa to parts of today's Europe.

While the majority of the population is Persian, other ethnic groups such as the Turks, Kurds, Arabs, and Baluchis call Iran home, too. Farsi, known also as Persian, is the official language of Iranians. It is an Indo-European language. Other dialects, including Azari, Kurdish, and Gilaki, are also spoken. The official religion of Iran is Shiite Islam, a type of Islam that is different from the more common Sunni sect.

During World War II, Iran, though declaring itself a neutral country, was occupied by the British to the south and the Russians in the north. In 1979 a popular revolution led by the Ayatollah Khomeini overthrew the government of the U.S.-supported Shah of Iran. This was the starting point for the

establishment of the first autocratic religious government, the Islamic Republic of Iran (IRI).

In 1980 the long and bloody war between Iran and its neighbor to the
east, Iraq, began. It lasted eight years. More than a million people were left
dead, and millions more were injured on both sides of the border. The war
caused major destruction in Iran and forced a large internal migration.
People migrated primarily from the border areas affected by the war to the
larger urban centers. Millions of Iranians were forced to leave their villages
and towns, some destroyed as a result of the war, to find a home in the large
cities, including Tehran, the capital city of Iran. They migrated in search of
safety and prosperity, leaving areas that offered few opportunities.

In Iran, the economic mismanagement by the government after the 1979
revolution, the costly war with Iraq, the declining price of crude oil, and
high levels of inflation have all contributed to a new poverty. The gross
national product (GNP) per capita was $1,780 in 1997 and the per capita
income was $5,718. These economic conditions are without precedence in
Iran. They are new in a country that was once one of the wealthiest countries
in the oil-rich Middle East, and one where crude oil remains the major
source of revenue. The main exports are oil, natural gas, carpets, pistachios,
caviar, leather, and dried fruit.

OVERVIEW OF CHILD LABOR

In Iran there is an ambivalence toward child labor. While there is a stigma
attached to children working outside the home, child labor has also been a
long-established tradition. Low-income families with many children have
historically looked to them as a source of labor that has the potential for
generating additional income for the family. In keeping with tradition, children from poor and low-income families begin working on farms and in
family or even non–family owned businesses once they are physically able.
Children also work in manufacturing and in factories. They are employed in
occupations such as rug-making, masonry, glass (window) making, foundry
and textile work, chemical production, auto repairs, heater manufacturing,
the sale of coal, farming, mining, construction, and in stores. Some children
work after school and as "seasonal helping hands" on farms and in fruit
orchards or in manufacturing; others work long hours at the exclusion of
education. The plight of children peddling on street corners is particularly
distressing.

The government has made genuine efforts to have all children, regardless
of their parents' income, work fewer hours and spend more time attending
free state-sponsored schools. In today's Iran, however, even with better
educational opportunities for school-age children provided by the IRI,
children continue to work to bring in income. In spite of advocacy by
children's rights organizations, the effort of the government to provide free

education, and legislation designed to protect children and punish greedy employers, thousands of children work nonetheless. According to unofficial sources, there are 1.8 million children nine through eighteen years of age working. The projection for the year 2000 by the International Labour Organisation was 265,000 economically active children; 149,000 girls and 116,000 boys from the ages of ten through fourteen (ILO, 1997). In Iran today, children younger than fifteen are not allowed, officially/legally, to work, while children from the ages of fifteen through eighteen can work as apprentices (Aamoli, 2002).

Most child workers are Iranian, but some are Afghani or Iraqi from the large refugee communities in Iran. They provide free labor as part of their contribution to overall family income. Children's rights advocates in Iran estimate the contribution to be 25 percent of the total family income (Shahabi, 2002).

The issue of child labor in Iran is unique in the region. Iran is an oil-rich country with a relatively high standard of living and a highly educated and skilled workforce. Located at the crossroads between Asia and Europe, Iranian society is more open than many in the region. It is a country with exposure to both the modern world and the Old World. Iranian women, for example, for decades have enjoyed many political and social rights. These include the right to attend a university, work outside the home, start businesses, inherit property, vote, and be elected to political office. These rights are unusual in the Middle East. Despite such openness and willingness to accept progress, Iranian society to this day continues to struggle with having a large number of its children working in difficult jobs inside and outside the home.

Vignette

Ahmad is a child weaver. He works up to sixteen hours a day in Qom, one hundred miles south of the capital, Tehran. It is a place where middlemen have traditionally arranged the "renting" of children ages seven through sixteen from families in the northern towns of Zanjan and Hamadan. The contracts have been low-paying, with an annual cost of 30 to 40 thousand toman (US$45) to sweatshop owners. The lives of these children are without health or happiness. The sound of the rug-making comb, the *dafe*, resonates in the rug-making sweatshops and in the lives of the children. Some owners of rug-making workshops, however, make an effort to hire only adult weavers.

Ahmad is thirteen and has been working in the rug workshop for three and a half months. He does not work there by choice; he was forced. The work is very difficult. Because he has to work, he doesn't even entertain an interest in going to school. The middleman and his parents receive money for his work, though he isn't sure how much. Ahmad himself never receives any pay. He has never been to the movies and is not able to visit his parents.

He did visit the doctor once when he had jaundice. Ahmad's middleman is paid 30,000 toman and his parents are paid 60,000 toman.

Ahmad reports that the children in the workshop are not happy. They are beaten and forced to stay because of advance payments paid to their fathers. At his last job, in Zanjan, he worked 3:00 A.M. to midnight. Here he only works from 6 A.M. to 6 P.M., and they give his father more money (Pourziai, 1999).

HISTORY OF CHILD LABOR

Traditionally there has been a cultural ambivalence in regard to child labor. On the one hand, the general exploitation of children was accepted by society in general. On the other hand, a stigma has been associated with children working for wages. While wealthy families sent their children to religious and private schools or home-schooled them, low-income and poor families expected their children to work. Sons might work outside the home to earn wages or apprentice within the family. Daughters, sometimes at an early age, were either sent to work as servants in the houses of the wealthy or married off, mostly in arranged marriage situations.

In accordance to old traditions, sons who inherit careers from their fathers have been required to work alongside their fathers to learn the craft. This work begins at an early age. In the case of girls, they have been expected to work alongside their mother and other elders in the extended family to manage the household as training for their future roles as homemakers.

The modern Iranian system of government, established in the late nineteenth century, gave birth to government-sponsored educational reforms. Education was made mandatory, and families were encouraged to send their children to school to receive a free education. Once the educational reforms became a reality, only the poor and those living in rural regions of the country continued to have their children work. Rigid cultural and social norms have made change difficult.

Child work in Iran follows two patterns. Many children work after school and/or during summer months to earn some wages. As seasonal workers they make a contribution to the family income by working a few hours during the school year and for a few months between school terms. Other children, however, work year round without the opportunity to receive an education. The joy of childhood is lost in long hours of backbreaking work. This work leads, in some cases, to work-related injuries and a life without the benefits of education.

Carpet Weavers

Throughout ancient and modern Iran, children, both girls and boys, some as young as seven, have worked long hours to weave rugs. They weave the

"Persian carpets" that are in demand internationally. They are expensive carpets, known globally for their high quality. Children are hired into rug-weaving workshops because their small hands make smaller knots, which create delicate carpets of increased value. The workshop owners, like other employers, receive an added financial "bonus" because the salary for the child worker is lower than that of an adult worker.

The hiring of children to work in rug-weaving workshops varies from one part of Iran to another. In most cases, particularly in regions of Iran where the finest carpets are manufactured, young girls and boys work in family-owned rug-making workshops. These workshops are set up inside the family compounds. In other cases children are "rented" from their parents for a large sum of money. Children "rented" to work at rug-weaving workshops are brought from their villages and towns by the middlemen. The middleman, for a fee, acts as the agent of the workshop owner. They scout the poor sections of towns and villages to locate families who are willing to send their children away to work. The children then work long hours in the workshops, where cruel punishment and abuse contribute to the terrible working conditions. They have to work for years in order to pay off the original purchase price or the high-interest loan that the family received.

While some rug-weaving workshops are licensed, many, however, are unlicensed and unauthorized. Licensed workshops are subject to regular government inspection and, as such, children working in them are somewhat protected from abuse. These workshops, for example, hire only children who are older and allowed by law to work. Generally these children enjoy official protection from abuse and wage discrimination that children working in unlicensed workshops are likely to experience. Unlicensed workshops are unmonitored and unregulated, leading to working conditions that are too often unhealthy and dangerous for the children "required" to work there.

Persian (Iranian) carpets continue to be popular and in high demand internationally. They make up the second-largest export item, next to crude oil. These carpets are made in workshops scattered across the country, concentrated in areas where the carpets are most famous. Although the use of children below the working age of fifteen is strongly discouraged by the Iranian government, ten of thousands of such workshops, some without licenses, continue to hire children as young as ten to weave carpets. Such children work fourteen hours a day under the worst health conditions.

During the past few decades, Iran, in line with other less-developed societies, has experienced a population shift. The population in rural areas has decreased while in urban environments it has increased. New national wealth tied to the export of oil began during the Shah of Iran's government in the early 1970s. Millions of Iranian farmers migrated to Tehran and other large cities in Iran, leaving their villages and the traditional life of farming in search of wealth and opportunities. The mass migration of these unskilled and mostly uneducated newcomers looking for jobs in factories and the service industry opened a new chapter in the social life of Iran. In addition, a large number of Iranians, Afghans, and Iraqis were displaced due to the Iran-Iraq War and the decades-old conflicts in Afghanistan and Iraq respectively. Many were forced to flee to larger urban centers in search of safety and better economic opportunities. The arrival of children in large numbers in Tehran and other cities as street beggars and peddlers made the issue of child labor a cause of national concern. It was new to witness so many children in the streets begging and selling goods. This shift moved the government of the Shah to action.

CHILD LABOR TODAY

The drop in population growth, increased entry of women into the domestic job market, more forceful enforcement of the existing labor laws, and improvement in education have contributed to a drop in child labor. Child labor practices continue, however, and a number of factors contribute. Old traditions, social habits, and customs passed from one generation to another slow the process of change. In Iran, family welfare comes first. The rights of individual members of the family, young and old, take a backseat. There is an ambivalence regarding children working outside the home. A transition is also occurring with the migration of unskilled and untrained rural workers to the cities, where the inhabitants have traditionally been well trained, skilled, and educated. Despite serious attempts by the Islamic Republic of Iran to enforce child labor laws, a large number of children are still working.

Economic instability has added to the ongoing increase in production costs, which encourages the use of children, who traditionally receive lower wages than adults. According to the Iranian Central Bank, 45 percent of the population in Iran is "low-income" as defined by their income being below the poverty line (Aamoli, 2002). Unfavorable conditions created by the high rate of poverty are aggravated by the all-time-high unemployment rate (unofficially at 16 percent nationally). Many low-income and poor families send their children to work despite the stigma associated with having a child work for wages in a society such as Iran. The poverty and general economic disparity faced by millions of Iranian families are significant contributors.

Other contributing factors include the population shift that has resulted in concentration of poor families in large cities. Here family financial concerns result in reliance on the income produced by the work of children. Even further, old traditions call for children of the poor to apprentice in a craft or establish a career so they will have a steady source of income as adults. Some children and families are placed at greater risk as a result of parental death, disability, and illness. The lack of either a safety net for the poor or national public policies to protect the rights of children are also factors. The existence of a global economy that demands a high rate of profit is another contributor.

Most street children in the cities of Iran, whether Iranian or not, are not homeless children as the term is generally used. They have families and a place to stay but use the streets as a place to peddle goods, from newspapers to drugs. They also offer services such as shoe-shining and cleaning cars. The problem is greatest for refugee children. The general poverty experienced by displaced foreign refugees, mostly Afghans, forces refugee families to send their children to work. In large cities throughout Iran, the children of Afghan and Iraqi refugees join other street children to peddle, selling newspapers, chewing gums, flowers, and even drugs and banned alcohol. According to advocates for "street children," in 2001, 65 percent of street children in Tehran alone were refugee children (Ghanbari, 2002). Although most refugee parents claim that their children, born in refugee camps in Iran and elsewhere, lack the required national identity cards required for them to attend public schools, it is often the poverty experienced by these families that interferes with their education.

Tehran and Iran's other large cities have a standard of living that is higher than that found in rural areas. Affordable housing is also harder to find in the cities. Further, local municipalities have not planned for this large influx of unskilled workers. This has created communities of slum-dwellers, and disenfranchised Iranians just outside the cities. Thus the new urban poverty, unseen in Iran until recently, has come to stay. Families had farmed and cultivated lands for centuries, sometimes lands their families have owned for generations. Now they were on their own, struggling to survive in cities that offered jobs demanding education and skills that the newcomers lacked. The larger families with more mouths to feed have no choice but to have every able-bodied member of the family, including the young ones, earning wages. This is needed to sustain the entire family.

POLITICAL VIEWS AND PUBLIC POLICIES

With the rise in children working on the streets, new laws were called for to protect the rights of children. In 1958 the Labor Law was approved in the National Consultative Assembly, which was the Iranian lower parliament of the Shah of Iran's government. The law prohibited children below twelve years of age from working, except in family workshops. In addition, the Law on Agricultural Work set the minimum age at twelve years. This law and similar laws were not implemented with force. The monitoring agencies, with the encouragement of the government, engaged in covering up the problem. They tried to avoid being called on by society to deal with the issue. In most cases, the owners of workshops were told to avoid employing children below twelve years of age, but no official instruction was issued and the matter was taken lightly (Labor, Law, 1999). Under the 1958 Labor Law, family carpet-weaving workshops were exempt from the child labor law that prohibited hiring child workers below the age of twelve. As a result, many loom owners set up workshops inside family compounds to escape the penalty.

In 1990, with a new government in power, there was a rise in number of street children due to economic mismanagement and internal displacement of a large number of Iranians. Soon the Expediency Council (a council of religious experts and elders with political power) agreed to raise the minimum age for the employment of children from twelve to fifteen years. Article 79 of the Labor Law forbids the employment of children under fifteen years of age and stipulates that a fine will be assessed for those who violate the law (Labor, Law, 1999).

In 1998 the reformists, led by the popular President Khatami, won a landslide election in Iran. Since that time awareness of the issue has been raised due to the efforts of Iranian children's rights advocates and international pressure. Pressure to reform laws designed to protect children has helped the Khatami government crack down on and punish those breaking the laws and exploiting children economically. In addition, Iran has ratified ILO Convention No. 182 (Convention on the Worst Forms of Child Labor).

Children as Soldiers

During the Iran-Iraq War of the eighties, the Iranian government was accused by international sources of using children as soldiers. According to the Iranian government's initial report to the Committee on the Rights of the Child, "The minimum employment age for the armed forces for the purpose of receiving military training is 16 years and the minimum age of employment for the Police Forces is 17 years" (Coalition to Stop the Use of Child Soldiers, 2001). There is evidence, however, that children as young as ten were drafted by the Basij, the Voluntary Army. Only children were drafted; adults went to war voluntarily. The children were mostly from more religious and conservative families, and from parts of Iran associated with the policies of the Islamic Republic. They went to war against a professional, better-armed and trained Iraqi army. While never proven, the Iranian government was accused of using children in battles, with high casualty rates. According to critics of the Islamic Republic, the children were sent to the front as waves of human shields to stop the advancing Iraqi Army. This use of child soldiers during the Iran-Iraq War was condemned by the United Nations and international human rights organizations. Unofficially, Iran's Basij, or Popular Mobilization Army, continues to provide a smaller volunteer peacetime reserve relying heavily upon youth in its recruitment (Global March, 1998).

THE FUTURE OF CHILD LABOR

General awareness of the issue of child labor and its implications for Iranian society are rising. The Iranian media, enjoying the openness provided by the

Reformists currently in power, cover the issue of child labor in a responsible and objective way. The sensitivity with which this issue is reported and dealt with by the readers supports the work of the local children's rights advocates.

The Iranian Reformist government has been responsive to both the critiques by internal commentators on its failure to address this issue and to international pressure to bring the practice of abusive child labor to an end. The employment of children has dropped dramatically over the last few decades. It has not increased even as the income per capita falls (Labor, Law, 1999). Since education and employment are linked for children and youths ten through nineteen years of age, it is a positive sign that the education level is increasing (Labor, Law, 1999).

According to the United Nations Child Labor Agency, the IRI continues work on improving the situation. Laws passed to protect the rights of working children are closely monitored. Violators are being punished. The minimum work age has been raised and educational gaps addressed. In addition, the government has made genuine efforts to educate the Iranian people on family planning. Families are being encouraged to have no more than two children.

It is seen that many of the issues of child labor will be unresolved until the economic picture of the whole country changes for the better and poverty as a social problem gets the attention it deserves (Bijani, 2001). The country is experiencing continued high unemployment due to population growth, distracting the focus from child labor onto other issues facing the country. Without a per capita increase in income, families continue the need for more family members to work (Labor, Law, 1999). Two additional factors are important to the reduction of child labor: improving the conditions of adult labor and increasing awareness regarding the importance of education (Bijani, 2001). A more educated and skilled workforce is one outcome. The carpet industry continues to use children as laborers, who are more likely to work long hours under unhealthy and difficult working situations for less money.

Many believe that creating and implementing consistent global standards is particularly important for a country such as Iran. But without global standards that prohibit children working in factories and manufacturing businesses, these jobs, jobs needed for the health of the economy and the family, will only be exported to other countries.

BIBLIOGRAPHY

Aamoli, A. (2002) *Bonyan*, April 8, p. 9.

Bijani, M. (2001) The high cost of child labor. *Sedaye Edalat Newspaper*. English translation by Zarin Shaghaghi. @2001. Retrieved September 2002 from http://www.iranianchildren.org/articles.html#sprcarticles.

Coalition to Stop the Use of Child Soldiers. (2001) *Global Report on child soldiers*. Retrieved July 1, 2003, from http://www.child-soldiers.org/cs/childsoldiers.nsf/.

Ghanbari, V. (2002) Street children or child labor? *Khorasaan Newspaper*, May 21, p. 11.

Global March. (1998) *The invisible soldiers*. Retrieved July 1, 2003, from http://www.globalmarch.org/childsoldier/invisible-soldiers.php3.

International Labour Organisation. (1997) *Combating the most intolerable forms of child labour: A global challenge*. Amsterdam Child Labour Conference February 26–27, 1997. Retrieved February 8, 1998, www.ilo.org/public/english/90ipec/conf/ams/laccleng.htm.

Labor, Law, and Child Rights in Iran. (1999) *Andisheye Jame'e* 7 (December).

Pourziai, N. (1999) A report on the condition of young children in rug-weaving sweatshops. *Sobeh Emrooz, Wednesday edition*. English translation by Zarin Shaghaghi. @2001. Retrieved September 20, 2002, from http://www.iranianchildren.org/articles.html#sprcarticles.

Shahabi. S. (2002) This deplorable condition is not the doomed fate of children. Etobicoke, Ontario, Canada: Children First. Retrieved September 20 2002, from http://www.childrenfirstinternational.org/.

United Nations. (n.d.) Information on the Islamic Republic of Iran. Retrieved September 20, 2002, from http://www.un.org/esa/agenda21/natlinfo/countr/iran/index.htm.

10

MEXICO

David Carey, Jr.

PROFILE OF MEXICO

Mexico is a multicultural nation of about 100 million people. It is a nation that enjoys rich resources, both human and natural, yet remains disadvantaged in the world economic order. Industrialized nations such as its northern neighbors and European countries often view Mexico as a source of inexpensive labor and extractable resources. While Mexico holds great potential, historically it has suffered from widespread poverty. Many children are forced to work to support themselves or their families.

The sixty-two indigenous languages spoken in Mexico reflect the diversity of its population and depth of its history. There is evidence that aboriginal peoples populated Mexico as early as 20,000 B.C. Nomadic hunter-gatherer tribes most likely began to inhabit Mexico between 12,000 and 14,000 B.C., and the earliest human remains are those of a woman dated to between 9000 and 8000 B.C., discovered northeast of Mexico City. By 5000 B.C. nomadic groups began to cultivate corn and establish sedentary communities. Around 1500 B.C. the Olmec civilization, ancestors of the Zapotecs, Maya, Toltecs, Mixtec, Teotihuacan, and Mexica civilizations, thrived in Mexico and Central America. These groups built on each others' achievements in astronomy, cosmology, writing, mathematics, extensive trading networks, and calendars. In 1518 the Spanish invasion and subsequent colonization interrupted and altered Mexico's rich historical trajectory.

Scholars estimate that 90 percent of Mexico's indigenous population was annihilated within the first fifty years of Spanish contact mainly because of epidemics such as smallpox. Mexico's indigenous people, who represent 10 percent of the population today, have been relegated to the margins of society for over five hundred years. After the destruction of indigenous populations, the Spaniards imported African slaves. Some free Africans accompanied Hernán Cortés and other Spaniards during the initial invasion, but the majority of Africans who settled in Mexico came via the Atlantic slave trade from the sixteenth through the early nineteenth centuries. Also among the early settlers in the New World were Jewish people expelled from Spain. Subsequent waves of emigrants contributing to Mexico's cultural milieu include Chinese, Italians, French, and Filipinos.

The transition to free market neoliberal economic policies in the mid-1970s has had a devastating impact on the majority of Mexicans. Real wages decreased by 34% from 1978 to 1988 at the same time that unemployment increased. In the early 1990s, 58% of the population lived in moderate poverty, surviving on less than two dollars a day. President Carlos Salinas de Gortari (1988–94) promoted neoliberal economic policies that culminated in the North American Free Trade Agreement (NAFTA) between Canada, Mexico, and the United States in 1994. While NAFTA was hailed as Mexico's new panacea, the income gap between rich and poor continues to grow, and increasing numbers of workers have been excluded because they lack necessary skills. The World Bank considers Mexico to be one of Latin America's most inequitable economies. Since the passage of NAFTA, Mexico has increased the imports of staple crops such as corn and beans. Yet much of its subsistence production has been converted to agricultural export goods. Indigenous people and rural inhabitants, the day laborers on these farms, have suffered most severely as a result of these economic reforms. Farmers produce 70% of Mexico's food, yet 46% of the rural population lives on less than one dollar a day. The increasing rural poverty feeds the cycle of urban migration as families and individuals move to cities in search of jobs. One of the consequences of neoliberal economic practices is a declining standard of living for the lower classes. Children often become one of the, if not the only, principal income producers for their families (Inter-American Development Bank, 1997; Mexico Solidarity Network [MSN], July 22–28, 2002; Nash, 2001; World Bank, 1994).

OVERVIEW OF CHILD LABOR

During the 1990s the participation of children in the labor force increased throughout Latin America because low-income families needed earnings from younger members of the household. About 20% to 25% of children age five to fourteen work in Latin America, many as wage earners who constitute an important part of the work force. Throughout Latin America child labor advances the cause of the elites while afflicting marginalized groups such as indigenous people and Afro-Latin Americans (Casa Alianza, 2002; CEPAL,

1999; Child Labor Today, 1996; Hallet, 1998; Himes, Colbert de Arboleda and García Méndez, 1994; Salazar, 1991; UNICEF, 2002).

The most pervasive cause of child labor in Mexico is the country's socioeconomic crisis. For example, in Tijuana, "the scarcity of work training for the economically active population in Tijuana and the inopportune availability of work for adult laborers, obligates some members of the family to contribute to the family income, which is the case for minors; they must develop a variety of jobs in the local economy" (Cabrera Núñez, 1989, pp. 13–14). On average 3.6 members of each nuclear family work. Likewise, a 1979 study of child vendors and service sector workers in Mexico City found that insufficient family income was the main motive behind most minors' decisions to work (Salazar, 1991).

The economic reforms of the 1980s and 1990s exacerbated the problem for poor families. The peso was devalued in December 1994, decreasing the income of poor Mexicans by nearly 50%—a devastating loss for families in extreme poverty who dedicate more than 60% of their income to food. With reduced earnings and rising unemployment, more families were forced to expect their children to work. The early stages of NAFTA saw increased numbers of minors working in export agriculture and the expanding informal economy. Joint ventures between Mexican and U.S. growers "are achieving greater competitiveness [in U.S., European, and Japanese markets] at the cost of children working in the fields" (Bacon, 1997, p. 19). Between 1992 and 1995, street children increased from 28% to 31.5%. The Mexican Secretariat of Public Education estimates that over 2.5 million children from the ages of six through fourteen do not attend school—many because it conflicts with the harvesting season. These children and their families are forced to choose work over education for survival (Arenal, 1991; Bacon, 1997; Estrada Iguíniz, 1999). Since 2000, more *(maquiladoras)* small U.S.-owned manufacturing companies that assemble goods for export have been closing and downsizing in the coffee-growing sector. This has forced more Mexicans to seek employment as undocumented workers in the United States.

Estimates of the numbers and percentages of child laborers vary considerably in Mexico; figures range from 400,000 to 11 million. UNICEF estimates that 8 million children (25.8 percent) under the age of fifteen are working, while the Mexican Statistics Institute (INEGI) puts the number at 11 million (34.4 percent) (U.S. Department of Labor, 1994). One of the greatest challenges to accuracy is the difficulty in counting the number of children who work in informal economies, often for parents or relatives. Mexico City's central market employs eleven thousand minors from the ages of seven through eighteen as cart pushers, vendors, and kitchen help. One study across twelve states found that children from seven through fourteen make up 30 percent of agricultural day laborers—evidence that agriculture is one of the largest culprits in employing minors (U.S. Department of Labor, 2002).

Vignette

Jun Ajpu', a twelve-year-old Mayan boy who lives in the highlands of Chiapas, Mexico's southernmost state, begins his day at 5:00 A.M. with a breakfast of beans, corn tortillas, and coffee. On some days he attends the local school because his parents would like him to learn to read and write Spanish, although they generally speak their native language in the home. The lad's school attendance is contingent upon the agricultural cycle; he rarely goes to school during the planting or harvesting season because his father needs his help on their farm. In fact, his parents have decided that this will be his last year of school because he is big enough now to dedicate his energies to the subsistence farming that maintains the family. On their three-acre farm they grow corn, beans, and squash. As he embarks on the two-mile walk to their land, Jun Ajpu' carries a hoe, machete, tumpline, and spray tube, which holds pesticide. The corn has been growing tall this year thanks to significant rainfall, but lately insects have been eating the leaves. Jun Ajpu' begins by pumping his tube and spraying the corn stalks with pesticide. Next he uses his hoe to weed and build up mounds of dirt around the cornstalks to help them withstand the strong winds. At noon, his mother and eight-year-old sister Ixchel arrive with a lunch of beans, rice, and corn tortillas in pots and baskets, which they carry on their heads. During the heavy labor seasons of planting and harvesting, his mother and sister would remain to help work on the farm. But today Jun Ajpu' and his father will finish the tasks on their own, so the women return to the village. Jun Ajpu' continues his work of weeding and building up the earth until late afternoon, when he begins to search for and cut firewood to bring back to their home. Once he gathers enough firewood, he straps his tumpline across his forehead to carry the load on his back. He and his father arrive back home around 6:00 P.M., where they enjoy a dinner of beans, eggs, and corn tortillas.

During the day Ixchel also has been working hard. She awoke with her brother at 5:00 A.M. to begin the process of making corn tortillas. Her mother soaked corn kernels in water with a bit of lime overnight so Ixchel could bring the corn to the miller at daybreak. Her mother reminds Ixchel that when she was Ixchel's age they did not have the luxury of a miller and she had to awaken at 3:00 A.M. to grind corn with a mortar and pestle. When Ixchel returns, she and her mother make corn tortillas for breakfast and heat a pot of beans on the hearth. After the family has enjoyed breakfast and the men have left for the hills, Ixchel retrieves water for the home from a nearby stream. When she returns, she helps her mother prepare lunch. By 9:30 A.M. the lunch is ready, so Ixchel and her mother set out for the community trough to wash the family's clothes. Often if they arrive at this hour they have to wait to get a spot at the trough or continue their journey to the stream, but today they are fortunate and find a vacant position. They return home to hang the clothes to dry and set out to deliver lunch. When they return around two in the afternoon, Ixchel and her mother set up their back looms and begin weaving. Ixchel is just learning, but is becoming very adept at this traditional skill. Because the family farm seldom produces a surplus, the potential income from the sale of her textiles is crucial to the family. Her earnings will allow the family to purchase other foodstuffs and clothes for her father and brother. At 5:00 P.M. she and her mother break to make fresh tortillas and prepare supper. After dinner, Ixchel may have a bit more time to weave, especially if the moon is full and lights up the family courtyard. She does not attend school partly because her labor, both paid and unpaid, is so important to her family's livelihood and because her parents believe that an education is not important for her since she will only get married and work in her husband's home. Ixchel laments that she does not have the opportunity to go to school, but hears from friends that attending class does not guarantee an education. Her friend Ixtz'unum began attending school this year and hates it because the teachers chastise her for not speaking Spanish and often relegate her to the kitchen to help prepare the school snack.

While life in rural Mexico is demanding for Jun Ajpu' and Ixchel, their counterparts in urban areas often suffer from a lack of housing, food, and familial support. Juan came to Mexico City when he was eight years old because his parents could no longer afford to care for him. Three years earlier his parents had told him that he could find work in Mexico City and support himself. At the open-air market at La Merced, he discovered that he could get paid to carry merchandise for people, help vendors set up and break down their stands, and clean the street. After saving a little money, he decided to go into business for himself; buying gum, he was selling it on the street and in the subway. He made little profit in this endeavor, so when he met a group of boys his age they easily convinced him he could do better washing cars stopped at red lights. Even though the earnings were poor and the occupation was dangerous, he appreciated the company of his new friends. One time they invited him to stay with them in the Terminal Centro de Norte bus station; it was better than living on the street, but they had to avoid the security guards, who were vigilant about removing them from their hidden living spaces in the terminal. These boys became Juan's family, and he began to inhale glue with them to help him forget his troubles. Eventually he seldom worked to earn money, but rather begged for food or gathered any scraps he could find. When a group of outreach workers from the Casa Alianza (a division of Covenant House in New York City) approached him to offer shelter, food, and the opportunity to attend school if he agreed to give up glue sniffing, he refused, not because of his drug addiction but because he was afraid to leave his new family. He has little trust in adults.

HISTORY OF CHILD LABOR

Children's work has been a reality in Mexico since its first inhabitants. Many aboriginal groups valued work as a natural part of a child's upbringing and a necessary preparation for adulthood. In a tradition that their descendants follow today, the classic Maya (circa A.D. 325–900) gave toys to newborn babies; these toys represented the children's future adult roles according to gender. Boys received a toy machete and hoe. Girls played with toys that resembled household or weaving utensils. Likewise, the Aztecs (circa A.D. 1000–1600) provided an extensive education for their children but also expected them to work. They believed that hard work and some suffering would prepare them for military battles. Children were in charge of collecting water and firewood, grazing and hunting animals, and farming and weaving.

The Spanish invasion and subsequent occupation of Mexico changed the face and reality of child labor. Spanish leaders argued that children should not work but rather dedicate themselves to study. Labor laws were passed that forbade children under fourteen from working except for shepherding. However, *("obedezco pero no cumplo")* "I obey but do not comply" was a common approach to the law in colonial Mexico. Government officials rarely enforced child labor laws, so children who spent their childhood and adolescence in servitude or even those who worked by choice had little protection, recourse, or hope for escape from their labor arrangements. Because most Spaniards on both sides of the Atlantic supported slavery, children of all ages were bought and sold in Mexico's slave markets. While historically, children worked because the elders believed they would benefit from the experience, now they worked because entrepreneurs needed cheap or free labor.

Mexico's independence movements (1810–21) brought little relief for child laborers. The emancipation proclamation in 1829 made Mexico one of the first nations in the Americas to abolish slavery, but children continued to be victims of forced labor. The newly independent nation passed a law in 1856 prohibiting children under the age of fourteen from working.

During the nineteenth century, society expected children to be industrious, not carefree and playful. Child labor was a common phenomenon in banana, coffee, and sugar plantations, small family farms, fishing boats, markets, private homes. It was not uncommon for children from the ages of six through twelve to be kidnapped and sold to *(haciendas)* large landed estates.

Since the early nineteenth century, adoption for labor was common. Foundling homes and orphanages often served as sources of young labor for middle and upper-class families, some of whom adopted multiple children. While most people looking for laborers preferred boys age eleven to fifteen, girls were more attractive to those looking for domestic servants. Many girls suffered rape at the hands of their masters and physical beatings from their jealous mistresses. The law gave these young women little recourse: the

1870 civil code considered employers of underage domestic servants their guardians with the power to discipline them. In places like Yucatán, where slavery persisted, boys often became perpetual indentured servants on *(henequen)* sisal plantations because they had inherited their fathers's debts.

Throughout President Porfirio Díaz's regime (1876–1911), children were essential contributors to his modernization plan; they developed infrastructure such as ports and railroads, which facilitated the exportation of Mexico's resources. Díaz's economic policies increased economic disparity and forced many poor families to seek sources of income from their children or surrender them to orphanages. Although not necessarily motivated by political reasons (many were conscripted), children also participated and died as soldiers and spies in the Mexican revolution (1910–17) that overthrew Díaz and ushered in democracy.

The Mexican revolution was a watershed event; the Constitution of 1917 promised liberty, justice, sovereignty, and equality. Laborers enjoyed increased rights and, most important, the freedom to organize. The Constitution outlawed forced labor and provided for an eight-hour workday, a six-day workweek, a minimum wage, equal pay for equal work, and the right to collective bargaining and striking. Children under the age of fourteen were prohibited from working. Those from fourteen through sixteen who had not finished their obligatory schooling could work only with the consent of a guardian. Other restrictions also applied depending on age and employment.

Concurrently, the 1917 Law of Domestic Relations legislated legal adoption, which required judicial approval. This law combined with the child labor restrictions nearly eradicated adoption for labor. As in the past, however, the letter of the law did not reflect its practice. Throughout the late nineteenth and early twentieth centuries, children migrated from their rural homes to the cities in search of employment. Most of the children were illiterate, had to settle for low-paying jobs, and were fortunate if they survived the infectious diseases and parasites of this time (Rodríguez Hernández, 1996; Boils Morales, 1979; Mendelievich, 1979).

Unions generally have not represented children. In some cases, however, children's work was so crucial that unions included them. For example, because of the proliferation of newspapers and magazines in Mexico City, the Union of Vendors, Vociferators, and Distributors of the Press was founded in 1923—by 1928 thousands of young vociferators (newspaper criers) had joined. Young boys dominated the profession of vociferator, and the leader of the union held them up as an example of the benefits of the union. He asserted that illiteracy among these criers had diminished because they were attending school and "their personal appearance had begun to improve [because]...they [the union] gave them denim clothes and underwear" (Aurrecoechea and Bartra, 1993, pp. 82–83).

By the beginning of the twentieth century, child labor's intensity had increased and its forms had changed. In 1960, 3.1% of the economically active population were from eight through fourteen years of age. In 1973, 20% of the children from five through sixteen in Mexico City were working. The number of minors who worked continued to grow in the 1970s. With the 1982 economic crisis, the increase was dramatic. By 1987 between 12 and 13.5 million youths under the age of eighteen were living in extreme poverty in the urban areas alone; between 7 and 10 million of them worked. Bear in mind that official estimates are notoriously low because of the inability to count the number of children working in the informal economy. Children worked in everything from agriculture to fishing, brick factories to bakeries, and markets to bands. As technology and other advances inundated Mexico, occupational hazards increased (Bensusan, 1979; Cabrera Núñez, 1989; Rodríguez Hernández, 1996). For example, the use of agrichemicals in farming, machinery in industrial plants, and toxic dyes in clothes manufacturing introduced new threats to young workers' health. A close look at Mexico today reveals that although the government and nongovernmental organizations (NGOs) have made important strides, childhood remains perilous for many Mexican youths.

CHILD LABOR TODAY

In the context of NAFTA, the United States and Mexico have embarked on joint studies to assess the situation in their countries. Although NAFTA countries can be fined for failing to enforce child labor laws, and Article 123 of the Mexican Constitution prohibits children under the age of fourteen from working, official statistics underestimate the number of working children. These laws are designed to protect children from work based on age and related physical capability and to preserve their childhood. Nonetheless, a special permit can be issued so that those under the age of fourteen years can work if their socioeconomic status warrants it. Adolescents from fourteen through sixteen can work if they have their parents' permission, however, they retain special protections by law. The law encourages those who have not finished the obligatory primary and secondary schooling to do so while employed—at the very least to attain literacy. Sixteen-year-olds may work only six hours a day, with a one-hour break, and cannot work after 10:00 P.M. The law requires employers to post a list of dangerous tasks that minors should not perform, limits overtime and holiday work, and outlines vacation rights. Professions that may be "dangerous or unhealthy" or that "may affect their moral or good behavior" (such as working in mines, submarines, and bars) are forbidden to minors. The responsibility for compliance falls upon employers, and offenders face stiff penalties with fines up to 155 times the minimum salary. Unfortunately, fines of this magnitude are seldom assessed (Bensusan, 1979; Dávalos, 2001; Estrada Iguíniz, 1999; U.S. Department of Labor, 1994).

Compulsory education plays a central role in eradicating child labor. (Fyfe, 1989; Himes, Colbert de Arboleda, and García Méndez, 1994; U.S. Department of Labor 2002; Weiner, 1991). National statistics show about 6% of the nation's eight to twelve year-olds are illiterate; 22% of indigenous children in this same age group are illiterate (U.S. Department of Labor, 2002). A study conducted in San Cristóbal de Las Casas, Chiapas, in 1998, found that 50 percent of indigenous children had never attended school because they had to help support their families (Figueroa Fuentes et al., 2000). In his 1980 study of San Cosme Mazatecochco, an anthropologist found that school attendance reduced child labor by the mere fact that children were not available to work for at least five hours a day (Rothstein, 1982). In much of rural Mexico, schools are abysmal in their physical structure and curriculum, and in many cases denigrate and discriminate against indigenous children whose only language is not Spanish. As a result, for many students the opportunities for advancement that these institutions provide are limited in spite of the sacrifices families make. Many students drop out of school because they have to work; others choose to leave school because they consider the endeavor fruitless. Factors that help attract and retain students include relevant curricula, flexible schedules, adequate resources, and competent teachers.

The Mexican government dedicates 20 percent of its total budget to education. In an effort to attract and retain students, the Mexican government provides over 4 million free breakfasts to schools (U.S. Department of Labor, 2002). It also has experimented to meet the needs of its target populations. For example, a plan was developed to allow migrant children to attend school in their home state and finish the school year in the state their parents migrate to. Other schools teach children in two shifts, morning and afternoon, which allows them to work in vegetable processing plants or surrounding fields part-time.

In August 1997 the Mexican government launched an innovative anti-poverty initiative called the Program for Education, Health, and Nutrition (PROGRESA), which offers improved schooling, nutrition, and housing to poor families and financial incentives such as grants and scholarships to parents who keep their children in school. Funds are awarded for good attendance, advancing in school, and receiving regular medical examinations. Financial assistance is also provided for school materials. The scholarships increase as students pass into higher grades and pay more for girls than boys at the secondary level. After only two years, one study showed that PROGRESA had increased the number of girls attending school, reduced male child laborers, and kept an additional one hundred thousand children from low-income families in school in 1999 alone. Already the program has been so successful that other nations are looking to PROGRESA as a model for increasing school participation and reducing child labor. By 2002, eight other Latin American nations had experimented with similar programs (Alarcón Glasinovich, 2000; Bachman, 1997; Becker, 1999; López-Calva, 2002; U.S. Department of Labor, 2002; U.S. Department of State, 2000).

The majority of government initiatives focus on rural areas because urban children are more likely to attend school than their rural counterparts (87.3 percent and 64.7 percent respectively). Nonetheless, poverty also inhibits educational opportunities in Mexico's cities. In response to this omnipresent crisis, the government's National System for Integral Development of the Family (DIF) provides about eight thousand stipends to poor urban families who keep their children in school.

SOCIAL VIEWS, CUSTOMS, AND PRACTICES

Child labor is most acute in agriculture, construction, and small businesses, especially those run by families. Large factories tend to reject underage workers. The laws are clear but seldom enforced. State governments are required to enforce federal labor laws except for certain fields under the jurisdiction of the federal government (automobiles, petroleum, metals, chemicals, textiles). State labor inspectors are overworked and underpaid. Many lack sufficient training or even means of transportation to work sites, especially in rural areas. In 1996 in Baja California, labor authorities uncovered hundreds of underage workers but refrained from fining the employer companies because the families were dependent on the income. Even when business owners are fined, the fines are too small to be effective. Seldom do the penalties coerce a change in business behavior. Labor leaders argue that the government allows some companies to violate child labor laws. In fact, President Vicente Fox (2000–2006) employed children as young as eleven years old to work on his family ranch and in freezer plants.

Like many of their Mexican associates, U.S. firms in Mexico often ignore child labor abuses. Spokespeople at Fresh Choice and Nunes Company were aware of child labor abuses on the farms that supplied their vegetables, but claimed no responsibility for the employment practices of their Mexican contract growers. Likewise, Green Giant and other U.S. canneries employ children in its fields and food processing plants (Bacon, 1997; Lee-Wright, 1990; U.S. Department of Labor, 1994). Traditional attitudes, poverty, a culture of acceptance, and the difficulty of replacing child labor with adult labor undermine child labor legislation.

Poverty is the most salient issue. Child labor is one of the diverse strategies that families use to guarantee their subsistence and improve their living conditions. Studies show that poor families depend on children's income. In Guadalajara, 80 percent of the children from single-mother households worked—a statistic that reflects a widespread phenomenon in Latin America. Additionally, single mothers need their eldest offspring to assume domestic duties—cooking, cleaning, child care—so that they may be employed. As a child feels increased pressure to provide for the family, work becomes incompatible with school. In some cases parents become so desperate that one or more of their children is sent away. Generally the oldest child begins working at a younger age than siblings, and boys are more likely to be sent out of the home to work than girls.

Gender is an important determinant of the type, intensity, and amount of work children perform. Mexican *machismo* dictates that women should be sheltered and protected. Boys are also more likely to continue with school while they work; girls often forfeit schooling to work and typically receive less education than their male counterparts. Girls begin working in the home at a younger age than boys and work longer hours. By the time a girl is five, she is learning household skills with her mother. Her brother may not begin his labor until he reaches seven or eight years of age (Becker, 1999; Comisión para el estudio de los niños callejeros, 1992; Estrada Iguíniz, 1999; González de la Rocha, 1988; Salazar, 1991).

Some parents encourage children to work as a means to learn how to make a living and prepare for life. These sentiments become especially acute during times of economic crisis. In this way child labor is part of the socialization process, especially among marginalized populations. Work does not necessarily impede the development of children; it can contribute to their self-esteem. However, many children surrender their childhood and educational opportunities because they must provide for their families and often seek or can find income only in abusive and exploitative settings.

Children most often secure work through their network of family and friends. Most children who work come from families whose parents and grandparents also worked as children, so this family tradition often becomes an inescapable cycle. Children whose parents work in a trade will accompany them; others pursue what their friends have established such as selling goods in the street, working in markets, or offering their services door to door.

Mexican society and especially the press demonize child street workers. Newspapers present them as useless beggars. Residents denigrate them as urchins, except when they need their services. The social stigma facilitates the police force's penchant to harass, abuse, and extort money from child street workers. The Minors in Distress (MESE) program seeks to ameliorate these conditions by assigning "street educators" to accompany child street workers in their daily lives. Likewise, in Mexico City, Casa Alianza provides a similar outreach in hopes of attracting street children to a more stable environment. While the vigilance of these programs protects some children, violence and exploitation against street workers continues.

Agriculture is the most common employer for children. The International Labour Organisation estimates that 90 percent of child laborers are rural residents who work in agriculture. This work comes with many dangers: exposure to harsh climates, sharp tools, heavy loads, and toxic chemicals (some of which have been proven to retard bone development).

Ten-to-twelve-hour workdays are the norm, with no overtime compensation. In addition, rural children often carry water and firewood, herd animals, and produce textiles (AFL-CIO, 1991; Bacon, 1997; Bensusan, 1979; Casa Alianza, 2002; Child Labor Today, 1996; Hallet, 1998; U.S. Department of Labor, 2002).

Throughout Latin America since the 1950s, in response to poverty and industrialization, people have migrated to the cities. Many live in shanty-towns and depend on their children's income for survival. Children's earn-ings tend to be 30 to 40 percent less than that of adults, even when they perform the same labor. Some children receive their payment in kind, such as a room and meals. Those who work in their families' endeavors are seldom financially compensated (Salazar, 1991).

A hierarchy of employment opportunities exists for children in urban areas. In most cases child laborers do not learn skills that will allow them to improve their economic position. At the top of the hierarchy are boys who bundle and carry packages for supermarket clients. They enjoy the safest working conditions and highest levels of education because they can arrange their job schedules to complement their schooling. They earn only tips because the supermarkets do not pay them, but since gratuities are a part of Mexican culture, they generally earn as much as their counterparts in the service and sales industries. Unlike children in the service and sales sector who contribute much of their earnings to their families, these boys tend to keep their money for themselves.

The service and sales sector positions in the informal economy are more hazardous because of the risk for exploitation. For example, in the Merced market, no regulations limit the maximum weight child porters can carry. Often supervisors abuse them and take their earnings under false claims of damage to wheelbarrows or other tools of the trade. Because these jobs demand longer hours, fewer of these children attend school, and those who remain committed to their education find it difficult to find time to study. The most marginalized among child laborers are the street performers, car washers, sex workers, and others who generally live on the streets. They keep all their earnings for their survival because most no longer live or even communicate with their families; school is a prohibitive luxury.

Most children are employed in simple tasks and services in small enter-prises, informal sector workshops, street markets, shoe and garment indus-tries, and brick factories. They wash and care for cars, run errands, transport goods in markets, shine shoes, sell gum, and disguise themselves as clowns and perform for cars at stoplights. In homes they make merchandise, textiles, or food that parents or adults will sell. More dangerous forms that ensnare children include the drug trade, prostitution, pornography, and military forces. Child prostitution has increased in Mexico City since 1994. In La Merced zone of Mexico City, girls sell sex in denigrating conditions. Agents who promise employment or marriage lure girls away from their families and turn them into sex workers.

Gender analyses of child labor reveal that girls are more vulnerable than boys. Domestic service absorbs the majority of female child laborers under the age of sixteen and exposes them to physical, mental, and sexual abuse. It is one of the most poorly regulated, inadequately compensated, and highly stigmatized forms of employment. Historically domestic labor has been one of the few options available to women, and many have resented it. Although women's opportunities have expanded, for girls from impoverished families, opportunity remains limited. Studies of domestic servants show that the majority of girls leave school to support their families and have their families's approval to work. Despite the fact that they had few rights—the homeowner established the more-than-ten-hour workday schedule and salary, and provided no medical services—most of the girls were happy to be working and helping their families.

Working conditions quickly erase any semblance of childhood for these girls. In most cases the distinction between salaried work and servitude is blurred; many domestic workers are paid in food, clothes, and housing—none of which allows any independence. Paternalistic employers view workers' benefits as privileges, not rights; the most dire consequence of this perception is that many men expect sex from their servants, and unequal and unregulated conditions make it difficult for girls to resist these advances. One UNICEF study found that many Latin American men have their first sexual encounter with domestic servants. In turn, young girls feel the wrath of their mistresses; often jealous wives beat or fire domestic workers for their husbands' infidelity (Hoyos, 2000; UNICEF, 1999).

Another area that predominantly affects girls is the *maquiladora* industry along the U.S.-Mexican border—more than 60 percent of *maquiladora* workers are young women. The majority of these laborers migrate from other parts of Mexico plagued by unemployment and depressed wages. Migrants earn less than half the average Mexican wage at most *maquiladoras*. Because these plants employ mostly women who often become the sole income earners of their households, these employment opportunities challenge *machismo*. Girls as young as twelve find it easy to secure employment in these factories, where they may be subject to hazardous materials, night shifts, and sexual abuse. Living conditions for *maquiladora* migrants are equally dismal; many live in shantytowns without piped water or electricity. Since the factories pollute the water wells, many communities' only source of water is delivered by a truck. Typically these communities are isolated from schools and hospitals. Despite the low pay and abusive working conditions, competition for these jobs is fierce because of dwindling opportunities. Between July 2001 and July 2002, 545 *maquiladoras* closed—most in search of even lower wages in places like China (U.S. Department of Labor, 1994; Mexico Solidarity Network 15–21 July 2002; AFL-CIO, 1991).

THE FUTURE OF CHILD LABOR

The root causes of child labor include poverty and lack of educational opportunities. Strengthening the family income is one of the best ways to eradicate child labor. PROGRESA provides stipends but not permanent increases in familial income; critics argue that sustainable solutions must be employed. Microenterprise development has enjoyed widespread success, but its benefits are limited. Modern technology offers greater potential because it can increase the productivity and income of adults in exchange for the cessation of child labor. This solution is especially attractive to brickmakers, miners, artisans, and farmers, who can realize immediate and significant benefits from technology. The larger goal is to replace child labor with adults, preferably from the same family, working for decent wages under fair labor conditions. This shift can begin through training, technology, and improved labor regulation, but endemic change cannot emerge solely from national efforts.

Mexico is not unilaterally responsible for its economic condition or child labor problem. Through NAFTA, agricultural and other consumer products made with child labor in Mexico are sold to industrialized nations. Consumers have the power to undermine exploitative practices by refusing to purchase goods made with child labor. U.S. labor unions and activists are pushing to have goods labeled so shoppers will be aware if child labor produced them. However, a shift from the misnamed free trade policies to fair trade approaches that provide just opportunities and living wages to workers in developing nations is more effective in eliminating child labor than boycotting certain imports. As one child labor scholar argues, "What makes our country [Mexico] attractive to U.S. growers is low wages, which are the product of economic policies of structural adjustment promoted by the government and financial institutions like the International Monetary Fund" (Bacon, 1997, p. 21).

The cures for economic crises, such as the 1994 peso devaluation, fall on the shoulders of the poorest citizens. In many cases children are most affected by these international mandates. Structural adjustment policies (SAPs) which the IMF, World Bank, and other international lending institutions advocate and impose, have increased child mortality, morbidity, illiteracy, and labor in many developing countries. These approaches to economic reform fail to adequately address these problems, and in most cases deepen poverty. As one anthropologist argues, "Reference to broad and ahistorical causes of the oppression of children such as poverty, illiteracy, backwardness, greed, and cruelty fail to go beyond the mere description of oppression and ignore the historical and social conditioning of exploitation" (Nieuwenhuys, 1996, p. 242). Many of Mexico's child advocates assert that real progress can come about only with fundamental social and economic change, and solutions will be successful only if leaders address the international and domestic causes of child labor in Mexico. To this end, industrialized nations that import child labor products and facilitate Mexico's disadvantaged economic position could reform their own economic policies.

Increased public awareness and activism contributes to the reduction of child labor. The Global March against child labor is exemplary in its efforts to inform the public, increase support at all levels from local to international, and mobilize public opinion and action against broader social, economic, and cultural injustices: discrimination against women and minorities, unfair distribution of land and resources, illegal labor practices, massive unemployment, southern nations' indebtedness to northern nations, SAPs, and unfair terms of globalization. Likewise, NGOs play a decisive role in disseminating information to raise public awareness and promoting creative solutions to the problem of child labor. Radio, television, press, posters, research institutions, public lectures, and other media can all promote awareness.

Mexico has a nascent child labor movement, which sent representatives to the Third International Congress on Child Labor in Guatemala in 1992, but it has much to learn from its counterparts in other Latin American nations. Child labor movements throughout Latin America today play an important role in ameliorating the effects of child labor and decreasing the number of minors who work. The mobilization of society can create institutional networks and collaborations between the congress, local committees, and NGOs. Parents and children who fully participate in a movement will find that empowerment is a right, not a privilege. Latin American child advocates emphasize that the goal is to create consciousness of rights, not dependency.

A holistic response to the crisis of child labor in Mexico includes consideration of cultural factors that impact perceptions of child labor. Gender, age, and kinship often dictate the type of labor performed by children and the value allotted to that work. In the diverse cultures of Mexico, these factors are not uniform or static so it is recognized that responses must be flexible and sensitive. Children are contributors to the economy in both paid and unpaid positions. It is seen that they must be respected for these roles or they will lose the inherent power in the creation and negotiation of value. A 1979 study of child vendors and service sector workers in Mexico City showed that child laborers were the most marginalized or despised group in Mexico City, yet most were working because they felt responsible for their families (Solórzano, 1979). Children already have proven their capacity to be independent actors in the economy and many prefer work to school. Scholars recognize that children who are viewed as rational beings are able to contribute to the complex issue of child labor. Including ideas, perceptions, and desires of children serves to create effective solutions to child labor.

CONCLUSION

Child labor permeates every corner of Mexico from its rural highlands to Mexico City's *zocalo* (central plaza). Jun Ajpu', Ixchel, and Juan personify the complexities in which child labor manifests itself. Education is an important tool to absorb children away from the labor market, and Mexico has initiated innovative techniques such as schools with flexible hours and schedules, scholarships, free breakfasts, and region-specific curricula. Mexico's socioeconomic situation, however, remains the most pertinent issue for child labor, yet conditions continue to deteriorate. In 2002, 1.3 million more people succumbed to poverty, raising the percentage of people who live in poverty to 53.7 (MSN, August 12–18, 2002). Increased family income and secure, living-wage job opportunities for adults will combat the crisis of child labor, but these changes cannot come about through Mexico's domestic policies and actors alone. Governments, NGOs, and individuals outside Mexico can work to adjust the economic imbalance that undermines the development of developing nations. U.S consumers can advocate for fair trade relations, equal economic opportunities, and a more equitable distribution of wealth between nations.

NOTE

I would like to thank Elizabeth KimJin Traver for encouraging me to pursue this project, Crystal Wilder for her tireless sleuthing as a research assistant, and Cathryne Schmitz for her insightful editorial comments on earlier drafts of this article.

BIBLIOGRAPHY

AFL-CIO. (1991, February 4) Free trade plan raises alarm on child labor abuses in Mexico. *AFL-CIO News* 36(3): 3.
Alarcón Glasinovich, W. (2000) El trabajo de niños y adolescentes en América Latina y el Caribe: Situación, políticas y retos en los años noventa. In G. Acosta Vargas, E. García-Méndez, and S. Hoyos, eds. *Trabajo infantil doméstico ¿Y quién la mandó a ser niña?* Santafé de Bogotá, Colombia: Tercer Mundo Editores.
Anales de la Asociación Médico Quirúrjica Larrey. (1876) Vol. 2. Mexico: Imprenta de Francisco Díaz de León.
Andrews, E. L. (2002, September 1). U.S. rebuked: slapping the hand that fed free trade. *New York Times*, p. 4
Arenal, S. (1991). *No hay tiempo para jugar... (niños trabajadores).* Mexico: Editorial Nuestro Tiempo.
Arenal, S., L. Ramos, and R. Maldonado. (1997) *La infancia negada.* Monerrey: Universidad Autónoma de Nuevo León.
Arrom, S. M. (1985) *The women of Mexico City, 1790–1857.* Stanford: Stanford University Press.
Aurrecoechea, J. M., and A. Bartra. (1993) *Puros cuentos. Historia de la historieta en México, 1934–1950.* Mexico: CNCA-Grijalbo.
Bachman, S. L. (1997, September 1) Young workers in Mexico's economy. *U.S. News and World Report* 123(8): 40–41.

Bacon, D. (1997, January 27) Mexico's new braceros. *Nation* 264(3): 18–21.

Becker, G. (1999, November 22) 'Bribe' Third World parents to keep their kids in school. *Business Week* 3656: 15.

Bensusan, G. (1979) Mexico. In E. Mendelievich, ed. *Children at work*. Geneva: International Labour Office.

Blum, A. S. (1998, July) Public welfare and child circulation, Mexico City, 1877–1925. *Journal of Family History* 23(3): 240–72.

Boils Morales, G. (1979, July–September) El movimiento de los trabajadores en Yucatán durante la gubernatura de Salvador Alvarado (1915–1917). *Revista Mexicana de Sociología* 41(3).

la Botz, D. (2000, November–December) Into the frying pan: Mexican labor faces its greatest crisis. *Dollars and Sense* 232: 29–30.

Brown, J. C. (2000) *Latin America: A social history of the colonial period*. Fort Worth: Harcourt College Publishers.

Cabrera Núñez, G. (1989) El empleo infantil en Tijuana. *Cuadernos de Economía* 4(3): 9–10.

Casa Alianza. (2002, 17 July) Child labor exploitation: The global march against child labor. Retrieved August 22, 2002, from http://www.casa-alianza.org/EN/human-rights/laborexploit/overview.shtml.

Castro Barrón, L., and A. Figuera Guzmán. (1982) *Estudio de 100 niños vendedores ambulantes en el Distrito Federal y su relación con el mercado de trabajo urbano*. Mexico City: Departamento de Sociología, UAM.

CEPAL. (1999) *Panorama social*. Santiago, Chile: United Nations.

Child Labor Today: Facts and Figures. (1996, June–July) *World of Work* 16: 12–14.

Coe, M. (1994) *Mexico: From the Olmecs to the Aztecs*. New York: Thames & Hudson.

———. (2000) *The Maya*. New York: Thames & Hudson.

Comisión para el estudio de los niños callejeros. (1992) *Cuidad de México: Estudio de los niños callejeros. Resumen ejecutivo*. México.

Cook, S. F., and W. Borah. (1971–79) *Essays in population history: Mexico and the Caribbean*. Vols. 1–3. Berkeley: University of California Press.

Dávalos, J. (2001) *Derechos de los menores trabajadores*. Mexico City: Universidad Nacional Autónoma de México.

Denevan, W. M. (1992) *The native population of the Americas in 1492*. Madison: University of Wisconsin Press.

El correo de los niños, 60. (1881, 20 May) Mexico. (Séptima época).

El escolar: Periodico dedicado a las niñasde las Escuelas Lancasterinas 1(10): pp. 2–3. (1872, October 27) Mexico: Imprenta en la calle de Santa Teresa.

Estrada Iguíniz, M. (1999, January–April) Infancia y trabajo. La experiencia de los sectores populares urbanos. *Estudios Sociologicos* 17(9) (Mexico City).

Figueroa Fuentes, P., J. Herrera Jácome, M. C. Manca, A. Hernández Cervantes, O. Sánchez Carrillo, and J. López Intzin. (2000) *Rumbo a la calle... El trabajo infantil, una estrategia de sobrevivencia*. San Cristóbal de Las Casas, Chiapas: Editorial Fray Bartolomé de Las Casas.

Fyfe, A. (1989) *Child labour*. Cambridge: Polity Press.

Gerhard, P. (1995) A black conquistador in Mexico. In D. J. Davis, ed. *Slavery and beyond: The African impact on Latin America and the Caribbean*, pp. 1–9. Wilmington, DE: Scholarly Resources.

Gibbons, T. (1992, spring) Tough trade-offs. *Human Rights: Journal of the Section of Individual Rights and Responsibilities* 19(2): pp. 26–31.

González de la Rocha, M. (1988) De por qué las mujeres aguantan golpes y cuernos: Un análisis de hogares sin varón en Guadalajara. In Gabayet et al., eds. *Mujeres y sociedad. Salario, hogar, y acción en el occidente de México.* México: El Colegio de Jalisco-CIESAS.

Hallet, M. (1998, February) Global update: Latin America. *Safety & Health* 157(2): 20.

Herrera Sánchez, R. (1991) *Los niños aprendices.* Morelia, Mexico: Impresos Hurtado.

Himes, J. R., V. Colbert de Arboleda, and E. García Méndez. (1994) *Child labour and basic education in Latin America and the Caribbean: A proposed UNICEF initiative.* Florence, Italy: UNICEF.

Hobbs, S., J. McKechnie, and M. Lavalette. (1999) *Child labor: A world history companion.* Denver: ABC-CLIO.

Hoyos, S. (2000) "¿Y quién la mandó a ser niña": El trabajo infantil doméstico desde una perspectiva de género. In G. Acosta Vargas, E. García-Méndez, and S. Hoyos, eds. *Trabajo infantil doméstico ¿Y quién la mandó a ser niña?* Santafé de Bogotá, Colombia: Tercer Mundo Editores.

Inter-American Development Bank. (1997) *Annual Report 1997.*

Klein, H. (1986) *African slavery in Latin America and the Caribbean.* Oxford: Oxford University Press.

Lee-Wright, P. (1990) *Child slaves.* London: Earthscan Publications.

Liebel, M. (1994) *Protagonismo infantil: movimientos de niños trabajadores en america latina.* Managua, Nicaragua: Editorial Nueva Nicaragua.

López-Calva, L. F. (2002) Social norms, coordination, and policy issues in the fight against child labor. *Serie Documentos de Trabajo* 2.

McNatt, R., and P. Magnusson. (2000, September 25). The sweat of small brows. *Business Week* 3700: 12.

Mendelievich, E. (1979) Introductory analysis. In E. Mendelievich, ed. *Children at work.* Geneva: International Labour Office.

Meyer, M. C., W.L. Sherman, and S. M. Deeds. (1999) *The course of Mexican history.* Oxford: Oxford University Press.

MSN (Mexico Solidarity Network). (2002, June 17–23). *Weekly News and Analysis.*

———. (Mexico Solidarity Network). (2002, July 22–28). *Weekly News and Analysis.*

———. (Mexico Solidarity Network). (2002, July 15–21). *Weekly News and Analysis.*

———. (Mexico Solidarity Network). (2002, August 12–18). *Weekly News and Analysis.*

Nardinelli, C. (1990) *Child labour and the industrial revolution.* Bloomington: Indiana University Press.

Nash, J. (2001) *Mayan visions: The quest for autonomy in an age of globalization.* New York: Routledge.

Nieuwenhuys, O. (1996) The paradox of child labor and anthropology. *Annual Review of Anthropology* 25: 237–51.

Oficina Internacional del Trabajo. (1998, June) Propuesta de nuevas normas internacionales sobre las formas extremas de trabajo infantil. Retrieved August 20,

2002, from http://www.casa-alianza.org/EN/human-rights/labor-exploit/
overview.shtml.

A report on child labor in Mexico and the United States (1993?). Mexico City:
Secretaria del Trabajo y Prevision Social/Washington: Department of Labor.

Restall, M. (1998) *Maya conquistador*. Boston: Beacon Press.

Rodríguez Hernández, G. (1996) *Niños trabajadores Mexicanos, 1865–1925*. Mexico
City: Instituto Nacional de Antropolgía e Historia.

Rothstein, F. A. (1982) *Three different worlds: women, men, and children in an
industrializing community*. London: Greenwood Press.

Ruiz González, E., and M. Díaz Barón. (2000) Las Niñas también trabajan. In
G. Acosta Vargas, E. García-Méndez, and S. Hoyos, eds. *Trabajo infantil
doméstico ¿Y quién la mandó a ser niña?* Santafé de Bogotá, Colombia: Tercer
Mundo Editores.

Salazar, C. (1991, March–April) Young workers in Latin America: Protection or self
determination? *Child Welfare* 70(2): 269–83.

Solórzano, A. (1979) *Estudio de mil casos de niños dedicados al comercio ambulante y
los servicios en la ciudad de México*. Mexico City: Instituto Nacional de Estudio
del Trabajo.

Stadum, B. (1995) The dilemma in saving children from child labor: Reform and
casework at odds with families' needs. *Child Welfare* 74(1): 20–33.

Taracena E., and M-L. Tavera. (2000) Stigmatization versus identity: Child street-
workers in Mexico. In Bernard Schlemmer, ed. *The exploited child*. London:
Zed Books.

UNICEF. (1999) *Innocenti digest: Child domestic work*. Florence, Italy: Child Development Centre.

———. (2002) *The state of the world's children, 2002*. New York: UNICEF.

U.S. Department of Labor. (1994) By the sweat and toil of children: Mexico.
Retrieved August 25, 2002, from http://www.dol.gov/dol/ilab/public/
reports/iclp/sweat/mexico.htm.

U.S. Department of Labor, Bureau of International Labor Affairs. (2002, August 1)
By the sweat and toil of children. Vol. 5. See http://www.dol.gov/ilab/media/
reports/iclp/sweat5/chap4.htm.

U.S. Department of State. Bureau of Democracy, Human Rights, and Labor. (2000,
February 25) 1999 Country Reports on Human Rights Practices: Mexico.
Human Rights Report. Retrieved August 25, 2002, from http://www.
state.gov/www/global/human_rights/1999_hrp_report/mexico.html.

Weiner, M. (1991) *The child and the state in India: Child labor and educational policy
in comparative perspective*. Princeton: Princeton University Press.

World Bank. (1994) *1994 Annual Report*.

11

SOUTH AFRICA

Catherine Stakeman

PROFILE OF SOUTH AFRICA

The Dutch established settlements in South Africa in 1652. They received intermittent or ineffective resistance from the nonwhites they encountered and experienced little opposition from European forces until the British took control of the Cape of Good Hope in 1806. Many of the Dutch settlers (the Boers) migrated north to establish their own republics. The discovery of diamonds in 1867 and gold in 1886 made some of the new settlers wealthy and intensified immigration. As immigration increased, so did the subjugation of the native black Africans. The Boers resisted British invasion but were defeated in the Boer War, which was fought from 1899 to 1902. The Union of South Africa was then created and apartheid was instituted. Institutionalizing racism, apartheid was a government policy of segregation and political and economic discrimination against nonwhite groups in South Africa. South Africa's first democratic election occurred in 1994. This ended almost fifty years of white minority rule, which had entrenched racial and cultural inequalities.

From the beginning, nonwhites were subjected to the labor needs of whites, first in agriculture then later in mining. Racially segregated nonwhite townships developed in which nonwhites were forced to stay. These were government-sanctioned parcels of land in which substandard housing was erected to house blacks, coloreds, or Indians who worked in the adjacent white communities. These townships often had inadequate sanitation and no infrastructure, such as schools, to support and education children. Children frequently did not accompany their parents to the townships, but were cared for by extended family members in their home community. South Africa helped maintain a society in which children, particularly black African children, had to work at a very young age to assure their own survival and contribute to the survival of their family.

South Africa has a land mass that is about twice the size of Texas, with its capital in Pretoria. There are eleven official languages, with Afrikaans and English being the most widely spoken. The gross domestic product (GDP) in 1999 was $296.1 billion, or $6,900 per person. South Africa's currency is the rand (R), which has an exchange rate ranging from six to eight United States dollars per rand.

The population of South Africa in 1996 was 43,421,021, with a labor force of 15 million people. A household survey conducted by the South Africa government indicated that in 1995, one year after free elections, the unemployment rate ranged from 47% in the Northern Province to just over 17% in the southernmost part of the country. Rural areas of the country experienced rates of unemployment of just over 56%, and for women the rate of unemployment was reported as high as 64% (Department of Education, 1995).

South Africans were most often employed in three occupational areas: 30% in agriculture, 25% in industry, and 45% in various kinds of service jobs. South Africa is divided into four ethnic groups: black Africans, who make up approximately 75% of the population; followed by whites, who make up almost 15%; then coloreds, 9%; and Indians, 3%. There is no clear definition of a colored person. Legally, coloreds are those who do not quite fit the other castes. Coloreds are the product of intermixing of whites, Africans, Asians, Malays, and Indian peoples, with color patterns running from near white to black (Martin, 2000; Vandenbosch, 1979). Black Africans comprise a clear majority of the population, yet the white government denied rights and privileges to compatriot Africans, coloreds, and Indians.

Today the life expectancies at birth for men and women are only 50.41 and 51.81 years respectively. The infant mortality rate for the year 2000 was estimated at 59 deaths per 1,000 births, with a fertility rate of 2.47 children born per woman. In 1995 it was estimated that the literacy rate for people ages fifteen and over was 81.7%. The predominant religious faith among South African people is Christian (68%) followed by Muslim (2%), Hindu (1.5%), and various indigenous beliefs and animist (28.5%) (CIA, 2001).

Elementary and secondary education in South Africa is in transition. As with many other lower and middle-income countries, the school dropout rate is significant. It was reported that in 1997, for example, only 73% of schoolchildren were likely to meet the government educational requirements to enter seventh grade (Lockhat and Van Niekerk, 2000). Which means that 27% of the children do not make the minimum grade requirements on a government-sanctioned standardized test and therefore must leave school. The government, however, is committed to giving all children from preschool through the ninth grade access to general education. The implementation of the "ten years of free and compulsory education" policy began in January 1995 (Department of Education, 1995). However, the costs of attending school, paying school fees, and purchasing the required uniforms is problematic for many families because of inadequate income.

South Africa today is a middle-income, industrially developing country with vast resources and a modern infrastructure to promote economic growth and a stock exchange that ranks among the ten largest in the world. Growth, however, has not been strong enough to decrease the 30 percent overall unemployment rate. In addition, economic problems remain from the apartheid era, especially the problems of poverty and lack of economic empowerment among the disadvantaged groups, particularly black South Africans (CIA, 2000).

OVERVIEW OF CHILD LABOR

The extent of child labor in South Africa varies according to the definition used, how a child is defined, and the age of the children reported in the data. Although the various sources that report on child labor practices are not uniform, the data clearly indicate that work is requisite for many South African children. Many South African children who work, work to earn pocket money or pay for school fees and often contribute to the family income.

Grasping the concept of child labor requires an understanding of how a child might be defined in some South African cultures. Common biological and sociocultural ways of defining a child are by: chronological age as defined by law; socially and culturally defined life phases; rites of passage; physical and mental development; and dependency on parental care. Among some South Africans, however, biological maturity is often reached after rites of passage associated with first menstruation for girls and circumcision for boys, which can be from the ages of eleven through thirteen. Others are considered adults and socially independent when they marry. This may occur before an individual reaches the legal age of eighteen. Traditionally or culturally, a married person is not considered a child, regardless of chronological age (Chirwa, 1993). Much of the data on child labor does not include work performed by married "children," most often females.

Children can be found working as part of the daily routine of family life, performing school maintenance, and working as farm laborers or in service jobs. Many of the jobs that children perform are neither harmful nor exploitative; others work in a myriad of exploitative or hazardous activities. Thousands of children, however, work in ways that risk their health and safety, rob them of their childhood, and thwart normal physical and mental development. Children work in a number of industries that expose them to harsh environments, unsafe chemicals and equipment, and long working hours. The lack of enforcement of child labor laws helps maintain a system in

which children fall victim to a myriad of abuses at the hands of their
employers. In the Northern Province, welfare organizations reported that
the working conditions faced by child workers, especially under white
farmers were brutal (Lockhat and Van Niekerk, 2000).

The vestiges of forced segregation in South Africa have had a major influence on where and what black South Africans can do for work. It has also
controlled the wages they can earn. This oppressive system has contributed
to the exploitative labor practices for African children, particularly black
South African children. The historic lack of standard wages for adults has
meant that the wages received were generally at the whim of the employer.
Adults frequently could not earn enough money to provide for their families'
most basic needs. The wages of children, regardless of how meager, were
sometimes needed to help sustain a family. Why and what children do for
work needs to be understood within the cultural context of South African
life, where often all members of a household are responsible for contributing
to the overall well-being of the family.

Demographics

Estimates based on the 1996 census indicate that 13.4 million children
ages five through seventeen were living in South Africa, and that 79% of
these children were black African, 10% were colored, 9% were white, and 2%
were Indian. Overall, more than half of South African children (54%) lived in
nonurban areas (International Labour Organisation [ILO], 2000a).

The number of working children under eighteen years of age is unclear
because of the lack of standardized methods of collecting data. The *Mail &
Guardian* (A third of our children are workers, 2002), one of the leading
newspapers in South Africa, estimated that more than 13 million of South
Africa's children work. The 1996 Green Paper report from South Africa's
Department of Labor estimates that over 400,000 children from the ages of
ten through fourteen are engaged in child labor (Department of Labor, 1996).
Other reports estimated that 500,000 children in the Northern Province (the
northernmost part of South Africa) alone were involved in child labor (*Mail &
Guardian*, 1999). In June 1993, UNICEF and the National Children's Rights
Committee (NCRC) reported that about 781,000 black South African and
colored children from the ages of five through fourteen years were used in child
labor, most of whom were believed to be employed in the informal and agricultural sectors (Lockhat and Van Niekerk, 2000). The number of white and
Indian children used for labor was reported to be negligible.

Vignette

Agricultural work is among the common forms of employment in which
children in South Africa engage. Farmers prefer to hire children because they

can pay them a lower wage than they would pay an adult doing the same work. Children have historically worked in the fields during school vacations to pay for school-related expenses such as books and uniforms, to provide additional income for their family, and to help pay school expenses for their younger brothers and sisters. Deloris, who is twelve years old, engages in a variety of work activities; some are exploitative and harmful while others are part of the daily routine of family life.

Deloris, a black South African girl, works on a farm in the western Cape. She works during her school vacation, which begins in December and ends in February, the summer months in South Africa. These months coincide with the peak of the harvest season. Deloris has worked on this farm during school vacations since she was nine years old. Attending school is important to her and her family because she hopes to one day become a teacher. The work is familiar to her and she has become accustomed to working the long hours her employer requires. Deloris lives in a township in a small modest three-room house with her mother, father, grandmother, and two younger brothers. Her home is modestly furnished and has no running water, but it does have electricity. Deloris's mother is too ill to work, and the income her father earns is not enough to meet the family's basic needs and cover the cost of the school fees for the three children. As with most South African children, Deloris works because she believes that it is her duty to contribute to her family.

Deloris's day begins at 4:30 in the morning and ends about 9:00 at night. Deloris rises early to complete her chores, which may include laundry, fetching water, making coffee, and doing the sweeping before meeting her friends to catch the morning lorry. She packs a modest meal, often just bread and a beverage, to take with her to the farm. Although there is a shop on her way to the bus, she conserves her money for things her family might need. The lorry ride to the farm takes about thirty minutes. Riding the lorry can be dangerous. The lorries leave the station at exactly at 6:00 A.M. and children and adults are crammed in like cattle. The driver does not wait for those running for the lorry nor does the driver slow to allow people to get securely situated, so Deloris arrives early to secure a place at the front of the line.

Adult and child farmworkers are often not provided with protective clothing. Therefore, Deloris has purchased a lotion to use on her face and hands to protect them from the rays of the hot sun and protect her from the pesticides that irritate her skin. Deloris labors at the farm standing in the hot sun from seven in the morning until six at night with only two short breaks to rest and for a light meal. The farmer oversees all the workers to be sure that they remain productive throughout the day. Once when Deloris was working too slowly because she was overcome by the heat of the day, the farmer reprimanded her and sent her home, costing her a day's pay. The lorry comes only once in the morning and again in the evening to pick up the workers, and it was too far for Deloris to walk home. She took shelter under shady tree, angry with herself for not keeping up the pace. Although she knows that she is treated harshly and she is exposed to hazards, Deloris continues to return to the farm because the work provides her family with much-needed income.

HISTORY OF CHILD LABOR

The history of child labor in South Africa parallels the colonial upheaval that caused massive displacement of people and dislocated farming economies. This upheaval ultimately reshaped the political landscape. During the 1880s the Bantus and the Boers (Dutch) expanded their occupied territories in southeastern South Africa. The continuing conflict over territorial boundaries caused a great many people to flee their villages and migrate to other territories (Atkins, 1993).

The black Africans came into greater contact and conflict with English and Boer settlers. As the black African population increased and the English and Boer settlements became more established, struggles over governance ensued. The English and Boer political agendas during this time were directed at securing the borders against incursions by black African military forces, regulating the number of black Africans entering the area, and harnessing a labor force for agriculture (Atkins, 1993).

During the 1840s the Boers continued to practice a system of apprenticeship. They established legal requirements for state control of African labor by apprenticing all orphan African children. Boys were required to perform services until they were twenty-five and girls until the age of twenty-one. The Boers also captured the children of black Africans and required them to work on farms and as domestic servants. Several years later statutes were amended to require all African children in tenant farming families to register for apprenticeships. Although these practices were challenged by the English magistrates, the apprenticeship system continued. Employers were required to guarantee that the children would be well treated, but serious abuses occurred (Atkins, 1993). The apprenticing of very small children was a common practice in other colonies as well. Very young children were taken to work in domestic service despite the protests of their parents. Children were the most likely targets for forced labor because the Boers, who had little success in preventing adult captives from escaping, could manage the minds of young children and make them conform to European institutions and customs (Atkins, 1993).

With the 1850s the Natal sugar cultivators were given priority in selecting from the pool of apprentices. Statutes were changed to require individuals under the age of eighteen to serve for five years. Masters were given the legal right to use corporal punishment to enforce their demands. Whipping as a means of control was liberally applied (Atkins, 1993).

Child workers were frequently used in agriculture. Evidence from the mid-1920s suggests that child laborers constituted a large portion of the plantation labor force. Accounts found in missionary journals indicate that child work was a significant part of the casual workforce on tea plantations as early as 1890. From 1930 through to 1950, economic conditions declined. Tea plantations could no longer afford to maintain a large workforce or continue to pay workers the standard wage. There was a shift to cheap casual labor, and children constituted a significant portion of that workforce (Chirwa, 1993).

By the early 1920s children ten or younger were regularly being employed in tasks such as herding animals and seasonal labor. The majority of children who worked on the European plantations in South Africa came from tenant families already living on the plantations in the surrounding villages. Tenant families were required to live and work on the plantation. One of the conditions of tenant farming was that the families were required to work two months out of each year without pay to cover the costs of taxes and rent for living on the land (Chirwa, 1993). In this arrangement, called the *somaar* system, tenant farmers had to be available at the whim of their landlords (Bradford, 1987). Other accounts suggest that the average *somaar* requirement imposed on the tenant farmers averaged 180 days (Nzula et al., 1979).

Monthly wages in South Africa were very meager, and there was no established system of wages. The wages of a tenant family were at the whim of the landowners. Some tenant farming families received in-kind payments of food and sometimes the discarded clothing of their employers at a discounted price (Nzula et al., 1979). Under these working conditions, tenant farmers rarely had enough money to pay their taxes or buy the goods needed to sustain their families. As a result, all members of the family, including young children, were expected to contribute their labor in some way for the survival of the family.

Women were expected to perform domestic work in the farmer's house. They also weeded, hoed, and reaped. It was the children, however, who were generally given these tasks to perform. Working conditions were very hard and the workday was limited by the rising and the setting of the sun (Nzula et al., 1979). There was little machinery, so all farming tasks were performed by hand. The annual work requirements varied greatly, often with quasi-feudal contracts requiring labor of either two to four days a week throughout the year or continuously for three, six, or twelve months a year. Since the agricultural work cycle was irregular, during planting and harvesting the workday could be as long as nineteen hours (Nzula et al., 1979). Children participated in work activities as part of the daily routines of family life. Since running water and electricity were very uncommon amenities, children often participated in gathering wood for cooking and fuel, fetching water for drinking and bathing, tending younger siblings, and other domestic chores. Younger children also had tasks to perform, which might include chasing birds and other small animals away from crops.

CHILD LABOR TODAY

In South Africa, child work is also a form of socialization and acculturation (Chirwa, 1993). Through participation in various work activities, children are integrated into community life and acquire skills and attitudes toward work. Families in poverty encourage their children to obtain paid employment and participate in informal income-generating activities to contribute to pooled resources used to meet basic survival needs. Child work in and of itself is not necessarily harmful or exploitative, but if minors are required to work in hazardous conditions or excessive hours, then work becomes exploitative and can harm the physical and emotional development of the child.

Understanding child labor in South Africa involves distinguishing between economic and noneconomic work activities (ILO, 2000a). Economic work activities involve work with or without pay that directly benefits the family. Any child under eighteen who works to help in a family business or assist in family farming or fishing, for example, is considered engaging in economic work activities. The products of the child's work activities just mentioned may result in the sale of goods or be used for the family's own consumption. Included in the economic work activities category are unpaid household chores in the child's home, fetching wood and/or water for the family, or begging for money or food in public. The aforementioned work activities can't be sold, but the family benefits from them nevertheless.

Noneconomic work activities for children consist of housekeeping and other chores in the home of a caregiver who is not a parent, and school maintenance such as cleaning classrooms and toilets, which are performed regularly on a nonvoluntary bases (ILO, 2000a). These unpaid activities, which are performed for others, are considered noneconomic because there is no direct benefit to the parents. Schools in South Africa are not fully supported by government funds, and families must pay a fee for their children to attend school. For many schools in South Africa, particularly schools attended by black Africans, school fees alone do not provide enough revenue to hire workers to do the routine cleaning and maintenance. Therefore, these tasks may be performed by the schoolchildren. While there are no international standards concerning the number of hours a child can work each week in school maintenance, the ILO (2000a) considers more than five hours a week performing school maintenance tasks excessive.

The results of a survey of nine hundred households in which at least one child was engaged in child labor activities are reflected in Table 11.1. The sample was drawn from both urban and nonurban areas. The findings

Table 11.1
High-Risk Working Conditions of Children Aged 5–17

Working Conditions	Children %
Hot work environment	31.6
Tiring work	26.6
Cold work environment	25.8
Dusty work	18.5
Long hours	17.7
Work before sunrise or after sunset	11.9
Very noisy work	7.5
Fear of being hurt	7.1
Dangerous machinery/tools	4.1
Dangerous animals	3.4
Bad light	2.7
Dangerous substances	2.4

Source:

International Programme on the Elimination of Child Labour.
Child Labor Statistics (ILO 1999).

indicate that 36 percent of the children surveyed from the ages of five through seventeen were engaged high-risk child labor (ILO, 2000b). The household survey of working conditions considered high-risk fall into several categories as listed in Table 11.1.

Many factors contribute to the need for child labor. A major factor is the high rate of adult unemployment. Due to this unemployment, the work of children is needed to supplement their family's income. Other factors include high school dropout rates, abandoned and homeless children, and a health crisis in the family. The unavailability of water and electricity in the household also contribute. The lack of electricity for cooking and heating creates circumstances in which a child's work contributes to the overall well-being of the family. Conditions are most severe in the eastern Cape rural area, where just over 81% of the rural population has no running water and almost 93% of the people have no electricity in their homes (South African Ministry, 1995). In one urban area about 43% had no electricity. Fetching water and firewood are common daily work activities in which children engage.

POLITICAL VIEWS AND PUBLIC POLICIES

Child labor is best understood in the context of societal values and cultural norms. South Africa has developed legislation for addressing the issues of child labor. The term child labor in South African government documents refers to the inappropriate or exploitative work activities of children. In 1998 child labor in South Africa was defined as "work by children under 18 which is exploitative, hazardous or otherwise inappropriate for their age, detrimental to their schooling, or social, physical, mental, spiritual or moral development" (ILO, 2000b, p. 1). The above definition includes household chores and activities in the household of the child's caregiver that are inappropriate for the child's age.

Proponents for the elimination of child labor recognize that children who engage in child labor are less likely to receive an education, may have their physical and social development compromised, or could experience working conditions that threaten their very lives. The African National Congress (ANC), the ruling party in South Africa, voices a commitment to the protection of its citizens, particularly women and children, from abuse and violence (ANC introduces legislation, 1998). Steps have been taken to address the child labor issue. This is evident in the 1997 Basic Conditions of Employment Act, which established a minimum age for employment and the conditions under which a youth can be employed (Mdladlana, 2002).

The child labor conditions of most concern both politically and socially are child workers under the minimum age or working in conditions deemed hazardous and abusive, including slavery, forced labor, and prostitution. When the definition of child labor includes all forms of children's work, 45 percent of all South African children are engaged in child labor (ILO, 2000). Abolishing child labor is part of a state plan in postapartheid South Africa. Levine (1999), however, asks pointed questions. How real is this renaissance for workers who still do not have the security of a minimum wage? And how can child labor be eradicated when adult exploitation and poverty persist?

SOCIAL VIEWS, CUSTOMS, AND PRACTICES

Traditionally the care of children who were poor and orphaned took place within the extended family. Being part of an extended family meant that there was a shared sense of duty and responsibility. Most traditional African cultures are built around patrilineal kinship systems, which can consist of three to four generations. Relationships among extended family involved reciprocal obligations—a favor for a favor (Foster, 2000).

Marriage arrangements also have implications for the welfare and well-being of children. When a couple marries, not only are the two individuals linked, but also the two families (Foster, 2000). The bride-price, which is paid to the bride's family, assured that children from that union became the responsibility of the father and his family. The extended family was the traditional social security system and its members were responsible for the protection of the vulnerable, care for the poor and sick, and the transmission of traditional social values and education.

Foster (2000) argues that the diminishing availability of land makes it difficult for larger families to be economically independent through subsistence agriculture. In more recent years, changes in labor migration, shifts to a cash economy, relocation from one geographic location to another, greater access to formal education, and increased exposure to Western culture have weakened extended families ties. These trends have resulted in fewer contacts with extended family and encouraged greater social and economic independence. The departure from traditional norms, in which possessions were more readily shared, burdens children. Families turn to their children to augment income. Children without parents are often left to support themselves.

Under the racial caste system, nonwhites were forced to live in segregated townships in substandard conditions. The tension associated with township life and the stress it placed on families led to an increasing number of children joining substitute families, such as criminal gangs, prostitution rings, and bands of street children (Lockhat and Van Niekerk, 2000). These youths must find a way to support themselves either through the formal or informal economy. In 1994, UNICEF estimated that about 250,000 children were homeless or living on the streets in South Africa in 1992 (Lockhat and Van Niekerk, 2000). Child abandonment is reported to be on the increase although reliable figures are not available (Lockhat and Van Niekerk, 2000). Among the homeless children are runaways, or "strollers." These are children under sixteen who have run away from family homes or school (Burman and Reynolds, 1987). Running away is often the result of the breakdown of traditional family forms caused by extreme poverty, joblessness, and apartheid.

AIDS has had a devastating effect on South African families, driving more children to become heads households, street children, and child laborers. South Africa is experiencing one of the worst HIV/AIDS epidemics in the world (Wilson and Loening-Voysey, 2001). Of children orphaned by AIDS throughout the world, 95 percent live in Africa. It is predicted that the number of new AIDS cases and the death rate from AIDS will continue to grow rapidly (Women's International Network News, 2001). In severely affected communities there will be an inevitable increase in the number of children who take on the role of primary wage earner and caregiver because their parents have either died or are too ill to work. Many of these children have an increased likelihood of being abused and exploited. They also have a greater vulnerability to HIV infections (Foster, 2000). The majority of these orphaned children will lose their right to a decent and humane existence (Wilson and Loening-Voysey, 2001).

THE FUTURE OF CHILD LABOR

The elimination of child labor is a complex issue. Thousands of families living in poverty depend on the wages of their children for their very survival. The AIDS epidemic that has ravished South Africa has left thousands of children either as orphans or the sole providers in households with sick and dying parents. The South African government recognizes that a comprehensive approach is needed to combat child labor. The proposed strategies include compulsory and free basic education for every child, social security and welfare provisions to relieve some of the pressures of poverty, continued economic development to increase earnings of adults, and programs to raise public consciousness about the exploitative and harmful effects of child labor. Improving the economic opportunities for adults reduces the need for children to work to supplement family income (Department of Labor, 1996).

Child labor in South Africa is driven by child and family impoverishment. The crisis is fueled by high unemployment and low wages. The AIDS crisis contributes as it robs thousands of children of a supportive family. Political apathy concerning the rights of children supports the status quo. In the government's discourse, child labor is synonymous with child exploitation because the activities of concern may be hazardous, interfere with the child's education, and be harmful to the child's health or physical, mental, or social development. Several conditions are important in reform: economics, politics, education, and addressing the AIDS crisis.

1. Rampant poverty in South Africa makes it possible for various employment sectors to gain significant profit from the labor of children. They are paid substandard wages and do not receive the benefits normally provided to adults. Impoverished children and families too often remain silent about abuses because they fear the loss of wages that are crucial to the family's survival.

2. Politically, the South African government has recognized that the exploitation of child workers is a problem. The government has declared a commitment to eradicating exploitative child labor practices. Child labor standards are proposed that delineate the number of hours and the kinds of work activities permissible by age. Enforcing existing child labor legislation is problematic because South Africa does not yet have the resources for adequate enforcement.

3. Elementary grade and secondary education in South Africa is in transition. The government has stated its commitment to providing access to general education for all children through the ninth grade. But many children work forty-plus hours a week, leaving them little time to go to school or attend to their studies if they are in school. Mandatory education is not free, which means many families are further burdened by paying for the necessary fees and supplies. The lack of an adequate education relegates many children to lifelong poverty and continued exploitation.

4. The AIDS crisis in South Africa has had a devastating effect on children and families. As a result, children are orphaned or given the responsibilities as heads of households. Too often, those orphaned become street children with no place to

call home. They are forced to engage in work activities that are both exploitative and harmful. Without extensive government and international support, the plight of South Africa's people is bleak and the future for its children defies description.

CONCLUSION

Levine (1999) argues that political change in South Africa has manifested itself in a number of complicated ways for poor people, including children. Although its white-only government has been replaced with a democratic government, extreme racism, poverty, and corruption continue to exist. The continuation of these oppressive conditions exacerbates child labor. As Levine (1999) aptly states, "Child labor [in South Africa] presents, perhaps, the most persuasive case in the modern world that economic and social inequality degrades human potential" (p. 152). Children in South Africa who work under conditions that are exploitative and hazardous experience this degradation of human potential. Hundreds of thousands of South African children will not experience the joy of a childhood that is safe and nurturing, a childhood without worry of hunger and extreme poverty, a childhood in which education is every child's right. Remediation requires a combination of economic growth, the elimination of poverty, a stable economy, enforcement of labor standards for children and adults, universal education, policies that promote and enforce the needs and rights of children, and the establishment of policies to address and combat the AIDS crisis.

BIBLIOGRAPHY

A third of our children are workers. (2002, May 31) *Mail & Guardian* archive. Retrieved June 05, 2002, from www.mg.co.za.

ANC introduces legislation to better the lives of women. (1998, August 7) *Parliamentary Bulletin* 41. Retrieved May 7, 2003, from http://www.anc.org.za.ancdocs/pubs./whip/whip41.

Atkins, K. E. (1993) *The moon is dead, give us our money! The cultural origins of an African work ethic, Natal, South Africa, 1843–1900*. Ann Arbor: University of Michigan.

Bradford H. (1987) A taste of freedom. *The ICU in rural South Africa, 1924–1930*. New Haven: Yale University Press.

Burman, S., and P. Reynolds, eds. (1987) *Growing up in a divided society: The contexts of childhood in South Africa*. Johannesburg: Ravan Press.

Central Intelligence Agency. (2001) *The world fact book*. Washington, DC. Retrieved October 12, 2002, from, www.odcia.gov/cia/publications/factbook.

Chirwa, W. C. (1993) Child and youth labour on the Nyasaland plantations, 1890–1953. *Journal of Southern African Studies* 19(4): 662–81.

Crackdown on child labour. (1999, April 9) *Mail & Guardian Archive*. Retrieved June 26, 2002, from www.mg.co.za.

Crankshaw, O. (1997) *Race, class and the changing division of labour under apartheid*. London: Routledge.

Department of Education, Parliament of the Republic of South Africa. (1995, March 15) *White paper on education and training*. Retrieved November 23, 2003, from www.polity.org.za/govdocs/white_papers/educ5.

Department of Labor of the Republic of South Africa. (1996) *Green Paper on child labour*. Retrieved November 2002 from www.gov.za/greenpaper/1996/labour.

Foster, G. (2000). The capacity of the extended family safety net for orphans in Africa. *Psychology, Health & Medicine* 5(1): 55–63.

International Labour Organisation. (2000a) *Definition of child labour*. Retrieved June 10, 2002, from www.ilo.org/public.english/standards/ipec/simpoc/southafrica/report.

———. (2000b) *Key Findings*. Retrieved June 10, 2002 from http://www.ilo.org/public/english/standards/ipec/simpoc/southafrica/report.htm.

———. (1999) International Programme on the Elimination of Child Labour/Statistical Information and Monitoring Programme on Child Labour (IPEC/SIMPOC). Retrieved June 10, 2002, from http://www.ilo.org/public/english/standards/ipec/publ/simpoc00.

Levine, S. (1999) Bittersweet harvest: Children, work and the global march against child labour in the post-apartheid state. *Critique of Anthropology* 19(2): 139–56.

Lockhat, R., and A. Van Niekerk. (2000) South African children: A history of adversity, violence and trauma. *Ethnicity and Health* 5: 291–303.

Martin, D. C. (2000) The burden of the name: Classifications and constructions of identity. The case of the coloureds in Cape Town. *African Philosophy* 13(2): 99–125.

Mdladlana, M. (2002) Speech by minister of labor on child labor. *ANC Today* 2(19): 10. Retrieved May 3, 2003, from http://www.anc.rog.za.ancdocs.anctoday.2002/text.at19.txt.

Nzula, A. T., I. I. Potekhin, A. Z. Zusmanovich, and R. Cohen. (1979) *Forced labour in colonial Africa*. London: Zed Press.

South African Ministry in the Office of the President. (1995, May 8) *Results of household survey for the nine provinces*. Retrieved October 2002, from www.polity.org.za/govdocs/pr/1995.

Vandenbosch, A. (1979) Brown South Africans and the proposed new constitution. *Journal of Politics* 41: 566–87.

Wilson, T., and H. Loening-Voysey. (2001) Approaches to caring for HIV/AIDS orphaned and vulnerable children: Essential elements for a quality service. *Southern African Journal of Child and Adolescent Mental Health* 13(2). Abstract.

Women's International Network News. (2001) HIV/AIDS: South Africa cases could total 7.5 million by 2010. *Women's International Network News* 27(4): 26. Retrieved October 25, 2002, from UN Wire: http://www.unfoundation.org.

12

SOUTH KOREA

Elizabeth KimJin Traver

PROFILE OF SOUTH KOREA

With a history over five thousand years old that is as rich as the most ancient of human civilizations, today's Republic of Korea, known as South Korea, can be understood as an evolution characterized by the ebbs and flows of occupation, resistance, and independence. According to archaeological and linguistic studies, tribes inhabiting the Altaic Mountains thousands of years ago began migrating eastward to Manchuria and Siberia. They came as far east as the coasts of the Korean Peninsula. Ethnologically now known as the Korean people, these people's heritages can be traced to the Turkish, Mongolian, and Tungusic peoples.

Korea (North and South) extends roughly 600 miles (1,000 kilometers) north to south between the 34th and 42nd parallels north latitude. From a wide base against the Asian continent, the peninsula narrows to only 120 miles (190 kilometers) at the 39th parallel, then widens to 160 miles (260 kilometers). Sheltered by the Sea of Japan to the east, Korea Bay to the northwest, the Yellow Sea to the southwest, and the Tumen and Yalu Rivers to the north, the Korean Peninsula is one of the most mountainous areas in the world. As mountains comprise nearly 70 percent of the land, traditional Korean life has been centered in the mountains.

Historically, Korea has too frequently been in the position of the small country caught between major powers, "a shrimp caught between two fighting whales," the Koreans say. This mountainous land bridge between North Asia and the outside world has always possessed great strategic importance. In peacetimes, Korea was a cultural channel between China to the north and the islands of Japan. The peninsula was united by the Shilla Kingdom in A.D. 668.

Known as the rabbit kingdom, the hermit kingdom, *Han'gŭk*,[1] or *Chosŏn*— the land of morning calm, Korea is a peninsula cut off from the Asian continent by seas and rough mountains. This isolation has served to reinforce a sense of unity and protect the peninsula from events on the Asiatic mainland or across the straits in Japan.

The necessary transition from a self-isolated, hierarchical society to a modern nation painfully began late in the nineteenth century when Korea again became a battleground of foreign conflicts over influence in North Asia. Russia and an expanding Japanese empire were struggling for economic control there while China sought to maintain the traditional status quo of feudal sovereignty. The Western powers pressured the international community for economic concessions in mineral and timber rights from the beleaguered five-hundred-year-old kingdom. In 1910 the nation was annexed by Japan, marking the onset of an oppressive and repressive foreign domination. With World War II's end in 1945, the Union of Soviet Socialist Republics and the United States agreed on an intended temporary division of one of the world's most homogeneous peoples into northern and southern zones at the 38th parallel. Manipulated by international politics, the peninsula would soon erupt with its own prolonged civil war. The Korean War was precipitated by a surprise attack from North Korea on June 25, 1950. The three-year war inflicted unspeakable suffering on the Koreans, north and south, leaving most of the land devastated. More than a million were killed or wounded in South Korea alone, and the 38th parallel was soldered into a permanent geopolitical division.

It was only in the 1960s that governmental reforms, burgeoning exports, and rapid industrialization—facilitated by massive Western foreign aid— called the world's attention to South Korea. It is a proud, progressive, and perseverant country with a vigorous, optimistic, and resilient people determined to shape their own destiny despite many sacrifices and hardships. Today the capital city of Seoul boasts the home of the Blue House, the seat of this republic's politics. Governing nine provinces and seven metropolitan cities, the current chief of state, President Roh Muh-hyun, took office February 25, 2003.

As of July 2002 the population of the Republic of Korea was estimated at 48.3 million. Children up to and including fourteen years comprise 21.4% of the total population. Of these children, males represent almost 53%. Of the total population, males slightly outnumber females, with 1.01 males for every female.

The population of this developed nation has become increasingly urban, with the farm population in 1984 accounting for 22.2% of the total. This urbanization is characterized by the dominance of Seoul over the life of the nation. Nearly 20% of the population lives in the capital city, which is the center of government, industry, education, and culture.

The percentage of the population living in absolute poverty in South Korea has drastically decreased due to rapid economic growth. Those in absolute poverty comprised approximately 40.9% of the total population in 1965, but within three decades it had decreased to less than 3.9% in 1995. Of the whole population, those people living in absolute poverty in 1995 equaled 1,755,000.

In 1985, national unemployment was at 4%. By 1995 unemployment had dropped to 2%. The government is currently implementing the livelihood protection system to secure the basic livelihood for persons who are not able to work while providing support for the self-reliance of persons who are unemployed but capable of working. In 1995, South Korea provided national unemployment insurance and inclusion of farmers in the national pension plan.

Korean is the primary language spoken and taught in all schools, while English is widely taught in junior high and high school. The Korean alphabet has enabled South Korea to have one of the highest literacy rates in the world, with a 98% rate. In South Korea, literacy is defined as the ability to read and write for those over the age of fifteen. Since 1986 the literacy rate of primary school students reaching grade five has been 100%.

OVERVIEW OF CHILD LABOR

Through minimum-age and compulsory education laws, South Korea has been successful in integrating and mainstreaming national efforts addressing the less egregious, nonhazardous forms of child labor. For the year 2000, the International Labour Organisation (ILO) projected in its 1997 Working Papers that there would be zero economically active children from the ages of ten through fourteen, and 411,000 economically active teenagers (those who held jobs) ages fifteen through nineteen. The U.S. Department of State Human Rights Report of 1999 confirmed that the Labor Standard Laws of South Korea prohibit the employment of persons under the age of fifteen without a special employment certificate from the Labor Ministry and observed no violations of these child labor laws. Thus Korea's national data support the effectiveness of recent national policies. Child work is rigidly monitored so that education and health remain primary for children's welfare. Korea, as an industrialized nation, shares an international commitment to the elimination of child labor.

Because of the illegal, immoral, clandestine, and usually invisible nature of the worst forms of child labor, it is difficult to secure definitive data speaking to the prevalence of these forms of child labor as defined in the 1999 ILO Convention Number 182. The "worst forms of child labour" defined in the convention include: 1) bonded or forced child labor; 2) compulsory military recruitment of children; 3) participation in the commercial sex industry through prostitution or pornography; 4) use of children in the drug trade and possibly other "illicit activities"; and 5) hazardous work (ILO, 1999, Article 3). How might the Korean government estimate or measure hazardous or other worst forms of child labor?

In recognizing that the plight of children's welfare is tied to the welfare of women, scholars attempt to infer the extent of worst forms of child labor from what is known about the plight of women in Korea. However, the research literature bears evidence to the conceptual and practical difficulties involved in the measurement of the female labor force (e.g., Anker, Khan, and Gupta, 1988; Dixon-Mueller & Anker, 1988). This literature emphasizes the underreporting and invisibility of female labor force activity, the lack of appreciation of women's economic and labor force contributions, and the reasons for this lack of knowledge. There is strong reason to believe that similar problems are involved in measuring both the child labor force and the female labor force (see Anker, 2000; Knaul, 1995; Levison, 1991). It is likely that underreporting on surveys of labor force activity is greater for measurement of the child labor force compared with that of the female labor force.

In Korea, women who are predominantly poor or of mixed heritage are coerced to enter and exit the country to work for the sex trade and in domestic servitude. Because of the free access and lack of monitoring of transit areas at international airports, South Korea is considered a major transit point for alien smugglers, including traffickers of Asian women and children destined for the sex trade and domestic servitude.

Young female job trainees in Korea disappear into underground exploitation, such as prostitution. In late March 1999 the Korean press reported on a Korean man who was arrested on charges of forcing forty Korean women, recruited as waitresses, into prostitution in Macao. Korean women are also trafficked to Hong Kong for prostitution.

Officials from the Overseas Workers Welfare Administration (OWWA) estimate the number of Filipinos in Korea's "entertainment" industry to be around 1,000 and those prostituted around the U.S. military bases to be around 600. The OWWA states that the women recruited are very young and mostly from central Luzon, in the Pinatubo area. Korea ranks seventh in terms of destination of deployed overseas Filipino workers. Illegal recruitment, allegedly for work abroad, has historically been exploited to bring women into prostitution or other forms of sexual exploitation in foreign lands. As a hidden industry with no regulations, the ages of these women are unknown.

Of major concern for children is their vulnerability to child prostitution. According to a 1993 Korean country report, it was estimated that approximately 18,000 registered prostitutes are serving 43,000 U.S. Army personnel stationed throughout Korea at more than forty bases.

Regarding child soldiers, in the November 30, 1994, Report of Korea to the United Nations Committee on the Rights of the Child, the country reported that "Korean men are liable for military service in the year of their eighteenth birthday and must attain the age of, at least, nineteen if they want to be in active service during the year of acceptance. However, a person aged seventeen or over who voluntarily applies for military service may be enlisted in the army, navy or air force" (United Nations, 1996). Because of conflicting information on recruitment age, there are no reliable statistics on males under eighteen in government armed forces.

In considering juvenile crime as a form of labor where children's crime is exploited by adults, Korea's general prison population in 1999 was 23.4 percent juvenile. National statistics indicate that the major activities juveniles are imprisoned for are aggravated theft, theft, robbery and violent theft, breaking and entering, and counterfeit currency offences.

Vignette

After folding and storing the bedding, sweeping the barren room, cleaning the few morning dishes, and hanging the week's laundry to dry, the young girl sat for a moment in a heavy silence on the floor. The floor's heat gently drifted upward as a warm reminder of the gift of a full night's sleep. Her infant brother remained sleeping on the pallet. Eight-year-old Jin Ae stared hypnotically through her roundish blue eyes and absentmindedly twirled her wavy dull brown hair into a knot. Wondering why the image in the broken mirror did not reflect the brown almond eyes and lustrous black hair of the neighborhood girls, Jin Ae prepared both body and soul to once more face the daily insults and slurs of a nation that has been slow to accept difference.

Jin Ae yearned to go to school, dreamed about having friends to play with, hungered to learn about the world and grow smart, craved to be like other kids she saw on the television screens in the store windows, and grieved for an imagined life that existed beyond her grasp. Her mother worked beyond the point of exhaustion six days a week at the factory to support her daughter and infant son. Struggling to contribute to the family's survival and to escape the stealth forces of poverty and homelessness, Jin Ae had to remain home to care for her six-month-old brother, Sook. Daylight hours imposed singular and solitary demands of the factory's production quotas on the hardworking mother, or *omma*. With stars, clouds, or moonbeams to accompany her, *omma* walked home each night from work wondering what kind of future awaited her precious daughter and blessed son.

With Sook bound securely to her back, Jin Ae walked to the market every day for her family's food. Often she saw the same man with the drooping cigar, wilted linen suit, and foul body odor wandering the familiar streets. Today was different. Today this man slithered up to and cornered Jin Ae and immediately thrust upon her a slew of private questions: name, age, parents, jobs. Worried that this man worked for the government and might take her away from her mother, Jin Ae barely escaped this predator's clutch to avoid answering dangerous questions.

She had heard stories about government officials searching for and removing kids from their homes because their mothers were single and too poor to feed their children. She had also heard stories about older girls going to live in a certain home and returning after six months to resume their previous lives. She had heard stories about the black-skinned orphans who go to live in American families. Word on the street was: go to the orphanages, go live in America, go find the land of opportunity. With her senses fine-tuned to the streets, she learned. Jin Ae fiercely resolved that none of this would ever happen to her. Today Jin Ae refused to answer the questions of strange men in suits. But what about tomorrow? What happens when the hunger pains too much? What happens when her brother cries too desperately? What happens when her mother's tears dry up? What happens when hope disappears too soon?

Omma entered the small one-room rental and found both Jin Ae and Sook asleep on their pallet, the threadbare cover molded around their thin bodies. Breathing a sigh of relief once more, the weary mother scrutinized her life over a steaming cup of diluted barley tea, *boh ree cha*. Her parents, who live in a town in the southern tip of this "rabbit kingdom," kept begging her to return home. The raw pain of losing family from the creation of North Korea thundered loudly in their hearts; her parents could not accept this additional dismembering of family. *Omma* continued to reject this offer, knowing all too well that the addition of three more mouths to feed would plunge her elderly parents into destitution. She knew all too well how her children, viewed as symbols of an impure mixture, would grow up as untouchables with labels bearing shame, hatred, and exclusion. At least in the city where there was industry, there was work. At least in the city, her outcast children could be invisible. And, at least here in the city, near the American army base, there was the hope that the children's father could be found. Perhaps he would welcome, after all, a son, if not a daughter.

Jin Ae tossed and turned on the padded bedding on the floor. Knowing that *omma* would arrive home soon, Jin Ae tried to soothe and comfort herself. Drowning in confusion, Jin Ae wondered to herself. "What do I do? What should I do? What can I do? Oh grandmother spirit, *samshin hal-mŏn-i*, please tell me what I must do! Today he sang me a song, he promised me money, he showed me heaven and hell. Money. Money. Money. I cannot sleep, sleep, sleep."

"Little one, you are pretty. Need money? Need money? Here's a secret just for you. I've got money, money, money. Easy. Fast. And with only a little pain. Don't worry, don't worry, I know you'll grow to like it. Most girls like you do. Girls like you. Most girls do. Come back here tomorrow. I'll be right here just for you. Hear me when I tell you—you can ease your family's burden. Do this for me once a week, just once a week, just once a week. I promise you'll feed your family from now on and every week. Maybe in the future you can go to school and learn. Trust me, little one. Only I can make this happen. Sleep on it, little one. Sleep. Sleep. Sleep."

HISTORY OF CHILD LABOR

The inadequacy of statistical evidence makes it extremely difficult to state with any confidence the level of child labor before, during, or after industrialization of South Korea. Tied especially to the implementation of international child labor treaties and the strengthening of education (compulsory schooling), the developed nation of South Korea would declare there is no problem of child labor. Indeed, a cursory look at the literature reveals that little has been written about industrial labor supplied by "children" as distinguished from "youths" and "women." Without established facts about child labor therefore, it is difficult to assess the supposedly ill effects of advancing industrialism and, more specifically, to evaluate the view that "compulsory primary education is the policy instrument by which the state effectively removes children from the labor force" (Weiner, 1991, p.3).

Korea is an industrialized economy where there are some working conditions that no one would condone. It marks a recent phenomenon. Child labor increased and became more exploitative in the initial stage of industrialization, a process captured in the images of children in mills and factories.

Prior to the forced transformation of political isolation, child labor in Korea, in its multiple forms of exploitation, was an invisible phenomenon. With Confucian mores undergirding a collectivist worldview, Korean life followed stable patterns of conduct and behavior. Deviant forms of behavior would have been observed in reference only to social norms. Understanding the emergence of the modern-day phenomenon of child labor as deviant behavior in Korea requires understanding the struggle of women to negotiate the role of parenting within women's rights and equality in an industrialized nation.

Prior to 1392, women seemed to have had a great deal more freedom than that limited by strict Confucian mores, which have influenced Korean culture. During the Shilla kingdom (57 B.C.E.–A.D. 935) there were three reigning queens, one of whom, Queen Sŏndŏk (r. 632–47), was credited with outstanding leadership and political ability. Beginning with the Yi dynasty (1392–1910), the role of Korean women was limited to the management of the large extended family and the producing of a male heir. In all other aspects of life she was expected to obey first her father and then her husband and sons. This concept has been so accepted in Korean culture that even today when family size has shrunk and women are well educated, many still feel guilty about wanting to work outside the home. Despite the limitation

on women during the Yi dynasty, there were many women who distinguished themselves in literature, the arts, scholarship, and household management.

Opportunities for women began to slowly open up at the end of the
nineteenth century, when Korea was opened to the outside world. The first
girls school in Korea, Ewha Haktang, was opened in 1886 with the enrollment of only one girl student, and from that small beginning, education for
women has gradually increased until today Korean girls have equal educational opportunities with their brothers. The *(Sunsŏng)* Adoration Society,
founded in September 1896 with the objective of establishing and operating
a girls' school financed by membership fees, announced in the same month
"A Letter on Girls' School Facilities." This document is evaluated as the
nation's first declaration of the rights of women with respect to education.
The Korean women's movement at that time was related to the country's
independence movement. It was strongly motivated to emancipate women
from ignorance through education as a means of building a strong country
and maintaining the nation's independence. Hansŏng Girls' High School,
the nation's first public school for women, was established in 1908.

Of the atrocities experienced by Koreans under various occupations from
invading nations, "comfort women" have epitomized the subjugation of
Korean women. Historians estimate that the Japanese abducted as many as
two hundred thousand Asian women, most of them Koreans, and forced
them into prostitution as "comfort women" for the Japanese army in World
War II.

Prior to the Korean War, women had second-class social status compared
with males. "Childhood" for all genders was life that occurred prior to
marriage. Poor families, who resided primarily in rural areas, relied upon
children's work to contribute to family subsistence. The forms of children's
work were varied and uncontrolled.

In the aftermath of the Korean War, not only economic but very serious
social and political problems appeared. Social disorders and hostility to the
government complicated the staggering social problems created by the war.
There were some 300,000 war widows, over 100,000 orphans, and hundreds of thousands of unemployed, whose numbers swelled as farmers left
their land to seek work in the cities. At the beginning of the 1960s, the
Republic of Korea had all the problems of a resource-poor, low-income,
developing country. The bulk of its population depended on scarce farmland
for bare subsistence.

During the four decades since, South Korea has been drastically trans-
formed, almost beyond recognition. This has been due largely to the successful implementation of five-year economic development plans launched in
1962. South Korea today is ranked as an industrialized country. How did
this happen, when the usual trend of widening income disparities emerges in

the early stages of industrialization? An important factor was the *(Saemaŭl)* New Community Movement.

In 1971, President Park Chung Hee introduced a nationwide movement know as *Saemaŭl Undong*, which has proved unique in terms of its impact on the modernization of a developing country. No program of other developing countries has mobilized so much social, administrative, and popular support or brought about such a dramatic impact on rural development and national integrity. *Saemaŭl Undong* originated in the negative consequences brought about in the agricultural sector as a result of the successful implementation and miraculous economic growth of the first and second Five-Year Economic Development Plans (1962–66 and 1967–71). During these periods the gap between the annual incomes of farm households and urban dwellers grew wider. In 1970 a farm household earned 61% of an urban wage earner's household. Farmers with less than one hectare of land constituted about 67 percent of Korean farmers, and they earned only half the income of urban wage earners. The deteriorating rural situation widened the gap between factory and farm and became a major cause for a rapid migration of the rural population into large cities. This population pressure on urban areas exacerbated many typical urban problems, among which the exploitation of children was observed. The quality of labor changed because mostly the aged and women remained in the rural areas. Therefore most villages were left without traditional leaders, since those who moved away were the relatively well educated young men.

Aware of this situation, the government policy for the third Five-Year Economic Development Plan (1972–76) emphasized "balanced growth between industry and agriculture" and the development of agriculture and fisheries. Under the *Saemaŭl Undong*, the agricultural sector made astonishing progress due to the promotion of the *Saemaŭl* spirit. In Korea, the *Saemaŭl Undong* is used as a training vehicle to enable people, communities, and villages to solve their own problems, requiring a great cooperative spirit. The urban *Saemaŭl* Movement, which began in 1974, emphasized the basic philosophy that no citizen should be excluded from a popular movement designed to bring about common prosperity. As a result, rural and urban communities participating in *Saemaŭl Undong* are characterized as having a cooperative attitude, a strong ethical sense, and the sound management of community life, which emphasizes maintaining order, helping less privileged neighbors, fostering friendship with neighbors, and the like.

CHILD LABOR TODAY

Schooling has questioned the moral basis for children's work within the family setting and has altered attitudes and expectations with respect to children's roles in South Korea. During the 1960s and 1970s, under the impulses of the five-year plans, schooling increasingly became part of "normal" childhood experiences.

Korea legitimizes a social division of labor that is essentially based on the subordination of females in society. The plight of children depends upon the equality of women—an ideology that is kept hidden and invisible in the perpetuation and promotion of the Western family values of industrialized nations.

POLITICAL VIEWS AND PUBLIC POLICIES

The Constitution of the Republic of Korea has been amended under various republics (administrations) since its adoption on July 17, 1948. In Article I the Constitution declares that the Republic of Korea is democratic, and that sovereignty is vested in the people. Specific to child labor, the Constitution guarantees the basic rights and freedoms of the Korean people, including equality before the law regardless of sex, religion, or social status. The Constitution emphasizes the right to a clean environment and the right to seek happiness, optimum wages, fair compensation, and protection of privacy. It recognizes economic rights, including the right to own property, the right as well as the duty to work, freedom of choice of occupation, and the right to collective bargaining.

The 1996 proposed legislation to establish a Law for Preventing Domestic Violence included a provision for dealing with violence against children. The only other national policies protecting children from the potential harms of child labor are the Declaration of Korean Children's Rights and the Public Child Welfare Law. Article 9 of the Declaration of Korean Children's Rights, which was revised on May 5, 1988, declared that "Children should not be maltreated or abandoned and they should not be used for harmful or arduous labor." In addition, Public Child Welfare Law (revised on April 13, 1981), Article 18, Section 9, prohibits abusive behaviors against children under penalty of a fine not exceeding US$2,500 or a maximum of two years imprisonment. The specific items in the Child Welfare Law pertaining to child labor include:

1. Exposing a handicapped or deformed child to public view for shows or other profit-making purposes.
2. Making a child beg or using a child in begging.
3. Employing a child under the age of fourteen in bars or other entertainment businesses.
4. Making a child perform obscene acts.
5. Influencing the upbringing of a child for money or other valuables without a legal right.
6. Making a child perform harmful entertaining activities, or letting him enter a place where these activities are performed.

7. Publishing, selling, distributing, giving, exchanging, narrating, or broadcasting books, periodicals, and other commercial message materials that may hurt children's nature.

However, this Child Welfare Law has not been enforced and lacks any obligation or provision for a mandatory child abuse reporting system.

Among the social and cultural guarantees are those providing for equal educational opportunities, welfare benefits for citizens incapable of earning a livelihood, and protection for working women and children. Women were given the right to vote, be elected, assume public duties, and participate in policy decision-making. Despite the increase in the number of women engaged in social and economic activities, it is not easy to resolve women's problems arising from traditional values and institutions that continue to be dominated by men.

The major emphasis of social welfare has been placed on children, the disabled, the elderly, and women who need special care. The government has continuously increased public support for child welfare facilities. Vocational training is provided at public training facilities, and job placement campaigns are carried out to help older children become self-reliant. Additionally, the government provides subsidies for the living and educational expenses of children who are heads of households. Although it has been established policy in both government and private organizations to encourage the adoption of children by Korean families versus out-of-country adoptions, the traditional value placed on blood relationships in family succession has been hard to transform.

Welfare programs for women are targeted at female heads of families, runaway women, unmarried mothers, women working at entertainment places, and other needy women. Support for maternal and child welfare facilities has been strengthened along with support for vocational training programs for young girls who run away from home, unmarried mothers, and other needy women.

SOCIAL VIEWS, CUSTOMS, AND PRACTICES

In Korean culture, children are taught to be obedient and to live up to adults' expectations, quietly carrying out their important duties, such as schoolwork. In such an adult-centered culture that has largely ignored children's opinions and perceptions, little public attention has been paid to children at risk of exploitation. In the past decade, children at risk of abuse and neglect have captured the public's attention, leading to a national public policy movement for preventing child abuse. In Korea as in the U.S., the welfare of children is overwhelmingly tied to the welfare of women.

The traditional life cycle of a Korean woman was characterized by her social and economic dependence on her father before marriage, her husband upon marriage, and her eldest son in her old age. However, under the rapid capitalist and industrial development in South Korea, the social relations that Korean women form have expanded beyond the patrilineal family into the market and other public spheres.

It is a well-known fact that the remarkable economic growth South Korea has achieved in the past four decades is in great part due to the contributions of female labor. Rural areas suffered a shortage in the labor force when males and young girls migrated to the cities and industrial areas. The gap created was filled by middle-age housewives. In urban areas, about 80% of female workers in the manufacturing sector are employed by the textile, clothing, electric, and electronics industries. These industries have led the nation's exports since the 1970s. While women ages fourteen through twenty-four accounted for 53.9% of the female labor force in manufacturing industries, women thirty and above occupied 84.3% of the female labor force in rural areas.

South Korean women have entered the class structure as major economic actors. They perform economic functions needed for the transformation of South Korean society. This transition, however, has not significantly changed their disadvantaged power relations with men. South Korean women continue to be the "first oppressed class" (Engels, 1942) in the capitalist social division of labor. The typical image of working women in Korea has been one of "permanent casuals" (Fuentes and Ehrenreich, 1983) without equal status with their male counterparts. Because of this marginalized position, they are susceptible to unconditional exploitation due to their unstable and unorganized nature of employment. Korean women's exodus from the patriarchal family seems to have resulted in a society-wide gender stratification under which their feminine characteristics are rationalized as the basis for social and economic discrimination.

Both Korean and foreign scholars have seen South Korean women suffering from male-dominant family relations. Structural obstacles bar their entry into modern economic sectors, there is and institutionalized segregation at the workplace (e.g., Chang, 1986; Cho, 1986; Greenhalgh, 1985). In particular, the Confucian tradition has had different implications for men and women because it envisions an explicitly gender-segregative social order. For example, phrases from Confucian classics, such as "Men are noble, women are lowly" (namjonyobi) and "Men and women should be differently treated" (namnyoyubyol) are still popularly remembered in South Korean society. Women continue to remain imprisoned within working-class or laborer jobs in a gendered occupational hierarchy (Chang, 1995).

On a final note, it is important to understand that South Korea's peoples are notably homogeneous in ethnicity, with the exception of about twenty thousand Chinese. This homogeneity is tied with traditional Confucian values about blood-ties and has resulted in a contemporary challenge for South Korea to embrace its citizens who bear the gifts of multiple racial/ethnic heritages. Relegated to an almost untouchable class status, biracial children in

Korea bear the scars of social ostracization and limited opportunities. These children's opportunities for survival depend primarily on their participation in the worst forms of child labor.

THE FUTURE OF CHILD LABOR

In 1998, several hundred foreign workers from Pakistan, Bangladesh, and the Philippines held a rally outside the Myong Dong Cathedral in Seoul to protest the IMF and Korean government economic policies. It was a sign of Korea's relative affluence that until recently tens of thousands of foreign workers were imported to do the hardest and dirtiest jobs. Similar to temporary foreign laborers in the U.S., now they're laid off and facing deportation. Ethnic minorities, although very small in number, face legal and societal discrimination.

According to the 1999 Country Reports on Human Rights Practices (2000), violence against women and physical abuse remain serious problems in South Korea, and there is still insufficient legal redress for dealing with them. Women continue to face legal and societal discrimination. South Korea is considered to be a major transit point for traffickers of Asian women and children destined for the sex trade and domestic servitude.

Vice crimes, including child trafficking, sex tourism, child pornography, and child prostitution, are notoriously difficult to effectively eliminate. Vice crimes are pervasive and appear, on the surface at least, as victimless consensual transactions. Some traditional societies customarily view prostitution with little or no moral or legal condemnation. These societies, such as Korea, hold a lax view of adult prostitution, and girls of sixteen or seventeen are regarded as adults capable of consenting to sexual relations. Negative publicity accorded child sexual victimization in recent years at the international level may cause Korea to create severe legal penalties for *child* prostitution and pornography. However, it is difficult to establish prostitution by sixteen or seventeen-year-olds as a heinous crime.

Recognition and elimination of the worst forms of child labor as an invisible, national, and systemic problem requires a multifaceted, organized approach involving the collaboration of respective governmental ministries that focus on children's welfare and women's rights. South Korea's Ministry of Health and Welfare is responsible for the policies concerning public welfare support, health insurance, and the national pension plan. Specifically, the National Welfare Planning Board established in 1995 is chaired by the Health and Welfare Minister and comprised of government bureaucrats, scholars, researchers, and welfare program managers. The committee plays a key role in constructing a new framework for welfare policies. This includes evaluating the health and welfare status of the country, making short- and long-term plans, and making a priority of various policies concerning health and welfare issues.

National strategies were reported by the Government of Republic of Korea to the United Nations Commission on Sustainable Development's Fifth Session, held April 7–25, 1997, in New York. Identified under Agenda 21, chapter 3 (Combating Poverty), the focus of South Korea's national strategies include: securing a minimum standard of living for the poor; improving work capabilities through occupational training, and increasing work opportunities for the poor; increasing welfare services for the elderly, the disabled, and children; supporting the procurement of housing (e.g., public housing for the poor); increasing the extent of medical insurance benefits; and increasing the maximum number of days covered by medical insurance to one full year for the elderly and the disabled.

Youth unemployment in South Korea has been aggressively addressed since 1960, with the national tasks of expanding educational and employment opportunities for adolescents. In more recent years, youth unemployment continues to reflect the 1960 initiative. Rates have dropped from 7.7 percent in 1992 to 6.3 percent in 1996.

In 1988 the Youth Development Act was promulgated to provide social and political foundations for healthy adolescent development. Of the four program areas established in order to ensure a brighter and healthier future for the youth and children of South Korea, the first two affect the prevalence of child labor: 1) increasing healthy activities for children, in an environmentally friendly lifestyle; and 2) improving delivery of welfare assistance to disadvantaged youth.

CONCLUSION

Eliminating child labor cannot occur without eliminating the demand for child labor. Korea is working to increase the costs and reduce the benefits of hiring child labor. Additionally, research is expanding on identifying the reasons for hazardous working conditions from the viewpoints of the various actors and institutions involved. This type of information will make it possible to devise effective awareness-raising activities among communities while increasing pressure on those who profit from hazardous and other worst forms of child labor.

The International Programme on the Elimination of Child Labour (IPEC) strives to support rather than supplant national efforts to combat child labor by emphasizing preventive measures and building sustainability into demonstration programs. Some 46 percent of IPEC programs are geared to prevention, which has proved to be more cost effective than remedial action. Programs that would facilitate Korea's efforts require identifying geographical areas, social groups, and conditions that favor child labor. Additionally, it is seen that it is critical to identify industry-specific or occupational factors that determine demand for and supply of child labor and intervene at policy and grassroots levels. IPEC provides evidence that market-based initiatives to combat child labor cannot address the root causes of the problem, where the slavery-like practices, child prostitution, and the devalued status of women place female children at highest risk of the most intolerable form of child labor.

NOTE

1. With a few exceptions, transliteration of Korean words from *han-gŭl* to the Latin alphabet follows McCune-Reischauer, the officially adopted system of the United States and the Republic of Korea. Korean words are italicized. Most exceptions are on personal names, which their owners often transcribe in a variety of ways. Hyphenation has been preserved where required by convention or where needed to facilitate pronunciation for foreign readers.

BIBLIOGRAPHY

Anker, R. (2000a) *Conceptual and research frameworks for the economics of child labour and its elimination.* Geneva: ILO/IPEC.

———. (2000b) The economics of child labour: A framework for measurement. *International Labour Review* 139: 257–80.

Anker, R., M. E. Khan, and R. B. Gupta. (1988) *Women's participation in the labour force: A methods test in India for improving its measurement.* Geneva: ILO.

Arat, Z. F. (2002) Analyzing child labor as a human rights issue: Its causes, aggravating policies, and alternative proposals. *Human Rights Quarterly* 24(1): 177–204.

Bishop, I. B. (1898) *Korea and her neighbors.* Seoul: Yonsei University Press.

Chang, K. (1995) Gender and abortive capitalist social transformation: Semi-proletarianization of South Korean women. *International Journal of Comparative Sociology* 36: 61–81.

Chang, P. (1986) Women and work: A case study of a small town in Korea. *Challenges for women: Women's studies in Korea*, ed. Chung Sei-wha, 255–81. Seoul: Ewha Women's University Press.

Cho, H. (1986) Labor force participation of women in Korea. *Challenges for women: Women's studies in Korea*, ed. by Chung Sei-wha, 255–81. Seoul: Ewha Women's University Press.

Committee for the Compilation of the History of Korean Women. (1976) *Women of Korea: A history from ancient times to 1945.* Seoul: Ewha Women's University Press.

Country Reports on Human Rights Practices. 1999 Bureau of Democracy, Human Rights, and Labor, U.S. Department of State, February 25, 2000.

Covell, J. C. (1985) *Korea's colorful heritage.* Seoul and Honolulu: Si-sa-yŏng-o-sa.

D'Amico, R. (1984) Does employment during high school impair academic progress? *Sociology of Education* 57: 152–64.

Dixon-Mueller, R., & Anker, R. (1988) *Assessing Women's Economic Contributions to Development Series:* Background papers for training in population, human resources and development planning, paper no. 6 Geneva. ILO International Labour Office. World Employment Programme, 1988.

Doe, S. S. (2000) Cultural factors in child maltreatment and domestic violence in Korea. *Children and Youth Services Review* 22: 231–36.

Fuentes, A., & Ehrenreich, B. (1983) *Women in the Global Factory*. Boston: South End Press.

Global Action for Women Towards Sustainable and Equitable Development. Retrieved April 13, 2003, http://www.un.org/esa/earthsummit/rkore-cp. htm#chap23.

Greenhalgh, S. (1985) Sexual stratification: The other side of "growth with equity" in East Asia. *Population and Development Review* 11: 285–314.

Hong Sa-woon. (1979) *Community development and human reproduction behavior*. Seoul: Korea Development Institute.

Howe, R. W. (1988) *The Koreans: Passion and grace*. Orlando, FL: Harcourt, Brace, Jovanovich.

Hughes, D. M., L. J. Sporcic, N. Z. Mendelsohn, and V. Chirgwin. (1999a) Jean Enriquez's Filipinos in prostitution around U.S. military bases in Korea. *The Factbook on Global Sexual Exploitation*. Retrieved May 26, 2003, from Coalition against Trafficking in Women (CATW) Web site, http://www. catwinternational.org/fb/Korea.html.

———. (1999b) Military prostitution in Korea, Coalition Report, 1993. *The Factbook on Global Sexual Exploitation*. Retrieved May 26, 2003, from Coalition against Trafficking in Women (CATW) Web site, http://www.catwinternational.org/ fb/Korea.html.

———. (1999c) Trafficking in women and prostitution in the Asia Pacific, 1996. *The Factbook on Global Sexual Exploitation*. Retrieved May 26, 2003, from Coalition against Trafficking in Women (CATW) website, http://www. catwinternational.org/fb/Korea.html.

Hyun, P. (1984) *Koreana*. Seoul: Korea Brittanica.

ILO. (1996) Child labour today: Facts and figures. *World of Work* 16: 12–17.

———. (1999) *Convention No. 182 concerning the prohibition and immediate action for the elimination of the worst forms of child labour*. Geneva.

ILO-IPEC. (1996) Children wage war on child labour. *Children and Work* 2: 10.

Kim, Byung-sung. (1984) *Schooling and social achievement*. Seoul: Korea Educational Development Institute.

Knaul, F. M. (1995) *Young workers, street life and gender: The effect of education and work experience on earnings in Colombia*. Unpublished thesis. Harvard University, Cambridge, MA.

Lee Chang-soo. (1981) *Modernization of Korea and the impact of the West*. Los Angeles: East Asia Studies Center, University of California.

Lee Jae-Chang. (1984) *Self-concepts and values of Korean adolescents*. Seoul: Korea Educational Development Institute.

Levison, D. (1991) *Children's labour force activity and schooling in Brazil*. Unpublished doctoral dissertation. University of Michigan.

Mattielli. S. (1977) *Virtues in conflict: Tradition and the Korean woman today*. Seoul: Royal Asiatic Society.

McKenzie, F. A. (1920) *Korea's fight for freedom*. Seoul: Yonsei University.

Nahm, A. C. (1983) *A panorama of five thousand years: Korean history*. Elizabeth, NJ, and Seoul: Hollym.

Solberg, S. E. (1991) *The land and people of Korea*. New York: HarperCollins.

United Nations. (1996) *Report of the Committee on the Rights of the Child*. General Assembly, Official Records, Fifty-first Session, Supplement No. 41 (A/51/41). New York.

U.S. Department of State. (1999) *Human rights report for Republic of Korea*. Retrieved May 26, 2003, from http://www.iet.com/Projects/HPKB/Webmirror/SD_HRP/southkor.html.

Weiner, M. (1991) *The child and the state in India*. Princeton: Princeton University Press.

Whang In-joung. (1981) *Management of rural change in Korea*. Seoul: Seoul National University Press.

Woronoff, J. (1983) *Korea's economy: Man-made miracle*. Seoul: Si-sa-yŏng-o-sa. Retrieved May 23, 2003, from www.globalmarch.org/worstformsreport/world/korea-rep.htm.

13

THAILAND

Lacey Sloan

PROFILE OF THAILAND

Thailand, known as Siam until 1939, is one of the few Asian countries that has never been colonized. Approximately 513,115 square kilometers in size, or about the size of France, Thailand is bordered by Laos on northeast and east, Kampucha on the east, Malaysia on the south, and Burma on the west. The population of Thailand is approximately 60 million, most of whom are Thai. There are other ethnic groups in the country, including Burmese, Chinese, Lao, and Khmer. Bangkok is the capital of Thailand, with a population of approximately 6 million. Buddhism is the state religion, with approximately 90% of the population practicing it, although there are also Muslims (6%) and Christians (2%). Thailand is considered a developing country.

Thailand has a 93% literacy rate for people over age six (Banpasirichote and Ponjsapich, 1992). Literacy rates for females (91.3%) is slightly lower than that of males (94.7%), which is largely due to historical inequities. Women have been important to Thailand's economic growth, with over 61% of Thai women in the labor force, including unpaid family agricultural work. Thai women have a high rate of participation in the recognized labor force (including unpaid family agricultural labor); over 78% of Thai men are in the labor force. These are important issues in considering the place that child workers and child labor plays in the economy of Thailand and her people.

OVERVIEW OF CHILD LABOR

In Thailand, "child labor" refers to all children under age eighteen who are employed (Banpasirichote and Ponjsapich, 1992). The term "legal child workers" is used for children under age eighteen who are legally employed under Thai and international law. "Child worker" will be used in this chapter to refer to all employed children under age eighteen, including both legal child workers and other child labor. National law prohibits the employment of children under thirteen years of age, falling under the International Labour Organisation (ILO) definition of the "most intolerable forms of child labor." Children ages thirteen through fifteen years can be employed in some occupations, but, like children ages fifteen through eighteen, they are prohibited from work that would present a physical, mental, or moral danger.

Approximately 3.5 million children are employed in Thailand. Almost half (44.4 percent) of children fifteen through nineteen years of age are employed, and 11.4 percent of children ages thirteen and fourteen are employed. These numbers probably do not include migrant children. Child employment is highest in rural areas and in the northeast (where the hill tribes reside). Younger girls are more likely to be employed than boys. The majority of child workers are engaged in agriculture (more than 60 percent), with most of the remainder employed in manufacturing, the service industry, and construction.

Bonded child labor is one of the situations most likely to be dangerous for children. In bonded child labor, parents are paid in advance for the wages the child will earn, so the child must work until the bond is paid off. Bonded child labor occurs most often with employment in small factories. These are jobs in which children work in hazardous conditions with dangerous materials or for long hours. Also included is involvement in the sex industry, including jobs that could lead to the sex industry such as some entertainment jobs. In times of economic downturns, children are at greater risk of child labor because other family members may not be able to stay employed and support the family. Therefore, income from child labor may be the only way for family members to support themselves.

Children from the hill tribes are considered to be at the greatest risk of becoming child laborers, because these tribes are isolated from the rest of Thailand. The hill tribes speak a different language, and even their Thai citizenship is questioned. Girls from the hill tribes are seen as being especially vulnerable to being employed in the sex industry, as parents may not realize the intentions of those who offer their daughters employment.

Vignette

Ma-Lee, age thirteen, is from the Karen (Kariang, Yang) hill tribe in northern Thailand. She lives in a bamboo house on raised stilts, beneath which live the family's chickens. Like her mother and older sisters, she is a skilled seamstress, dyeing her own cloth to make the beautiful patterns in the colorful sarong she wears. Her long, dark hair is pulled back in a bun and covered with a white scarf.

Ma-Lee and her family are not considered citizens of Thailand because her parents cannot prove that they were born in the country. Not being able to prove they are citizens, the family is denied government welfare services such as health care, and they cannot own land, work legally, or own a vehicle. Therefore, her family earns a meager living, surviving on about 12,000 baht a year (approximately US$290). Her father often leaves the family for eight or nine months a year to work in the rice paddies in central Thailand. Her fourteen-year-old brother goes with their father to work in the rice paddies. However, her sixteen-year-old brother, having learned in school that his village is considered primitive, never returned from the central region after his first season of migrant work, feeling ashamed of his own culture.

Ma-Lee attended school for a few years but eventually left to work beside her mother at home, tending to the younger children and making clothing for the family. Recently a man from Bangkok came to Ma-Lee's village looking for girls to work in his garment factory in Bangkok. He offered to pay 3,000 baht (approximately US$72) in advance, for one year of work from each girl. Ma-Lee and her eleven-year-old sister felt obligated to repay their parents for raising them and willingly left with the man. When they arrived in Bangkok, they found the working conditions harsh. Their sleeping quarters is a crowded room with over twenty other young girls, each of whom have only a small space on the floor to sleep. Ma-Lee and her sister work as many as twelve hours a day, with only short breaks to eat and use the bathroom. The garment factory is hot and loud. The girls try to comfort each other, but dream of returning home someday.

After more than a year of working in the garment factory, the girls had not yet repaid the money given to their family for their work. The factory pays low wages, and then charges the girls for room and board. The owner of the garment factory offers Ma-Lee an opportunity to work in a restaurant in the neighborhood, and transfers her debt to the restaurant owner. The restaurant is actually a bar, and Ma-Lee soon learns that she can earn much more money if she entertains the predominantly male customers. In exchange for sex, the men buy her drinks and food and tip her more than she could earn in a week at the garment factory.

Ma-Lee continues to work at the bar for several years. One of the girls with whom she works is fired when it is discovered she has AIDS. Ma-Lee realizes she needs to find another way to support herself or she will end up like her friend. Then one day she learns about the Child Labour Club, an organization that provides shelter, education, and health care to children. She contacts them and is able to get help. The Child Labour Club provides her shelter and she is able to return to school (Banerjee, 1980). Ma-Lee never returns home, but she is alive and believes that one day she will be able to find safe work to support herself and her family.

HISTORY OF CHILD LABOR

Child labor is not a new social issue in Thailand. There is a strong cultural tradition in Thailand that expects children to "pay back the breast milk," that is, to pay their parents back for the "trouble and cost of raising them" (Banpasirichote and Ponjsapich, 1992; International Labor Organization, 1998). Children, no matter their socioeconomic status, were expected to work. These beliefs are considered a major factor in children's continued participation in child labor, often in abusive and dangerous conditions. Poor children worked in agriculture, as domestics, or later, in factories. Children from wealthier families might have been sent to work with royalty, but nonetheless, they were away from their families at young ages, working long hours for meager wages (Banpasirichote, 2000).

Historically there were at least three occupations in which children labored in Thailand. Perhaps the oldest tradition was that of children being employed as domestic workers. Child domestic workers usually worked long hours for little pay (Child Workers in Asia, 2002; Poonyarat, 2001; Thailand Foundation for Child Development, 2002). They were frequently isolated from their families under the control of comparatively better off house owners. Too often they were denied healthy food, education, and emotional comfort. One of the dangers of domestic work for children is that they are in private homes, where they are hidden from the view of the public. This makes them vulnerable to physical, emotional, and sexual abuse (Child Workers in Asia, 2002; Poonyarat, 2001; Thailand Foundation for Child Development, 2002).

Another occupation in which children were commonly employed was agriculture. In the 1800s, along with adult migrant workers, children traveled to the central region of Thailand to work in the rice paddies. Today child laborers still migrate to the central region to work during the rice season. This seasonal work takes children away from their families for most of the year, denying them the opportunity for education and family support.

Another tradition for young Thai children was to work alongside their parents to learn a trade. While this was not considered abusive at the time, by today's standards much of the work they performed would be considered dangerous or exploitative. Laws enacted in the twentieth century suggest that children were employed in a variety of other occupations. For example, a law in 1916 prohibiting rickshaw drivers from being under age eighteen suggests that children under this age were employed as rickshaw drivers (Banpasirichote and Ponjsapich, 1992; International Labor Organization, 1998). In 1947 the ILO recommended that children under the age of ten not be employed, presumably in response to the fact that children under that age were employed.

CHILD LABOR TODAY

Today the belief that children should work continues, even if that work is in violation of Thai law. One study (Banpasirichote, 2000) found that only 30 percent of families sending their children to be child workers considered themselves poor. "She found that these households did not value higher education, thought their children would gain from the experience of work-ing, as well as helping the family economically, and that while they were aware of problems encountered by child workers, they thought these could be transcended or were not significant" (Bennett, 1998).

It is the most intolerable forms of child labor that receive the most at-tention, such as the sex industry and pornography. The government estimates that 22,500 to 40,000 children in Thailand are engaged in the sex industry, almost all of whom are female. Many jobs are considered to place children at high risk of eventually entering the sex industry, such as certain jobs in the entertainment industry. In some instances, employers who solicit girls to work in the sex industry tell families that the girls will be employed as do-mestics or in other aspects of the service industry. Other potentially dan-gerous forms of child labor include manufacturing, the fishing industry, the construction industry, and working with parents at rubbish dumps or col-lecting materials for recycling.

Other children considered to be at high risk of exploitation are migrant workers and street children. It is estimated that there are 2000 to 10,000 street children in Thailand. These children survive by begging, selling gar-lands, washing windshields at intersections, and other marginal work. All of these children are extremely vulnerable to abuse and exploitation.

POLITICAL VIEWS AND PUBLIC POLICIES

Thailand has ratified the United Nations Convention on the Rights of the Child, 1989 (CRC); the Convention for the Suppression of Traffic in Persons and the Exploitation of the Prostitution of Others; and the Convention on the Elimination of Discrimination against Women, 1985 (CEDAW). Despite the ratification of the Convention on the Rights of the Child, it took more than ten years for antiprostitution provisions to be passed (International Labor Organization, 1998).

Although the child employment laws in Thailand are not necessarily well known and may not have a lot of support from the community, there are laws governing the employment of children. Some of the provisions of Thai law include:

• The prohibition of employment of children under age thirteen years.
• Children ages thirteen through fifteen can work without permission in certain service occupations such as delivering newspapers or other items that weigh less than twenty-two pounds.

- Children ages thirteen through fifteen can work with special permission as long as the work is not considered dangerous for the child.
- Children ages thirteen through eighteen may not be employed in hazardous occupations such as "metal melting or molding; work with excessive heat, cold, noise, light and vibration; with dangerous chemicals or infectious substances; with toxic or inflammable substances (except at gas stations); or, in slaughter houses, casinos, adult entertainment places, massage parlors and similar places."
- The minimum wage for children is the same as that of adults.
- Children are entitled to receive their own wages. (Bennett, 1998)

The last two aspects of Thai law do not receive much support from the community. In addition, enforcing the laws can have negative consequences for the children themselves. Despite sometimes dangerous conditions, some children may still be better off illegally employed than they would be at home with their families.

SOCIAL VIEWS, CUSTOMS, AND PRACTICES

In general "there is no public consensus that children under 15, or even under 13, should not be working, a view that is also reflected among officials and non-government workers, many of whom still feel that there are many cases when these children's welfare is better protected by allowing them to remain in work" (Bennett, 1998). One specialist noted that "a lot of experts say eventually we want to stop children from working, but that is very much against the feelings of the local people. Particularly at this time [of economic difficulties], families need the supporting income and you cannot expect much serious labour inspection and enforcement, as if you place too much pressure on employers, they can just threaten to close down the company" (quoted in Bennett, 1998).

The one exception to these attitudes is toward the most intolerable forms of child labor, particularly child prostitution and pornography. Since antiprostitution legislation was passed in 1996, there has been a lot of pressure on police to penalize those who solicit children into the sex industry. And for the children, there are increasing services to help them move out of the sex industry. Because of international pressure and Thai law, child prostitution has become less visible. It is unclear whether there is actually less child prostitution or whether it is simply out of the view of the public.

THE FUTURE OF CHILD LABOR

Many factors need to be addressed to successfully address the issue of child labor in Thailand. Ideally children remaining in school to be educated for employment in occupations enable them to support themselves and their

families. Cultural norms do not currently support children remaining in
school. Many parents are not aware of the dangers children face in many
forms of child labor. Enforcement of child labor laws allows identification
and prosecution of employers who violate child labor laws. Children who are
already working illegally can be offered alternatives, including safety and
resources. And once rescued from illegal child labor, children can be
returned to their families and protected from reentering the labor market.
There are no such coordinated efforts under way in Thailand.

Both government and non-government agencies broadly have considerable difficulties in providing long-term follow-up of the cases of children for whom they
may have cared after they were rescued from intolerable working conditions. In
many cases these children may ultimately return to conditions similar or even the
same as those from which they were originally rescued, and an NGO or government agency is unlikely to be aware of this. (This problem is particularly acute in the
case of undocumented migrant children, such as girls working in the commercial
sex industry, who frequently may be returned to the border and only a few days later
be back at the same or related business from which they were rescued.) (Bennett,
1998)

Many projects, however, are working on solutions to pieces of the problem.
Below, various components considered necessary for successful prevention
and intervention in child labor are discussed.

Awareness

One of the first components in a successful campaign to address child
labor is to make parents, teachers, and the community aware of the problems
that can be encountered by children in the labor marker, particularly those in
the most intolerable forms of child labor. Awareness campaigns have been
conducted in some areas of Thailand, with radio announcements, programs
targeting teachers, and education of the public about child labor laws.

Children have been taught to feel responsible for the fiscal support of their
families. Preventing them from working may be harmful to their emotional
well-being. Similarly, prohibitions and enforcement may push child workers
further underground, making them more vulnerable to the most intolerable
forms of child labor.

Education

One of the most important ways to combat child labor is through the
provision of high-quality education and training. Thailand has worked to
increase compulsory education from six years to nine years, in recognition of
the skills needed to have a viable workforce that can compete in the global
marketplace. However, given the economy and aforementioned cultural

beliefs, keeping children in school is a challenge (International Labor Organization, 2001).

A recently instituted program provides 1,000 baht from the Public Welfare Department to help families keep their children in school. Schools must inform the Public Welfare Department about families who need this assistance, but it is unclear that this program has been publicized. Also, since the amount of money is very small, it is unlikely to be a major factor in a family's determination of whether or not to send their child to school.

The Ministry of Education offers scholarships that pay for the cost of school and living expenses to help children remain in school. Again, however, lack of awareness of the program and how it works may prevent children and their families from taking advantage of it. These scholarships also do not address the problem of the child's financial contribution to the family. It is likely that children who are poor or from isolated areas are unlikely to know about these scholarships and/or be able to take advantage of them (International Labor Organization, 2001).

Enforcement

Questions emerge regarding prosecution of employers of child laborers through the court system in cases of repeat offenders or cases of serious abuse of children. This requires the involvement of the police. Simple cases of first-time offenders are usually dealt with by an internal tribunal, which has the power to decide limited penalties. Yet dealing with the issue of child labor is outside the experience of most police and not generally regarded as a central part of their work. To tackle this issue, IPEC (International Programme on the Elimination of Child Labour) has launched a project to mobilize police, piloting it in the Police Bureau Seven Region (covering eight provinces surrounding Bangkok). This is very much an early, pioneering effort.

The Child Protection Unit in Bangkok operates a hot line service, which is advertised through radio programs and paid radio advertisements, pamphlets, stickers, posters, and so on. These are designed to encourage members of the public to report cases of child labor they encounter. These indicate that in provincial areas, the police or provincial labor office should be contacted. (The pamphlets also contain a brief outline of the legal provisions controlling the employment of child labor.) The Bangkok hot line records an average of about ten calls per month, about 50 percent of which prove to be verifiable cases of abuse of child workers.

Welfare and Income Replacement

The Public Welfare Department is primarily responsible for caring for individuals in immediate crisis situations in Thailand, including the children. They may provide immediate help for a child rescued from child labor by providing bus fare home. They also have the responsibility for ensuring the welfare of children in their care, including those who have been victims of the commercial sex industry. However, the Public Welfare Department is seriously limited in its ability to fulfill this monitoring task due to inadequate funding and resources.

Family Reunification

The Child Protection Unit in Bangkok instituted a project to reunite parents of working children who have lost contact with their offspring or who are concerned about their welfare. The Child Protection Unit attempts to locate the children and check their circumstances. Approximately one-third of the applications for assistance have resulted in cases.

International Response

The Department of Labor's (DOL) Bureau of International Labor Affairs (ILAB) is responsible for monitoring and oversight of all department-funded international child labor projects. Since 1995, ILAB has administered approximately $195 million for technical assistance programs designed to combat and prevent abusive child labor around the world. ILAB awarded a $703,000 grant to the International Justice Mission (IJM) to conduct a program to combat child trafficking and sexual exploitation of girls in Thailand through prevention, removal, and rehabilitation activities (ILAB, 2002).

BIBLIOGRAPHY

Banerjee, S. (1980) *Child Labour in Thailand*. Report No. 4, London: Anti-Slavery Society.

Banpasirichote, C. (2000) Rapid economic growth: The social exclusion of children in Thailand. In B. Schlemmer, *The exploited child*, pp. 135–45. London: Zed Books.

Banpasirichote, C. & Ponjsapich, A. (1992) Child workers in hazardous work in Thailand. Bangkok, Thailand: Chulalongkorn University.

Bennett, N. (1998) *Thailand country study: Toward a best practice guide on sustainable action against child labour*. ILO-IPEC. See www.journ.freeserve. co.uk/child/child2.html.

Child workers in Asia. (2002) Cwa.loxinfo.co.th/task_force_on_child_domestic_ work/tf_on_cdw_page%201.htm.

ILAB (2002) Child trafficking in Thailand target of Labor Department grant to faith-based group project designed to counter sexual exploitation of girls. Washington.

International Labour Organisation-International Programme on the Elimination of Child Labour. (1998) The situation of child labour in Thailand: A comprehensive report. Bangkok: ILO-IPEC (IPEC Thailand paper No.2).

———. (2001) *Good practice in action against child labour.* Bangkok: ILO-IPEC.
Poonyarat, C. (2001) Rights Thailand: Child workers are half family, half servants. IPS. See oneworld.org/ips2/june01/15_31_046.html.
Thailand Foundation for Child Development (FCD). (2002) Mapping of Child Domestic Workers' Programs in Asia. [Available from author: 143/109-111 Moo Ban Pinklao-Nakhonchaisri, Bangramru, Bangkok-noi Bangkok 10700 Thailand].

14

THE UNITED STATES

Pamela Pieris

PROFILE OF THE UNITED STATES

With 9,629,091 square kilometers, the United States is the third-largest country by size, behind Russia and Canada. It is located in the central part of the North American continent with Canada and Mexico as its immediate northern and southern geographic neighbors. Two states, Alaska and Hawaii, lie beyond this portion of the continent. Puerto Rico, the U.S Virgin Islands, American Samoa, the Northern Mariana Islands, and Guam also come under the territorial jurisdiction of the United States.

The climate is primarily temperate except for tropical Hawaii, arctic Alaska, and the arid or semiarid Great Plains and the Great Basin of the Southwest. It is a country rich in natural resources, agriculture, and industry. Air and water pollution are growing problems, with the U.S. as the largest carbon dioxide emitter in the world. Natural freshwater is scarce in the West, requiring careful oversight. The gross domestic product (GDP) in 2000 was $9,872.9 billion (International Association of Insolvency Regulators [IAIR], 2002).

With a tumultuous history marked by conquest and immigration, the U.S. has struggled in its evolution as the oldest democracy among the world's nations. Prior to early settlement, first by Spain and then the Western European countries, hundreds of Native American populations thrived on the North American continent with customs, languages, spiritual beliefs, and cultural and political systems specific to their respective nations. These nations treasured their children. Through disease and violence, the native population was reduced from 10 million to 1 million (Zinn, 1995).

The U.S. economy was propelled forward during the early eighteenth, the nineteenth, and the twentieth centuries. In the antebellum South, the wealth was built from the work of slave laborers brought to the U.S. from African nations. Men, women, and children abducted from Africa were the necessary source of forced labor in the expanding plantation economies of the Southern states. In the East and Midwest, immigrants, including children, arriving from Europe in the nineteenth century were a critical labor source in building the industrial sector of the U.S. In the West, the contributions of the early Chinese immigrants marked the success of the railroad industry as well as a renegotiation of race and ethnic relations. Later on, waves of immigrants and refugees from Africa, Latin America, and Asia contributed to the growing economy through the provision of cheap labor. Characteristic of life in the U.S., new groups brought in to fill labor needs became vulnerable to discrimination and exploitation. Mexicans were displaced as the U.S. claimed its lands. More recent immigrants from Mexico, Southeast Asia, Eastern Europe, and the Pacific Islands again contributed multiple resources.

Migrant labor, predominantly from Mexico and Puerto Rico, has emerged in the past thirty to forty years as vital to commercial agriculture's labor needs. Migrant workers' children exist as a silent, invisible workforce who are victims of exploited labor. Today the U.S. boasts of 280 million people who contribute a richness in ethnicity, culture, language, religious and faith traditions, political orientation, and lifestyles. The population is 77% white, 13% African-American, 4.2% Asian, 1.5% Amerindian and Alaska native, and .3% native Hawaiian and Pacific Islander. It is a country rich in choices in regard to religion: 56% Protestant, 28% Catholic, 2% Jewish, 4% other, and 10% none (CIA, 2002). Among the many other religions practiced are Buddhism, Hinduism, Islam, and indigenous religions and spiritual practices.

Poverty rates vary widely. According to the 2002 U.S. Census, the overall rate of poverty is 11.3% for individuals and 9.6% for families. The rates vary by age and race. For white non-Hispanics it is 7.5% while it is 22% for African-Americans, 11% for Asians and Pacific Islanders, and 21% for Hispanics. The poverty rate for the U.S. population under sixteen years of age is 16% (U.S. Census Bureau, 2001). Again it varies by race; for white non-Hispanic youth it is 9.4%, 31% for African-American youth, 28% for Hispanic, and 14.5% for Asian and Pacific Islander youth (Children's Defense Fund, 2003).

OVERVIEW OF CHILD LABOR

The term child labor is commonly used to denote employment that is harmful to a child's physical, cognitive, emotional, social, and moral development. In the United States, work that is detrimental to children's well-being is called *oppressive child labor* in the Fair Labor Standards Act (FLSA) of 1938. This is the main legal instrument ensuring the safety and protection of child workers (Pignatella, 1995). The use of the term child labor in the United States means work carried out by teenagers (Manser, 2000).

While there is a general consensus that oppressive child labor is not present in contemporary U.S. society, recent studies and media stories provide evidence that it does exist. It is predominantly prevalent in the agricultural sector, with few federal and state laws for protection. Children in the non-agricultural sector are subject to health and safety hazards as well as illegal employment. Although the prevailing opinion is that children work because of their desire to acquire material items, researchers have found that children work in order to supplement their families' income; some even work at two jobs. A recent study reported additional reasons for children working: a) for fun; b) to occupy time; c) to keep out of trouble, and d) to help people in need (Pieris, 2003).

Estimates from a 1997 longitudinal study indicate that 50% of youth twelve years of age are engaged in some employment activity. Estimates increase to 57% at age fourteen, and at age fifteen it is 64% (Rothstein and Herz, 2000). Other studies reported that 2.9 million adolescents in the fifteen through seventeen-year-old age group were employed during the school months and 4.0 million during the summer months of 1996–98 (Herz and Kosanovich, 2000). The number of adolescents in farm work in the U.S. is not known. The United Farm Workers Union estimates that 800,000 children are employed on family owned farms and as hired workers (Human Rights Watch, 2000).

It is difficult to track child labor with any accuracy. In the U.S., the Bureau of Labor Statistics (BLS) collects data on persons fifteen years and older, but these estimates are not used in official government figures. In addition, U.S. child labor laws allow children under fifteen years of age to work within family-owned farms and businesses as well as in other selected jobs, including as news carriers. The Current Population Survey (CPS) excludes this data from its estimates (Committee on the Health and Safety Implications of Child Labor, 1998). As a result, child labor statistics represent conservative underestimates.

Vignettes

Fourteen-year-old Alejandro went into a panic attack, screaming and yelling one day at school just before taking a midterm test. After putting in forty hours of work at two jobs to supplement his single mother's meager income, Alejandro had reached the end of his rope. In despair, frightened, and worried, he asks himself, how can he succeed in school and work to provide necessary income for his family?

Tyrone, fifteen years old, is involved in selling illegal drugs and sometimes weapons. He belongs to a local gang and is known to be "quite rich." Obedient and loyal to his gang, Tyrone never questions the gang's thirty-two-year-old leader, who directs the drug operations from his prison cell. Disowned by his family and lacking any belief that his life has value away from the drug culture, Tyrone enjoys the instant yet temporary gratification from his work.

Jaime, thirteen, and his sister Monica, eleven, had to move to another state for the harvesting season. Their parents depend on their children to work with them harvesting seasonal fruits and vegetables, to take care of the twins, and to cook. With every new move, they never know if they will return to school. Recently Jaime had sliced his fingers while working at a farm. His parents were afraid to take him to the local hospital, afraid that the government would take him away.

Victoria, fifteen years old, poses as a model for pictures that will go on the Internet. She receives a lot of cash. Shocked by the instant reward of money, Victoria is anxious to keep her modeling job a secret. The adult who takes her pictures threatens Victoria if she tries to tell her parents. Victoria has dreams of moving to New York to be a model.

HISTORY OF CHILD LABOR

Before the U.S. became an independent sovereign nation, children worked alongside other family members and were considered an integral part of the workforce (Hobbs, McKechnie, and Lavalette, 1999). Children were socialized to contribute to the maintenance of the family through apprenticeships. This arrangement exemplified the child's relationship to both work and family in preindustrial society (Weiner, 1991). In the precolonial and postcolonial U.S., children worked both on family farms and in cottage industries. Children in the agricultural and industrial sectors worked for long hours and in conditions that were detrimental to their physical and mental health. For parents and children, education was of secondary importance to supplementing the family income.

The idea that people are responsible for their poverty and misery is rooted in the English poor laws. Many of the early settlers from Europe, including the Puritans, brought religious beliefs establishing a strong work ethic. They believed that social and economic degradation could be prevented by hard work and prudent saving. These beliefs provided the impetus to justify child employment, instilling in parents and employers that it was their role to prepare their children for adult life by teaching them positive work habits (Hawes, 1991; Hobbs, McKechnie, and Lavalette, 1999; Zinn, 1995).

Early in the history of the U.S., children who were destitute and neglected were placed in private homes as domestic workers; in other instances, by court rulings, they were bound as apprentices. Boys were apprenticed until the age of eighteen or twenty-one, and girls until they were eighteen years old or in marriage. Work was considered training that provided children with skills in certain trades and occupations. Many children, however, received little or no training, and their education was ignored. They carried out menial tasks and were underfed and inadequately clothed (Trattner, 1999).

The child labor of children of color is sparsely documented. For example, we know that some children born to parents in slavery were sold into servitude (Kerschner, 2000). Prior to the Civil War, most African-American children who were enslaved worked on farms and plantations; approximately 5 percent worked in mines and factories (Cambell Bartoletti, 1999). During the antislavery period, children's apprenticeships bore striking similarities to forced bondage. Apprenticeships continued through the nineteenth century, especially in the Southern states. Whites in the Southern states used apprenticeships as a way to further enslave young African-Americans and secure a cheap source of labor (Trattner, 1999).

Industrialization increased rapidly, with New England leading the nation in the beginning of the nineteenth century. Towns emerged around newly constructed mills and factories, and populations in the major cities along the East Coast and in the Midwest increased as people abandoned their farms. The entry of underage boys and girls to the industrial workforce was seen as early as the completion of Samuel Slater's first spinning mill in 1790. His first workforce employed seven boys and two girls from the ages of seven through twelve (Cambell Bartoletti, 1999).

New immigrants arrived from Europe and were marginalized along with people of color (Trattner, 1999). They were compelled to sign contracts with mill owners committing them to involve their families, including the children, to work for a certain period of time. Workers were paid in scrip and lived in tenement slums owned by the same companies for whom they worked. The scrip could be used only in the company-owned stores, and if their manager considered their work unsatisfactory, they were evicted from their housing. Preference was given to employing new immigrants because they could be easily controlled. Their newness to the country left them vulnerable and disoriented due to clashes of culture and shifting identities. Families with several children and widows with children were highly favored (Zinn, 1995). Immigrant women and children worked long hours for low wages, scarcely sufficient to supplement family incomes. The children worked both as apprentices and as regular factory labor.

Child labor was considered a cheap and manageable workforce (Kerschner, 2000; Trattner, 1999). The cities provided a wide array of employment opportunities for children. Girls and boys were engaged in similar jobs, although more boys were engaged in street type occupations. More girls on the other hand worked at home helping their mothers in household tasks such as cooking, cleaning, laundry, ironing, mending, sewing, and caring for younger siblings. Some girls worked in textile mills and factories as spinners and weavers. They sent their wages home or saved their pay for education, job training, or a marriage dowry (Campbell Bartoletti, 1999).

In the early twentieth century, when most crop planting and harvesting was performed by hand, more children were engaged in farmwork than any other occupation (Freedman, 1994). A belief at that time was that farmwork was good for children's health. Some children moved from farm to farm with their families, carrying out the same backbreaking tasks as their parents. Entire migrant labor families, most of whom were African-American and other ethnic minorities, worked in the fields; this included children as young as three and four years old. Some families spent the entire year following the crops, staying at locations for just a couple of weeks. Migrant farmworkers and their families were denied access to health and welfare services and, in certain areas, their children were not allowed to attend the local schools. Even if the children were allowed to attend school, work always came first. Many families who lived in the city would get involved in agriculture work during the spring and summer months (Freedman, 1994).

The 1879 U.S. Census included estimates of child workers for the first time. In 1880, 1 million children from the ages of ten through fifteen were in the workforce; by 1890 the number had increased to 1.5 million, and by the 1900 census it was at 1.75 million (Weiner, 1991). This data does not include eight- and nine-year-old children in the workforce (Hobbs, McKechnie, and Lavalette, 1999) or African-American working children. Although child labor declined to less than 5% of ten- through fifteen-year-olds by 1930, significant disparities existed in geographic region and among people of color. In Rhode Island, 3% of children from the ages of ten through fifteen were employed, whereas in the state of Mississippi, 24% were employed because African-American child labor was cheap (Axinn and Levin, 1997).

In 1938 the FLSA was passed, defining child labor in the United States. Labor in occupations deemed hazardous for children under sixteen was then considered by the Children's Bureau to be oppressive. Of the 850,000 children under sixteen years of age in employment, only 6% of them were in jobs that protected them according to this law (Hobbs, McKechnie, and Lavalette, 1999).

Birth of a Child Labor Movement in U.S. History

Both children and adults were involved in opposing oppressive child labor. Contrary to commonly held stereotypes of child workers as docile employees, Campbell Bartoletti (1999) provided empirical evidence that children working in the industrial era were courageous and demanded what was rightfully theirs.

[It is] the story of kids who discovered power when they banded together for a common cause . . . the children fought abuses and demanded social justice and human dignity. They developed a common understanding from their shared living and working experiences. Even though they didn't share the same language, traditions, or customs. Kids on strike made a difference. (p. 193)

On July 19, 1899, the New York newsies rose against two millionaire publishers, William Randolph Hearst, owner of the *New York Journal*, and Joseph Pulitzer, owner of the *New York World*. They organized and after a two-week strike agreed to a partial win. In the 1912 Lawrence, Massachusetts, strike, the most militant and well organized in the history of labor, sixteen children provided testimony to both a House committee and President William Howard Taft about work. As a result, their testimonies helped win the strikers' demands (Campbell Bartoletti, 1999).

Significant adult advocates in the emerging child labor movement came from multiple arenas. Mary Harris Jones, a famous labor advocate for the Industrial Workers of the World and also known as Mother Jones, organized a children's march to Washington, D.C., in 1903 in support of ending child labor. She also organized the Kensington, Pennsylvania, workers' strike of June 14, 1903, where, out of 75,000 workers, 10,000 were children (Cambell Bartoletti, 1999; Hobbs, McKechnie, and Lavalette, 1999). Lewis Wickes Hine chronicled child labor with his photography, in defiance of mill and factory authorities, between 1908 and 1924. He traveled extensively across the U.S. to document child labor in canneries, coal mines, glass factories, textile mills, furniture and shoe manufacturers, homes, and farms (Campbell Bartoletti, 1999; Freedman, 1994; Hobbs, McKechnie, and Lavalette, 1999).

Jane Addams, who pioneered the Settlement House movement in Chicago in the late 1880s, worked with others to bring about social and economic change for immigrant women, children, and families. She fought against child labor and worked to raise public awareness of the issue. She argued that employment of young children lowered wages for all workers and contributed to illiteracy (Hawes, 1991). She was a founding member of the National Child Labor Committee in 1904. Addams was awarded the Nobel Peace Prize in 1931 (Hawes, 1991; Hobbs, McKechnie, and Lavalette, 1999).

Florence Kelly, also a social reformer of the Settlement House movement, was instrumental in the fight against child labor. She investigated the "sweating system" in which disadvantaged laborers worked long hard hours for very little pay (Hobbs, McKechnie, and Lavalette, 1999). She worked to abolish child labor as a member of the Illinois Consumers' League; helped establish the National Federation of Consumers' League in New York City in 1899; and was instrumental in starting the first nationwide committee, the National Child Labor Committee (NCLC) on April 15, 1900 (Hawes, 1991; Hobbs, McKechnie, and Lavalette, 1999; Trattner, 1999).

The original purpose of the NCLC was to abolish child labor. This organization viewed compulsory education as a strategy to remove children from the labor force (Hawes, 1991). The NCLC began an educational campaign, introduced several pieces of state legislation, and developed a Federal Children's Bureau. Support for this proposal came in 1909 from the first White House Conference; opposition came from several children's agencies and Southerners, who feared the possible regulation of child labor. In 1912 the U.S. Congress passed a bill, which President Taft signed into law, creating the Children's Bureau. One of the objectives of the Children's Bureau was to abolish child labor.

The NCLC helped draft the first federal child labor law in the U.S. in 1916. However, it was found unconstitutional in 1918 after the Southern Cotton Manufacturers contested its validity. They successfully argued that child labor is a matter to be dealt with by the states. In 1924 a constitutional amendment was submitted that incorporated child labor; however, it was not ratified.

Today the NCLC continues to take an active role in contemporary, oppressive child labor issues (Hawes, 1991; Hobbs, McKechnie, and Lavalette, 1999). In 1946 the Children's Bureau was partitioned, and its various functions were distributed among several other government entities (Hawes, 1991; Hobbs, McKechnie, and Lavalette, 1999; Trattner, 1999; Weiner, 1991).

CHILD LABOR TODAY

Child employment in the U.S. is acceptable within the parameters of the FLSA of 1938 and various state labor laws. The FLSA defines a child as a person under eighteen years of age. Terms such as teen employment, youth employment, adolescents in employment, and child employment are commonly used in documents to refer to the twelve-through-seventeen-year-old age group. Child employment in the U.S. does not carry the negative connotations that are associated with child labor in other industrialized countries. However, the incidence of oppressive child labor in the contemporary period is now greater than in prior years, especially in the apparel industry, the restaurant and grocery industries, in door-to-door candy selling, and among migrant farm communities (Pignatella, 1995).

POLITICAL VIEWS AND PUBLIC POLICIES

Oppressive child labor is prohibited by the FLSA of 1938. The standards of the FLSA Non-Agricultural Employment, Minimum Age and Work Hours are:

1. Minimum age for employment is age sixteen.
2. Children aged fourteen and fifteen may be employed outside school hours. The employment should be in jobs that the Secretary of Labor has determined will not

interfere with the child's health or well-being. Employment may be found in nonhazardous, nonmining, and nonmanufacturing areas.

3. Hours of work for ages fourteen and fifteen: three hours per school day, eighteen hours per school week, eight hours per non–school day, and forty hours per non–school week. Work is restricted to between 7:00 A.M. and 7:00 P.M., with the exception when evening hours are extended to 9:00 P.M. June 1 through Labor Day.

4. Youth ages sixteen and seventeen may work in nonhazardous jobs for an unlimited number of hours.

5. Persons age eighteen and above may perform in any job hazardous or otherwise, with no hourly restrictions, but in agreement with minimum wage and overtime requirements.

Individual state laws may or may not adopt the same federal standards. For example, New York has the same standards for fourteen and fifteen-year-olds but less stringent standards for youths in the sixteen and seventeen-year-old age group. In Washington state, stronger standards were adopted for all age groups than what is specified by federal law (Committee on the Health and Safety Implications of Child Labor, 1998).

The FLSA standard for child labor in the agriculture sector is less stringent than in other areas and lacks adequate protection. This looseness in policy creates opportunities for oppressive child labor among youths of color and migrant child populations. The standards of the FLSA Agricultural Employment, Minimum Age and Work Hours are provided below (Committee on the Health and Safety Implications of Child Labor, 1998; Pignatella, 1995).

1. Minors of any age may hold jobs on farms owned or operated by their parents.

2. Children age fourteen and fifteen may work at any nonhazardous farm job outside school hours.

3. Children age twelve and thirteen may work at nonhazardous jobs outside school hours at the same farm as the parents, or be employed elsewhere with written parental consent.

4. Children under age twelve may be employed by a parent in nonhazardous work out of school hours, or with parental consent may work at nonhazardous jobs outside school hours on farms not covered by minimum wage stipulations.

5. Children ages ten and eleven may work as hand-harvesting workers for no more than eight weeks in a given calendar year, and must be subject to a waiver from the Department of Labor.

6. Children age sixteen and older may work at any job, hazardous or otherwise, with no hourly restrictions.

SOCIAL VIEWS, CUSTOMS, AND PRACTICES

In contemporary U.S. society, children's work is viewed as being in two classes: informal or freelance work, and formal or employee-type jobs.

Freelance or informal work refers to work such as babysitting and yard-and-deck work. Because freelance jobs are not regulated by the FLSA of 1938, youths do not have restrictive hours and are permitted to hold a job at any age without parental consent (Gardecki, 2001). Formal work or employee-type jobs are ones where children work for an employer. Many children work during both the school and summer months in a variety of occupations including farming, harvesting, yard-and-deck work, the food industry, babysitting, entertainment, the arts, teaching, and entrepreneurship. *Young Biz* magazine celebrates each year the top one hundred child entrepreneurs from the ages of eight through eighteen. Children are involved in multiple entrepreneurial organizations as well as other occupations such as teaching languages and computers, teacher's aides, hairstylists, and mobile disc jockeys (Collins, 2002; McCarroll, 2002; Pieris, 2003).

According to Human Rights Watch (2000), child farmworkers age seventeen and younger are found in several states. Migrant farmworkers and children follow the crop patterns, moving through the agricultural states.

Children come to agriculture work at varying ages. Reports of children as young as four or five working alongside their parents are not uncommon.... Farm work is low paid, exhausting, stigmatized, and often dangerous. Agricultural workers labor under extreme weather conditions from pre-dawn cold to intense desert heat, where temperatures are commonly well above 100 degrees Fahrenheit. Their work is physically demanding, requiring sustained strength, endurance, and coordination. (Human Rights Watch, 2000, p. 11)

The hazardous work conditions that children encounter on family farms leave many children mutilated and dismembered. Family farms are known to be unregulated, and the exact numbers of accidents and deaths are not reported. Migrant children work from dawn to dusk stooped in the fields. They are sometimes sprayed with various pesticides. School attendance is sporadic, with children frequently missing school. Although the situation of working children on family farms and migrant child labor is different in many ways, what is common to both is oppressive labor, with the opportunity of injury and death to the child (Pignatella, 1995).

Sweatshops in the garment industry in cities such as San Francisco and New York, are another major arena of oppressive child labor. In New York, where fifteen hundred sweatshops thrive, children as young as eight years of age are found to be employed. In San Francisco sweatshops, children, mostly immigrants, can be found working for low wages in unsafe work environments. These children work from early in the morning to late in the evening.

Mostly middle-class adolescents are employed in the restaurant and grocery industries. Child labor advocates speculate that these jobs increasingly require more responsibilities, compelling work hours that exceed the legal limits. Too often such work results in injury and even death. Grocery stores are considered the most persistent violators of the FLSA. One company had over nine hundred child labor violations and employed fourteen and fifteen-year-old youths who worked more than the legally stipulated number of hours during prohibitive times. Also, the company allowed employees younger than eighteen years old to use equipment considered hazardous by law. Door-to-door candy-selling is a growing industry that has large numbers of child labor violations. Children, some as young as seven, are forced to work until late at night. They are driven in vans to various neighborhoods to sell candy; in one instance children were taken 160 miles from home. These children face the dangers of mistreatment and abuse, including child molestation (Pignatella, 1995).

Many children risk the worst forms of child labor, for example, in drug dealing, pornography, and commercial sexual exploitation. Such oppressive labor is documented mainly among runaway adolescents or at the point of arrest (Committee on the Health and Safety Implications of Child Labor, 1998). Yet, as in all countries, clandestine occupations where children are exploited are hard to detect.

Socioeconomic and racial characteristics are important factors in a child's ability to secure employment. Youths from low-income families living in disadvantaged communities have fewer opportunities to secure paid jobs while they are in high school. The retail sector provides the greatest number of first jobs for adolescents. It also employs a significant number of minority workers for the most undesirable service positions. Low-income child workers of color are more likely than their white counterparts to obtain employment in agriculture, manufacturing, and construction, which are considered hazardous industries. The participation of children who have disabilities in the workforce is considered to be very low. Typically parents or caregivers postpone the disabled child's entry into the workforce (Ahituv et al., 1997 and U.S. General Accounting Office, 1991; as cited in the Committee on the Health and Safety Implications of Child Labor, 1998).

THE FUTURE OF CHILD LABOR

A consensus exists in the U.S. over the need for uniform standards in the FLSA for child labor. The Committee on the Health and Safety Implications of Child Labor (1998) has made several proposals to make the workplace a safe and healthy place for the child worker. The committee's four guiding principles direct the efforts to abolish oppressive child labor in the U.S. and other countries.

Guiding Principle 1. Education and development are of primary importance during the formative years of childhood and adolescence. Although work can contribute to these goals, it should never be undertaken in ways that compromise education or development.

Guiding Principle 2. The vulnerable, formative, and malleable nature of childhood and adolescence requires a higher standard of protection for young workers than accorded to adult workers.
Guiding Principle 3. All businesses assume certain social obligations when they hire employees. Businesses that employ young workers assume a higher level of social obligation, which should be reflected in the expectations of society as well as in explicit public policy.
Guiding Principle 4. Everyone under 18 years of age has the right to be protected from hazardous work, excessive work hours, and unsafe or unhealthy work environments, regardless of the size of the enterprise in which he or she is employed, his or her relationship to the employer, or the sector of the economy in which the enterprise operates. (pp. 213–14)

Discussions on oppressive child labor place responsibility on adults for making the workplace a safe and healthy place for children. It is seen to be equally important, however, to educate child workers regarding their human rights (Collins, 2002). Other than those children who are given opportunities and recognized for their entrepreneurship, most children whose labor is exploited are not aware that they have any rights.

CONCLUSION

In 1999 the United States made financial contributions of $37.1 million to improve the lives of working children in the developing countries and a further commitment of $30 million to the International Labour Organisation (Kerschner, 2000). The United States supports work to eliminate exploitative child labor in developing countries, however, such advocacy has yet to be seen in this country.

Oppressive child labor exists in the U.S. Working children in the eighteenth and nineteenth centuries fought for rights in the workplace, winning partial achievements. Child workers in contemporary U.S. society have protections and opportunities far greater than child laborers in the industrial period and far greater than their counterparts in other nations. Increased public awareness along with more effective enforcement of child labor laws are seen as ways to help diminish oppressive child labor in the United States. Social programs and policies addressing poverty, particularly of oppressed populations that are vulnerable to hazardous employment, are also recognized ways to move the United States toward a society that has permanently eradicated oppressive child labor.

BIBLIOGRAPHY

Axinn, J., and H. Levin. (1997) *Social welfare. A history of the American response to need.* 4th ed. New York: Longman.

Cambell Bartoletti, S. (1999) *Kids on strike.* Boston: Houghton Mifflin.

Central Intelligence Agency. (2002) *The world factbook, 2002.* Retrieved June 29, 2003, from http://www.cia.gov/cia/publications/factbook/geos/us.html.

Children's Defense Fund. (2003) *Every child deserves a fair start.* Retrieved June 30, 2003, from http://www.childrensdefense.org/fs_cptb_child00.php.

Collins. (2002) Colorado Department of Labor & Employment, October 1997. Know your rights. A young person's guide to employment.

Committee on the Health and Safety Implications of Child Labor. (1998) *Protecting youth at work: Health, safety and development of working children and adolescents in the United States.* Washington, DC: National Academy Press.

Farson, R. (1974) *Birthrights.* New York: Macmillan.

Freedman, R. (1994) *Kids at work: Lewis Hine and the crusade against child labor.* New York: Clarion Books.

Gardecki, R. M. (2001, August) Racial differences in youth employment. *Monthly Labor Review:* 51–67.

Giampetro-Meyer, A., T. Brown, and N. Kubasek. (1994) The exploitation of child labor: An intractable international problem. *Loyola of Los Angeles International and Comparative Law Annual* 16(3): 657–74.

Hawes, J. M. (1991) *The children's rights movement: A history of advocacy and protection.* Boston: Twayne Publishers.

Herz, D., and K. Kosanovich. (2000, November) Trends in youth employment: Data from the current population survey. In A. M. Herman, ed. *Report on the youth labor force,* pp. 30–38. Washington, DC: U.S. Department of Labor.

Hobbs, S., J. McKechnie, and M. Lavalette. (1999) *Child labour: A world history companion.* Santa Barbara, CA: ABC-CLIO.

Human Rights Watch. (2000) *Fingers to the bone: United States failure to protect child farmworkers.* New York: Human Rights Watch.

International Association of Insolvency Regulators. (2002) Member profile: United States. Retrieved June 29, 2003, from http://www.insolvencyreg.org/members/profiles/unitedStates.html.

Kerschner, A. (2000, November) Child labor laws and enforcement. In A. M. Herman, ed. *Report on the youth labor force,* pp. 3–13. Washington, DC: U.S. Department of Labor.

Manser, M. (2000, November) Introduction. In A. M. Herman, ed. *Report on the youth labor force,* pp. 1–2. Washington, DC: U.S. Department of Labor.

McCarroll, C. (2002, June, 24) Beyond babysitting. *Christian Science Monitor.*

Pieris, P. (2003) *What under-aged children in the United States work force say about their employment experience: A qualitative multiple case study.* Unpublished dissertation. University of Denver, Graduate School of Social Work.

Pignatella, M. A. (1995) The recurring nightmare of child labor abuse: Causes and solutions for the 90s. *Boston College Third World Law Journal* 15(1): 171–210.

Rothstein, D., and D. Herz. (2000, November) A detailed look at employment of youth aged 12 to 15. In A. M. Herman, ed. *Report on the youth labor force,* pp. 14–21. Washington, DC: U.S. Department of Labor.

Trattner, W. I. (1999) *From poor law to welfare state: A history of social welfare in America.* 6th ed. New York: Free Press.

U.S. Census Bureau. (2001) *Poverty in the United States, 2000.* Washington, DC: U.S. Government Printing Office.

Weiner, M. (1991) *The child and the state in India: Child labor and education policy in comparative perspective.* Princeton, NJ: Princeton University Press.

Winfrey, O. (2001, March 5) *More smart kids in the Oprah Winfrey show.* Harpo Productions, Inc., Chicago, IL (Transcript produced by Burrelle's Information Services, Livingston, NJ).

———. (2003, March 9) *Smart kids in the Oprah Winfrey show.* Harpo Productions, Inc., Chicago, IL (Transcript produced by Burrelle's Information Services, Livingston, NJ).

Zinn, H. (1995) *A people's history of the United States, 1492–present.* Rev. and updated ed. USA: Harper Perennial.

15

ZIMBABWE

Otrude Moyo

PROFILE OF ZIMBABWE

Zimbabwe is in southern Africa. The country covers 390,308 square kilometers. It is an elevated savanna over 1,200 meters in altitude. The great dike runs from northeast to southwest through the center of the country, with both sides sloping from midlevel (900 to 1,200 meters) to low level (below 900 meters). The borders are marked mainly by large rivers, with the Zambezi in the north and the Limpopo in the south. Along the great dike, granite outcrops and hills characterize the landscape; otherwise, the land is fairly flat. Mountains are found along the eastern border with Mozambique.

The climate is subtropical, warm throughout the year, and has a rainy season lasting from November to March; winter is dry and cool and extends from May through August. The eastern highlands receive more than 1,200 millimeters of rain annually; otherwise two-thirds of the country receives less than 800 millimeters. The country is often plagued with droughts.

Colonial occupation of Zimbabwe by white settlers in the late nineteenth century was part of European imperialism. The growth of capitalism in Europe spurred the need for markets for European products as well as a search for raw materials and a quest for investment opportunities (Nelson, 1983). Before colonial rule, a number of societies existed including the Great Zimbabwe. In these early societies, the primary food production consisted of livestock—mainly sheep and goats. Cattle emerged later. The hunting of wild animals and gathering of wild fruits and vegetables for food continued alongside the domestication of stock throughout the Iron Age. Archaeological findings indicate that the economies of these early African societies were based on iron, and gold smelting.

Today the population of Zimbabwe is estimated to be 11.5 million (Zimbabwe Census Bureau, 1997), with fluctuations because of emigration and mortality from the AIDS pandemic. Beginning with colonial occupation, estimates of the white population in Zimbabwe have been 250,000. Colored (persons of mixed ancestry) and Asians constitute 2% of the population; 97% of the total population is African. Zimbabwe is an ethnically diverse country with various ethnic groups and languages. As an accident of a colonial history, the missionaries in the late nineteenth century, in their efforts to translate the Bible, unified several ethnic languages and groups. To this day, however, linguistic features still distinguish dialects.

Today Ndebele and Shona are the two official indigenous languages in Zimbabwe; the major nonindigenous language is English. The Shona with several dialects is a first language for 60% of the population; Ndebele is a first language for 30%. There are several recognized minority languages and a number of indigenous languages that are also spoken in neighboring countries.

The ideology of colonialism was the racial subordination of Africans who attempted to resist this subordination throughout the colonial period and the subsequent periods. European settlers in Zimbabwe confiscated land and pushed indigenous societies onto reserves. This occupation stripped indigenous Zimbabweans of resources, disenfranchising them in human, political, and economic rights. Africans and their families were incorporated into the free market system as cheap migrant labor for the white settlers' enterprises. The urban formal sector was designed to cater to the needs of white settlers, not the well-being of all Zimbabweans. Colonial occupation resulted in a lopsided economy comprising an underdeveloped rural sector where most Africans resided and a well-developed (in terms of amenities and services) urban sector where whites resided. Without financial capital to extend economic activities, many Zimbabweans have had to provide work for themselves whenever possible.

Upon independence in 1980, the African-led government assumed a somewhat larger role in developing an inclusive economy. Education expanded, increasing enrollments in primary school and growing substantially in secondary education. However, the expansion in human capital development was not met with an expansion in labor opportunities. Thus, those who left school without completion suffered the highest unemployment. There were marked improvements in health care, environmental sanitation, water access, and the development of preventive health care. These improvements have deteriorated with the economic hardships facing the Zimbabwean economy today.

Because of a history of colonial occupation, which racialized the political economy by using race as the determining factor in all relations, exploitative administration in the economy became an established rule. Within this system of social stratification, anybody considered white had the highest status, followed in descending order by Asians, coloreds (persons of mixed race), and Africans; this system was preserved and enforced as law from the 1890s until Zimbabwe's independence in 1980. African labor was supposed to serve white interests. Most Africans were confined in the reserves in rural areas with no property rights to the land. They were allowed to enter urban and commercial areas only through the "pass law" system. Circulatory labor migration emerged where adults, males oftentimes, sought wage employment in the urban areas and returned to their families periodically. These workers maintained ties to the rural areas where their families resided. To this day more than 60 percent of Zimbabwe's population resides in rural areas; the circulatory connections between urban and rural have prevailed.

After independence, Zimbabwe established a diversified economy that included private enterprises in agriculture, manufacturing, mining, tourism, and banking, and a strong public sector largely dominated by education, health, and military services. There were also historical state/private enterprises in energy and transportation. Economic restructuring and political issues, however, led to the collapse of the Zimbabwean economy in the 1990s.

Zimbabwean society has always been pressured by the youth bulge. Current population estimates of children vary widely owing to the impact of the AIDS pandemic and emigration, but it is generally agreed that they account for approximately half of the population. According to the Zimbabwe Census Bureau (1997), out of a population of 11.5 million, there were 4,667,599 children. For many children, the first problem is survival. This is especially the case during the first five years of life, when mortality rates remain high. For those children who survive, survival for themselves as well as their families remains an ongoing concern.

Reports on the level of poverty have shown that more than 50 percent of households in Zimbabwe live on less than US$1 per day. The prices of basic necessities, however, have continued to rise phenomenally. According to the 2001 Human Development Index, Zimbabwe has one of the three economies where general living conditions have slipped to pre-1980 levels. In 2002, Zimbabwe ranked 128th out of 173 countries, with a Human Development Index (HDI) of 0.5514; this compares to 0.5700 at independence. The reason for this fall has been attributed to the worsening economic and political crisis. Political violence has often resulted in widespread dislocations of people throughout Zimbabwe. Often times it is the children who are most vulnerable.

OVERVIEW OF CHILD LABOR

Because of the large youth population, there has been an increasing emphasis on education. The Zimbabwean economy has never been large enough to accommodate all children who exit school into the workforce. In order to survive, many young people languish in the private sphere of domestic help. These children often live in families that have never had a steady flow of income. All members, including the children, have to work. Recently many youths have been pressed into the National Youth Service, which has enabled them to become part of the pro–ruling party militias, nicknamed "Green Bombers" for the uniforms they wear. This has unleashed more critical issues in the exploitative use of children as paramilitary, including the crimes that children commit.

Like most social issues affecting the African population, the economic exploitation of children has only recently emerged as an issue of concern in Zimbabwe. Accurate statistics are not available. Frequently quoted "statistics" on child labor in Zimbabwe are mostly guess-estimates (Chinyangara et al., 1997). Child labor in Zimbabwe is connected to poverty, population demographics, capitalism, and the vestiges of colonial occupation. Both poverty and child labor exist within a context of colonialism that disenfranchises Africans.

There is no universally accepted definition of child labor. Various definitions are used by international organizations, governments, nongovernmental organizations, trade unions, and other interest groups. Definitional problems increase the difficulty in accurately assessing the numbers of children engaged in child labor. This is the case of children on the streets, who for most of the 1990s have been estimated to number 12,000 nationwide and "increasing." On March 22, 2002, the *Zimbabwean Herald* reported that "nearly 5 million children in Zimbabwe between the age of five and 17 years are being forced to work in several sectors of the economy against their will." This statistic has been used by the Global March against Child Labor to emphasize the struggle for survival. Sectors where children work, for example, in the domestic sphere, have not been areas of focus and are excluded in statistical indicators (Chinyangara et al., 1997). The economic definition frequently used suggests that child labor is labor performed by children believed to be too young chronologically. This definition encompasses the assumption that children's work unduly reduces future income capacity, through shrinking their future choice sets or capabilities (Andvig, Canagarajah, and Kielland, 2001).

Child labor in Zimbabwe, like other parts of Africa, is perceived to be largely nonwage labor, including labor performed in the household (Bourdillon, 2001). Even with this definition, very few studies have shown how children work in this sphere. A few studies have addressed domestic maintenance work, caring for others, food production, and making handicrafts for sale—activities that involve the work of children (see Moyo, 2001; Reynolds, 1991). The major issue in these studies is that while all children tend to be engaged in some economic activities, female children tend to be inundated with food production, domestic, and caretaking work (Moyo, 2001).

In a recent book edited book by Michael Bourdillon (2000), *Earning a Life: Working Children in Zimbabwe*, the plight of children's work is examined from the lens that the work that children do is critical to survival: theirs and their families. This work necessary for survival includes: work in informal trading enterprises, assisting their parents' or operating their own trading activities, work in small-scale agriculture in family plots, work in exchange for schooling, work in small-scale mining, or caretaking for the sick, younger children, and elder relatives.

In Zimbabwe, children have played and continue to play a significant economic role in the formal sectors of the economy, mainly in mining and commercial agriculture (Grier, 1994; Lowenson, 1981; Sachikonye, 1991; van Onselen, 1976). In these sectors children work alongside family members or on their own under verbal contracts (Levine, 1999). They primarily pick cotton, tea, and fruit while remaining invisible appendages to parents and guardians. Grier (1994) captures the use of child labor in commercial farming areas of Zimbabwe vividly. African families seeking employment have been allowed to settle on a farmer's land while providing labor to that farmer. Oftentimes farmers avoided paying for labor at all costs. Additionally, in a study of children in mines, van Onselen (1976) reported that young boys in the rural areas of central Africa were recruited by *chibaro* (for bonded labor). Bound by contract, these children shouldered the responsibility of cooking for the adult workers making the long march to the mines.

The duality of the economy—the mixing of the formal and informal sectors—has meant that child labor occurs in the informal economy as well. For example, in informal mining children are found on the streams of rivers panning gold. Other examples of children's labor in informal sectors include: service work, being totes in the emergency taxi businesses, domestic work, hustling, hairdressing, illegal work such as prostitution and thieving in open air/flea markets, or work in garages, markets and all the other small businesses that spring up with food/fuel/foreign currency shortages. With the restructuring of the economy in the 1990s, employment standards loosened, contributing to the likelihood that children would be pushed into more exploitative work.

The issue that has dominated the focus because of developmental and safety issues is the plight of "street children" (Bourdillon, 2000; Muchini and Nyandiya Bundy, 1991). Some of the street children have homes to return to, others do not. Other examples include street children peddle goods or services or beg for money and return home at night to maintain contact with family and other relatives. They contribute their earnings to the survival of their families. Some street children are orphaned children who are left to take care of siblings. Others are homeless and live and sleep on the streets in urban areas. These street children are totally on their own, living with other homeless children and adults. They oftentimes lack the emotional and psychological support of parents and other family members. Some have been abandoned or rejected by families; others were forced to leave families due to problems at home. All have developed coping mechanisms for surviving in unsafe environments.

Vignette

Mwale is a thirteen-year-old boy who grew up on a commercial farm in Somabhula, about one hundred kilometers from Bulawayo. He is the oldest of four children. Originally, Mwale's family had come from Malawi in the federation of then Rhodesia(s) and Nyasaland to work in the asbestos mines in Zvishabane. When they were laid off, they moved to the farm as squatters.

Mwale's father and mother are farmworkers for a commercial livestock ranch and live as "squatters" on the farm. Their farm wages are very little. Sometimes his father and mother are paid only in alcohol for their work on the farm, which forces Mwale and his siblings to find food on their own. Sometimes his family is paid in rations, and they get food and some clothing from the local store owned by the farmer. Mwale's family is forever in debt and can not leave the farm because of the money owed to the white-owned store.

Mwale used to work alongside his mother and father on the farm before he moved to the city to live with his grandmother in a township in Bulawayo. Even though Mwale's days at the farm were miserable, his life has not changed much for him at his grandmother's place. Mwale attends school erratically because his grandmother can not afford to pay the fees. Because of the late payment of fees, Mwale is not receiving his school progress reports. Hardship keeps his grandmother from addressing Mwale's school problems. Oftentimes Mwale skips school to work on the streets—hustling, selling cigarettes in the beer garden, and sometimes as a "tote" for the emergency taxis. Sometimes he returns to his grandmother's home with money, food, or whatever he has found. When the rains are good, Mwale and the other children in his grandmother's house cultivate the city's open lands to supplement their erratic food sources. However, Mwale does not do much of the routine domestic chores because there are several "girl" cousins in his grandmother's house. They are responsible for those chores (Vignette derived from Moyo, 2001).

HISTORY OF CHILD LABOR

The realities of poverty and historical social relations have resulted in massive socioeconomic inequality in Zimbabwe. The socioeconomic structures sculpted by colonial capitalism have created an ordering of society that affects children. The structures ushered in by colonial capitalism have been so pervasive that they have persisted into the postindependence era (Grier, 1994).

Colonial capitalism in Zimbabwe established an ideology of racializing people by using white supremacy to subordinate African economies and ways of life. European settlers in Zimbabwe replicated and built the economies of their countries of origin by securing and extracting African resources. Too often the securing of these resources required the use of violence. During the later years of colonial capitalism, the state gained access to children's labor through coercive measures, poll taxes, relocation of peoples, and reconstitution of social relations with institutionalization of the patriarchal system of *kraal* heads and tenancies (Grier, 1994). This assisted in keeping count of and policing African movements and controlling where Africans and their children worked as laborers through restricted and poor wages.

African families were disrupted in their economic activities and prohibited by law from settling in urban and commercial areas. The precarious nature of employment made it impossible for families to migrate together. As a consequence, child labor has always been critical for the survival of children their families. Colonial capitalism ushered in poverty and socioeconomic inequality based on the creation of racial oppression. This racial oppression served as a powerful deterrent against full integration of African families into the political economy of Zimbabwe. Every African, including every child, was forced into hard and degrading labor to assure survival.

Since labor, land, and capital are key factors in economic development, these became the major devices for enforcing colonial capitalism. Forced migrations and confinement of African laborers into reserves (environments where people could not meet their basic needs) precipitated circulatory migration for some family members. Other members, including children, worked to survive—using whatever ways they could manage.

During colonial rule, no laws existed to protect African children and their "childhood." There was very little investment in the infrastructures of education, human services, and health care to support the well-being of African children. Instead, exploitation instigated by colonial capitalism undermined the social relations and local economies of Africans. White settlers became the owners of all African labor and determined how many and which Africans could enter the white settler cities and commercial areas. White households often employed Africans as farm and domestic workers. Many children worked on farms in return for a place to stay, oftentimes without wages and after being dispossessed from the land.

Rural areas became the holding pools of the labor reservoirs. African men and women were forced into the emerging commercial centers to seek paid employment. Here they were barred by law from living as families and/or migrating with their families. This forced children, the elderly, and some women to take on full responsibility for their own survival in an economic system that awarded less-than-survival wages for their labor.

CHILD LABOR TODAY

The debates surrounding child labor as a current social issue have intensified in Zimbabwe. Differing opinions abound regarding the definition of child labor, what differentiates child work from child labor, what explanations are put forward to understand child labor, and what actions should be taken to address this issue (Brazier, 1998; Levine, 1999; Otis, Pasztor, & McFadden, 2001). The history of colonial occupation and the socio cultural context of work and well being in Zimbabwe remain powerful divisive forces over understanding and addressing the issue. Not surprisingly, emotions run high on all sides of this issue leading to complications, especially in the area of the choices made and/or not made to address child labor (Levine, 1999; Otis, Pasztor, and McFadden, 2001). It is the nature and condition of children's work that determines whether work is exploitative, necessary for survival, or an opportunity for discretionary income (Brazier, 1998).

Poverty emerges as an important factor in explaining child labor in Zimbabwe (Bourdillon, 2000; Lowenson, 1981; Reynolds, 1991; Sachikonye, 1991) as does the cultural use of children's labor in the domestic arena (Andvig, Canagarajah, and Kielland, 2001). The local context as well as the desire to help children are equally important factors in understanding the complex issue of child labor in Zimbabwe. However, what is necessary to understanding child labor in Zimbabwe today is the global political economy that has excluded, devalued, and prevented African labor from realizing its potential. Child labor in Zimbabwe as a social issue is defined and framed within international politics. These politics are entwined with global economic inequality, enmeshed in the politics of the global child labor movement (Levine, 1999).

Over the years, counterproductive neoliberal policies accompanying globalization have pushed for structural adjustment policies (SAPs) favoring the interests of foreign enterprises and disregarding local needs. In Zimbabwe like elsewhere in the poor world, the conditions that the International Monetary Fund (IMF) and the World Bank set for lending have no regard for human well-being (Arat, 2002). SAP-driven government policies regard the provision of people with meaningful work as a function mainly of sustained economic growth spurred by foreign interests and investments. The results have been that wages for adults declined precipitously, and government spending in education and health has been reduced substantially. This collapse of the economy plunged Zimbabwe into profound poverty. Since children's well-being depends on adults working—increased poverty has forced children to labor to stave off starvation.

The collapse of the Zimbabwean economy not only increased the number of poor households but also increased the informal sector activities. The SAPs in Zimbabwe spawned environments conducive to child labor, including the exploitation of children's labor in economic activities outside governmental regulations and enforcement. As the cost of living increased, so did the work of children—families more and more needed the labor of all members to get by (Moyo, 2001). In addition, government cuts in social spending hit education hard. Spending per student declined dramatically and fees were added. This dramatic cut in educational spending adversely affected children's education. Some families were forced to rearrange their priorities to add payment of school fees and supplies. In an attempt to cope with shrinking family incomes, poor households stopped sending children to school. For those children who remained in school, increased work after and before school became the norm. In some families, children were moved to rural areas because of tuition/fee waivers. The rural schools, however, have historically been the most deprived; schools are too far away and often lack books and other educational resources. Moreover, after completing their high school and college education, children in Zimbabwe were not able to find employment let alone have the resources to create work for themselves. Many of these children today swell the streets hustling, begging, trading, doing anything to survive, their hopes and expectations shattered.

The HIV/AIDs pandemic has impacted the crisis as the numbers grow. The effects ripple through the Zimbabwean society, leaving many children orphaned. Deaths from AIDS-related illnesses continue to increase with the breakdown of the health care system following the SAPs. All too often these children are forced to fend for themselves. In Zimbabwe the principal mode of HIV infection is through heterosexual transmission. Deaths from AIDS-related illnesses primarily affect women 20 to 30 years of age and men 25 to 35, and very young children born of infected mothers (Barnett and Blackie, 1992). The number continues to increase. Moreover, the separation of couples and families for long periods of time due to the colonially established labor migration has contributed to heterosexual transmissions. Often the responsibility for care of the ill is transferred to children and women with children—who must take care of the sick as well as look for the means to survive. In some cases children are withdrawn from school to care for sick parents/guardians; they may also be forced to work outside the home. Home-based care is extremely demanding when there is no support. Many children confronted with these circumstances endure the hardships alone, tucked away in the privacy of their homes; their plight emerges as a social issue only when they are found on the street.

POLITICAL VIEWS AND PUBLIC POLICIES

Since independence, the government of Zimbabwe has, at least on paper, committed itself to support the welfare of children. With independence in 1980 the government of Zimbabwe set out to rectify the imbalances caused by colonial capitalism. Significant improvements in education were made between 1980 and 1991, both in the number of schools and student enrollments, which more than doubled under a government policy aimed at achieving the goal of universal primary education. Considering the socio-demographic conditions of Zimbabwe, this commitment was inevitable. After independence, education was free until rising government budget deficits and the conditions for borrowing set by the SAPs forced the government to impose school fees in 1992. Only some schools provided students with books; parents had to buy their children's school supplies and uniforms.

Some urban schools are overcrowded, forcing them to run morning and afternoon shifts. The split schedule, however, can be beneficial in accommodating the work schedules of some students. Rural schools continue to lack infrastructure, personnel, and educational materials. On commercial farms, education has historically been provided haphazardly for children in farm schools, which are usually paid for and operated by the farm owner. Parents generally cannot pay the necessary fees, and many commercial farm owners force children to work in return for their education. Schools are closed during the harvest season. With the recent crisis in agriculture and land reforms, it is now likely that more children will be left without any access to education.

According to the International Labour Organisation (ILO) report of 1999, the government of Zimbabwe attaches great importance to the rights of children. Child welfare has always been one of the priorities on the national development agenda. The government has ratified major regional and international covenants and instruments that have a focus on the welfare and rights of the child, such as the United Nations Convention on the Rights of the Child (1989); the ILO Convention No. 138 on Minimum Age (1973), ratified in June 2000; and the African Charter on the Rights and Welfare of Children (1990), ratified in 1995 (Chinyangara et al., 1997).

Child labor is governed by the statutory instrument SI 72 of the Labor Relations Employment of Children and Young Persons' Regulations 1997 as amended by SI 155 of 1999, and promulgated in terms of the Labor Relations Act, Chapter 28.01. This legislation is in sync with ILO Convention No. 138 on Minimum Age (1973). In Zimbabwe, violations of the convention are subject to punishment. Children performing household activities as part of their socialization process are safeguarded in the Children's Protection and Adoption Act. In pursuit of these goals, the Ministry of Public Service, Labor and Social Welfare (MPSLSW) works with other relevant departments, nongovernmental organizations, and international organizations to develop and implement programs for improving the welfare of children and also sensitize the general population on the rights of children (Chinyangara et al., 1997).

In late 1993 the Zimbabwean government launched a Child Labor Task Force Committee composed of representatives of several ministries including:

Education and Culture; National Affairs, Employment Creation and Cooperatives; Public Service Labor and Social Welfare; Health and Child Welfare; Lands, Agriculture and Water Development; and Local Government and Rural and Urban Development. This committee has been charged with defining child labor, determining problem areas, and suggesting legislation to alleviate the problems. All these policies on paper affirm the Zimbabwean governments' strong commitment to children's rights and welfare. This concern on paper, however, is not reflected in terms of the actual well-being and life chances of Zimbabwe's children.

SOCIAL VIEWS, CUSTOMS, AND PRACTICES

In Zimbabwe like in other African societies, children are a blessing and a gift that link past and future. Children belong to the extended family, carry the family names, and connect the dead with the living. The cultural themes regarding raising children emphasize these connections and responsibilities. In this regard, children are to be protected and guided. However, all too often children end up in the background reflecting the saying "Children are to be seen and not heard." These cultural attitudes impact the ways in which child labor is perceived, defined, and created (Chinyangara et al., 1997). Additionally, African cultures value children's contributions to the family. Work is part of socializing children so they learn responsibility, acquire an appropriate work ethic, and appreciate the value and the dignity of work (Chinyangara et al., 1997).

Debates and discussions on child labor are generally based on the assumption that children are exploited only by their employers. These debates tend to reflect protective attitudes toward children and emphasize the harmful effects of child labor but neglect the poverty that engulfs these children and their families. In Zimbabwe there is an assumption among government officials that there is no child without a home, loving parents, and an extended family to provide support during difficult times (Chinyangara et al., 1997). Yet because of poverty it is becoming evident that some children are being exploited by their parents. It is usually assumed that the parents have the best interests of their children at heart. Thus the idea that parents might exploit their own children is presumed culturally unacceptable. The work of children continues to be important to the survival of children and their families. Zimbabwe's challenge is to eliminate child abuse in the form of exploitative and dangerous child labor while honoring children's work.

While the cultural ideal today is that "childhood" should be protected and preserved through play and education, in reality this experience is a privilege. Most children in Zimbabwe do not have a chance to enjoy this privilege because of the precarious nature of their lives. Because of the historic concerns about inequality in commercial farming areas, public officials have raised concerns about children laboring in commercial farming areas. The Global March against Child Labor exposed children whose labor tends to be hidden away from the public eye.

Since the 1990s the problem of street children has been highlighted. It is presumed that no child is without family support and that, based on cultural norms, no child would run away from home because of parental abuse and overwork. As a consequence, these children are generally perceived as a nuisance at best and as delinquents at worst who pollute the streets and flagrantly violate the law and therefore need to be locked away. The perception by public officials and authorities is that these children paint a negative image. They are frequently rounded up and tucked away from the public eye (Chinyangara et al., 1997).

THE FUTURE OF CHILD LABOR

Children in Zimbabwe labor to survive. Heated debates about what is child labor and the explanations regarding the causes of child labor have too often complicated issues. These debates assume that the wealthy nations can and should dictate policies to the poorer nations. These debates frequently overshadow the socioeconomic inequality that underpins capitalist relations regarding who can work and the value of their labor. Within this context, the goal is to improve the well-being of children and address factors that interfere with their welfare.

One of the pressing issues in child labor today is the continued devaluing of their parents'/adults' labor. Today those nations that enjoy better wages and high standards of living seem to be trapped in the destructive pattern of devaluing African labor. These are the conditions and attitudes propagated and sustained by colonial capitalism—a world where the struggles for survival of Africans are generally accepted and tolerated as normal, everyday occurrences. By centering the problem of child labor in Zimbabwe within the context of improving the work and quality of well-being for adults, the well-being of children can be improved. Addressing the nature and conditions that devalue and exploit adult labor can improve the well-being of children who are dependent upon their parents and guardians.

The vestiges of colonial capitalism and the ideology of racial subordination continue to perpetuate discrimination, poverty, employment, housing, and labor patterns in Zimbabwe today. Due to issues of racial subordination families and children are placed in situations that require the labor of children for survival. Children flourish with a focusing on developing economic programs and policies addressing high unemployment and poverty, changing the exploitative nature of adult work, and increasing funding to education. Collaborative national and international efforts are a component of raising awareness and eliminating hazardous child labor and its accompanying abuses of children.

BIBLIOGRAPHY

Andvig, J., S. Canagarajah, and A. Kielland. (2001) Issues in child labor in Africa. *Africa Region Human Development Working Paper Series*. Washington, DC: World Bank.

Arat, Z. (2002) Analyzing child labor as a human rights issue, its cause, aggravating policies and alternative proposals. *Human Rights Quarterly* 24(1): 177–200.

Barnett, T., and P. Blackie. (1992) *AIDS in Africa: Its present and future impact*. London: Belhaven Press.

Bourdillon, M. (2000) *Earning a life: Working children in Zimbabwe*. London: Zed Books.

Brazier, C. (1998) Issues on Child Labor. *New Internationalist* 292 (July).

Chinyangara, I., I. Chokuwenga, R. G. Dete, L. Dube, J. Kembo, P. Moyo, and R. S. Nkomo. (1997) *Indicators for Children's Rights. Zimbabwe Country Case Study*. Harare: University of Zimbabwe. http://www.childwatch.uio.no/cwi/projects/indicators/Zimbabwe/ind_zim_ch3.html. Retrieved October 24, 2002.

Dhlembeu, N. (2001) *Ministry of public service, labor and social welfare: Statements and technical reports on child labor and child exploitation*. Harare, Zimbabwe: Government of Zimbabwe Publications.

Drenovsky, C. K. (1992) Children's labor force participation in the world system. *Journal of Comparative Family Studies* 23(2): 183–95.

Feagin, J. R., and C. B. Feagin. (2003) *Racial and ethnic relations*. New Jersey: Prentice-Hall.

Grier, B. (1994) Invisible hands: The political economy of child labor in colonial Zimbabwe, 1890–1930. *Journal of Southern African Studies* 20: 1–27.

Human Development Report. (2002) *Deepening Democracy in a Fragmented World*. New York: United Nations Development Program.

Levine, S. (1999) Bittersweet harvest: Children, work and the global march against child labor in the post-apartheid state. *Critique of Anthropology* 19(2): 139–56.

Lowenson, R. (1981) The health status of farm worker communities in Zimbabwe. *Central African Journal of Medicine* 27(5): 88–91.

Moyo, O. N. (2001) Dealing with work in its context: An analysis of household work and provisioning strategies in Bulawayo, Zimbabwe. *Dissertation Abstracts International* (UMI No. 3015035).

Muchini, B., and S. Nyandiya Bundy. (1991) *Struggling to survive: A study of street children in Zimbabwe*. Harare: University of Zimbabwe.

Nelson, H. D. (1983) *Zimbabwe: A country study*. Washington, DC: American University Foreign Area Studies.

Otis, J., E. M. Pasztor, and E. J. McFadden. (2001) Child labor: A forgotten focus on child Welfare. *Child Welfare* 80(5): 611–25.

Reynolds, P. (1991) *Dance civet cat: Child labor in the Zambezi Valley.* Harare, Zimbabwe: Baobab Books.

Sachikonye, L. M. (1991) Child labor in hazardous employment: The case of Zimbabwe. *Consultancy Report, Series No. 18.* Harare: Zimbabwe Institute of Development Studies.

UNICEF (1997) *State of the world's children: Report on child labor.* Retrieved July 11, 2002, from http://www.unicef.org.

Van Onselen, C. (1976) *African mine labor in Southern Rhodesia, 1900–1933.* London: Zed Books.

Zimbabwe Census Bureau. (1997) *Inter Census Demographic Survey Report.* Harare: Government of Zimbabwe.

INDEX

ABOUT THE EDITORS
AND CONTRIBUTORS

B. J. BRYSON, Ph.D., MSW, is an Associate Professor at James Mason University Department of Social Work in Harrisonburg, Virginia. Her primary areas of interest are in any aspect of oppression and diversity, especially involving women and children. As a qualitative researcher she seeked to understand meaning behind the numbers.

TINA BRYSON, BA, is a high school Spanish teacher in the Atlanta City School District. Her primary interests are in the educational experiences of all children. She has traveled extensively in the Caribbean and Latin American countries.

DAVID CAREY, Jr., Ph.D., is Assistant Professor of History and Women's Studies at the University of Southern Maine. He teaches courses on the history of women, indigenous peoples, Africans, and the environment of Latin America. His publications include *Our Elders Teach Us: Maya-Kaqchikel Historical Perspectives. Xkib'lj kan qate' qatata'* (2001), *Ojer taq tzijob'äl kichin n' Kaqchikela' Winaqi'* (A History of the Kaqchikel People) (2004), and *Engendering Mayan History: Mayan Women as Agents and Conduits of the Past, 1870–1970* (forthcoming).

ADAM DEFAYETTE is a graduate student at the Pratt Institute and the Brooklyn College of Law. His interests include sustainable development, community organization, and environmental justice. He is the 2003 winner of the James Mapstone Essay Award at the State University of New York-Plattsburgh.

SHELLEY FELDMAN, Ph.D., is Professor of Development Sociology and former Director of the South Asia and the Gender and Global Change programs at Cornell University. She has lived and carried out research in Bangladesh for more than two decades exploring topics that include gender and fundamentalism, NGOs and civil society, globalization and EPZ production, rural subsistence and provisioning, and differential access to health, education, and credit, publishing widely on these themes.

REZA JALALI, MHSA, is the Director of the University of Southern Maine's Stone House. As a human rights advocate he has participated in UN-sponsored international conferences. He is a former member of Amnesty International's board of directors and writes and speaks nationally on Islam and the politics of the Middle East.

DAVID KEYS is Associate Professor and Chair of the Sociology and Criminal Justice Department at State University of New York-Plattsburgh. He is the author of several books on the death penalty and 20th Century American sociology.

DESI LARSON, Ph.D., is an Associate Professor of Adult Education and Women's Studies, and the Coordinator of Adult Education at the University of Southern Maine. Her research interests focus on the role of education in promoting social justice for women, children, and other oppressed groups.

SHIZHEN LU is the President of China Youth University for Political Sciences (CYUPS) in the city of Beijing of China, vice chairman of China Youth Research Association and vice chairman of China Social Work Education Association. She is a professor at the Department of Social Work of CYUPS. Her research interests include juvenile social work, social work education and family counseling.

OTRUDE MOYO, Ph.D., MSW, has lived and worked in Zimbabwe and the United States. She teaches and practices in the areas of international development, social change and globalization, international migration and refugees, social welfare policy, evaluation research, understanding work and provisioning strategies of families, rural communities, and human service delivery systems to disadvantaged communities globally.

PAMELA PIERIS, Ph.D., is an independent consultant with a Masters in International Administration and concentrations in human services and training of trainers. She has a background in international social development and has worked in Sri Lanka, Columbia, Bolivia, India, and the United States.

CATHRYNE L. SCHMITZ, Ph.D., ACSW, is a Professor and the Director of the School of Social Work at Radford University in Virginia. Her practice, teaching, and research interests center around the needs of high risk children and families. She has focused her career on understanding and dismantling oppression nationally and globally.

LACEY SLOAN, Ph.D., MSW, is a Research Associate in the Muskie School of Public Service, Institute for Child and Family Policy in Portland, Maine. She has studied extensively in the area of social policy. Her areas of expertise include the sex industry and the issues of violence against women, children, and minority populations.

CATHERINE STAKEMAN, DSW, MSW, is the interim Executive Director of the Maine Chapter of the National Association of Social Workers. Her primary areas of interest include oppression and diversity, particularly involving women and children, and African American single parent families. She has traveled in South Africa researching some of the social issues that affect women and children.

XIAOJUN TONG, Ph.D. candidate, MSW, is a faculty member of the Department of Social Work of China Youth University for Political Sciences (CYUPS) in the city of Beijing of China. Her research interest includes international adoption policy, the practice of adoption and foster care in China, youth and their families, and the education and practice of social work ethics in China.

ELIZABETH KIMJIN TRAVER, Ph.D., MSW, teaches undergraduate and graduate research, public policy, multicultural social work courses at the University of Southern Maine's School of Social Work. Her areas of practice include clinical social work with international adoptees and their families, strengthening multicultural communities, culturally competent research and evaluation, and eradicating poverty.

NONA TSOTSERIA, MD, MPA, MPPM, is the Country Director in Georgia, for the Overseas Strategic Consulting, LTD (Philadelphia, PA) and oversees health programs funded by the USAID and the Global Fund to Fight Tuberculosis, HIV/AIDS and Malaria. She has extensive experience as a medical doctor and health care expert.

RAUL ZELAYA, Ph.D., is the Senior Research Officer for the Learning Systems project in Honduras of the Canadian International Development Research Center (IDRC). His main area of work has been as director of Education for Rural Development in Central America.